Gender, Caste and Social Justice

Gender, Caste and Social Justice

Dr. Anji A, Dr. A. Ranjithkumar

KALPAZ

First Published, 2019

Published by

Kalpaz Publications
C-30, Satyawati Nagar,
Delhi – 110052
Ph.: 011-47034999, 9811692060
www.kalpazpublications.com
E-mail: kalpaz@hotmail.com

Printed at: G. Print Process, Delhi

Cataloging in Publication Data—DK
Courtesy: D.K. Agencies (P) Ltd. <docinfo@dkagencies.com>

Gender, caste and social justice / [editors], Dr Anji A,
Dr A. Ranjith Kumar.
pages cm
Contributed articles.
ISBN 9789353240400

1. Social justice—India, South. 2. Women employees—India, South. 3. Women—India, South—Social conditions. 4. Women—India, South—Economic conditions. 5. Women in rural development—Government policy—India, South. 6. People with social disabilities—India, South. 7. Caste—India, South. I. Anji, A., editor. II. Ranjithkumar, A., editor.

LCC HN690.S68G46 2019 | DDC 303.37209548 23

CONTENTS

List of Contributors

B. P. Pereira: Soft Skills/HR Trainer, Speech Point, Madurai – 625018

Anandakumar. S: PhD Research Scholar, Department of Science, University of Kerala, Kerala – 695 034.

Dr. Manzoor Hussain: Senior Assistant Professor, Department of Sociology, University of Kashmir, Srinagar – 190 006.

Gousia Yaseen: Ph.D Research Scholar, Department of Sociology, University of Kashmir, Srinagar – 190 006

Dr. Anji. A: Teaching Assistant, Research Centre of Women's Studies, Karnatak University, Dharwad – 580 003.

Dr. A.Ranjithkumar: Research Associate, Centre for the Study of Social Exclusion and Inclusive Policy, National Law School of India University, Nagarbhavi, Bangalore – 560 072.

Dr. P. Dhanalakshmi: Coordinator, Axis Bank, Saibaba Colony, Coimbatore, Tamil Nadu – 641011.

Dr. Prabudha S. Kamble: Teaching Assistant, Department of Studies in Anthropology, Karnatak University, Dharwad, Karnataka.

Dr. Shilpa M. Sangam: Lecturer, Department of Women's Studies, B.V.V.Sangha's Akkamahadevi, Women's Arts Science and Commerce College, Bagalkot – 587 101, Karnataka.

Raju Kamble: Ph.D Research Scholar, Dept. of Studies in Mass Communication & Journalism, Karnatak University, Dharwad – 580 003.

Dr. S.M. Malagatti: Assistant Professor, Dept. of Studies in Mass Communication & Journalism, Karnatak University, Dharwad – 58 0003.

Dr. Hiranniya Kalesh P: Assistant Professor, Department of Local Governance, Rajiv Gandhi National Institute of Youth Development, Sriperumbudur 602105

Dr. Jitendra Wasnik: Assistant Professor, Department of Public Administration and Local Self Government, TM Nagpur University, Nagpur.

S. K. Asha Begum: Ph.D Research Scholar, Department of Economics, Acharya Nagarjuna University, Guntur, Andhra Pradesh – 522 510.

Dr. M. SREEVIDYA: Post Doctoral Fellow, Department of Anthropology, Sri Venkateswara University, Tirupati, AP, India-517502

V. Pragati: Associate Professor, Department of Anthropology Puducherry Institute of Linguistics and Culture, Puducherry.

P. Jayapradaban: Assistant Professor, Department of History, Madras Christian College (Autonomous) Tambaram, Chennai – 600059

Devi Prasad: ICSSR, Doctoral Research Scholar, Department of Sociology, SSS, University of Hyderabad, Hyderabad.

Savita Yadav: Post Graduate Student, Department of Hindi, School of Humanities, University of Hyderabad, Hyderabad.

S. Genani: Assistant Professor, Centre for Women's Studies, Gandhigram Rural Institute – Deemed University, Gandhigram – 624 302. Dindigul District, Tamil Nadu.

Sunita Meena: Research Scholar, JNU, New Delhi

Mr. Balraju Rajaram: (Research Scholar) Center for Lifelong Learning, Gandhigram Rural Institute – Deemed University Gandhigram – 624 302. Dindigul (Dist). Tamil Nadu (State).

Dr. S. Vedapurieswaran: Guest Lecturer, Dept. of Sociology, Bharathidasan University, Tiruchirappalli-620 024, Tamil Nadu.

Himadri Dutta, B.S. Mipun: Department of Geography, North-Eastern Hill University,Shillong, Meghalaya.

FOREWORD

Marginalization is a multi-dimensional, multi-causal, historical phenomenon. There are no general laws to understand and comprehend- the complex nature of marginalization. The nature of marginalization varies in different setting. The religious, ideological systems, patriarchy, political economy of the country and over all social system have an impact on the marginalization of the specific groups or an individual. The most vulnerable marginalized groups in Indian Society are: dalits, women, tribals, and people with disabilities, aged, poor, and other deprived sections of society. These groups are deprived of adequate access to the basic needs such as health, education, food, security, employment and equity. Despite many attempts to improve their status by government, they are not come up in main stream development. Hence this work provides a platform to understand the issues of marginalized groups and their intricate relation with gender age, socio-economic dimensions and caste. The articles in this edited volume, will open new discourses on the issues of marginalization to the academicians scholars as well as students. ***I appreciate the efforts of the editors for bringing this volume and wish them all success.***

Dr. (Smt), Shakuntala C Shettar
Professor and Head
Department of Sociology &
Han. Director of Research Centre for Women's Studies
Karnatak University, Dharwad

INTRODUCTION

— *DR ANJI. A, DR A. RANJITHKUMAR*

Social Justice is a multidisciplinary and revolutionary concept which provides for just social order to everyone through rule of law and legal provision. Justice Srinath Sahay rightly pointed out that Social Justice is an expression which has found its way in the vocabulary of the Constitution and has become a part of the Constitutional terminology (Srinath Sahay: 1996). Hence Constitution of India assures social justice to all. The concept of social justice is not new, it is an old concept. Even various western political philosophers supported to social justice. Plato argued that justice would be achieved when each person received those goods they deserved based on their prescribed place in the social order. Unequal would be treated as unequal. Social justice would not involve efforts to transform or transcend existing societal structures, but rather would guarantee that existing institutions would continue to work as intended (Michael Reisch: 2002).

Social justice can be achieved through legal provisions, at the same time legal providing does not properly addressing to social justice. Indian Constitution gives three kinds of justice, namely, political, economic and social. India is a welfare state and people are treated as equal under law without any discrimination. But our constitution gives special protection to special groups like Scheduled Caste and Scheduled Tribes. Article 14 of the Indian constitution assures that "The State shall not deny to any person equality before the law or the equal protection of the laws within the territory of India". This article gives there are two equality, one is equality before the law and it is a negative concept. Second one is equal protection of the laws and it is a positive concept. The concept of equal protection of laws requires the state shall give special treatment to persons in different situations to set up equality among all.

John Rawls, 'A Theory of Justice' (1999) argues that justice is two principles, namely the principle of equal liberty and the difference principle. He pointed out that there are two principles of justices; 1. Each person is to have an equal right to the most extensive scheme of equal basic liberties compatible with a similar scheme of liberties for others. 2. Social and economic inequalities are to be arranged so that they are both (a) reasonably expected to be to everyone's advantage, and (b) attached to positions and offices open to all. The first principle deals with egalitarian, and it distributes extensive liberties equally to all persons. The second principles (2b) are also quite egalitarian, since it distributes opportunities to be considered for offices and positions in an equal way and (2a) is not egalitarian, but makes benefit of some (those with greater talents, training, etc.) proportionate to their contribution toward benefiting the least advantaged persons.

Henry S. Richardson explained that John Rawls's principles of justice address two different aspects of the basic structure of society. The First Principle speaks about the essentials of the constitutional structure. It holds that society must assure each citizen an equal claim to a fully adequate scheme of equal basic rights and liberties, which scheme is compatible with the same scheme for all. The second principle addresses instead those aspects of the basic structure that shape the distribution of opportunities, offices, income, wealth, and in general social advantages. The first part of the second principle holds that the social structures that shape this distribution must satisfy the requirements of fair equality of opportunity. The second part of the second principle is the famous-or infamous Difference Principle. It holds that social and economic inequalities are to be to the greatest benefit of the least advantaged members of society. Each of these three centrally addresses a different set of primary goods.The First Principle concerns rights and liberties; the principle of Fair Equality of Opportunity concerns, opportunities; and the Difference Principle primarily concern income and wealth.

Will Kymlicka's Multiculturalism is closely associated with identity politics, the politics of difference, and the politics of recognition, all of which share a commitment to devaluing disrespected identities and changing dominant patterns of representation and communication that marginalize certain groups. He further said that the traditional model of citizenship as rights have been challenged from two directions. The first directions emphasized the need to supplement the focus on rights with greater attention to civic virtues and active political participation and second directions emphasized the need to supplement the focus on the common rights with greater attention to cultural pluralism and group differentiated rights which reflects a broad ranging movement not only in political philosophy, but also in real world politics (Kymlicka 2017:327).

There is a vast gap between theory of social justice and practice of social justice. Social justice may be implemented through public policies and welfare policies. Public policies have divided into three types, Theodore Lowi highlighted three kinds of policies are; regulatory, distribution and redistribution. Regulatory policies are concerned with the regulation and control of personal conduct by coercive techniques. These policies deal with the regulations of trade, quality of education and safety measure. Distribution policies grant goods and services to specific interest groups of the population and all public welfare programs are distributed. Redistributive policies are aiming at redistributing resources from one group to another which is the main goals of such policies is to set up an fair society through redistribution of social and economic rewards (Bidyut Chakrabarty and Prakash Chand 2016: 25).

Man made inequality can be abolished through public policy which leads to social order. At the same time public policy has properly not executed and implemented in a proper way and not good yield. Everyone has equal under law without any discriminations and but few people like SC/ST, women, transgender, child, and minorities have been neglected from mainstream development. Many scholars have made an attempt to addressing against discriminations. Due to economic and social hierarchy the solutions have not come out. Liberal and social democracy are always too far way for vulnerable communities. The problem of injustice is everywhere too threatening of a just social order. In the contemporary era, many injustices are being practiced all over the Indian states. We quote Martin Luther King Jr. statement about injustice and he said that "Injustice anywhere is a threat to justice everywhere. We are caught in an inescapable network of mutuality, tied in a single garment of destiny. Whatever affects one directly, affects all indirectly". From these perspectives, we feel that many scholars are trying to work in addressing social injustice but no result. Hence we also try to discuss about gender justice, problems of aging persons, sub-caste problems, migration and so on. This book is closely looking at three aspects are gender, caste, social justice and it are broadly divided into three categories. Twenty one research papers have been collected and discussed in this book.

The first paper is 'social justice: A Critics' which is written by B. P. Pereira. His paper deals with concept of social justice. He said that the legally enforceable fundamental rights that the Indian Constitution guarantees every citizen will remain empty words unless these rights are recognized as human rights. He argues that social justice can possibly through legal perspectives and it is based on the concepts of human rights and equality. An article on Democratic Justice through Electoral Reforms written by Anandakumar and he argues that the electoral reforms are built just social order and election commission is major role play to demonstrate democratic justice.

Manzoor Hussain and Gousia Yaseen talk social-cultural Mobilization through Welfare Programme with reference to the Indira Awaas Yojana Scheme in Kashmir valley. His study is carried out in order to note the social implications at the ground level and they said Indira Awaas Yojana (IAY) Scheme is the very beneficial scheme and has many advantages for an uplift of people living in the society especially poor. The main focus of the scheme has been to raise the poor families Above Poverty Line (APL) by fulfilling one of the basic needs of their life.

The problem of transgender is being discussed by Anji and he examines the Socio-Economic Status of Transgender in Karnataka. His paper states that the proper measures should be taken up to provide medical care to TGs in the hospitals and also provide those separate public toilets and other facilities. Steps to create public awareness should be taken so that TG's feel that they are also part of the society, regain their respect and are not to be treated as untouchables. The solution to their problems requires concerted efforts to mainstream them and adoption of an inclusive approach in all spheres of life. Author critically examines and understood about micro level problems faced by transgender.

Dhanalakshmi critics on problem of old age women towards Inclusive Perspectives and inclusive policy. She rightly pointed out that family members of old aged women feel that they are problematic due to they do not earn any money not helping their family. This study suggests that guidance and counselling should be given to the family members, neighbours and youngsters protect the elder's women with the help of NGOs, school and college.

The issues of child rights are a contemporary problem among the all communities and in this aspect Prabudha and Kamble's articles deals about Child Rearing Practices among the Mahar Community in Karnataka state. In this paper says that the breastfeed is the first fundamental right of the child and Child Rearing practices are a major determinant of morbidity status of infants. The study pointed out that the breastfeeding is fundamental for survival, growth and development, health and nutrition of infants. The study is observed that Illiteracy and low socio-economic status were found to be the influencing factors behind these faulty practices Child Rearing. A paper on Women's Reproductive Health by Shilpa M. Sangam discusses women's reproductive health is basic rights of women, which is assured by the state. This discussion sexual and reproductive health are the most important sources of women's empowerment and third generation of human rights are discussed by the author and study conclude that the reproductive health can be maintained and achieved through the proper usage of reproductive health care methods and reproductive rights.

Mass media is one of key actors to promote gender justice and social justice. Raju Kamble and Malagatti write on Mass Media and Participation of Women in Agriculture. This paper deals with two kinds of concepts, namely the impact of media, women's participation in agricultural and mass media. This study illustrates that Women have an important role to play in all economic and productive activities. Their contribution in the agriculture sector is very significant in farming activities in small and small land holdings. The women are the backbone of agricultural workforce, but worldwide her hard work has mostly been unpaid. This paper brings out that mass media is main role play to participation of women in agriculture sectors and allied services and mass media is communicating from a rural population to global population about rural agricultural products.

Their contribution in the agriculture sector is very significant in farming activities in small and marginal land holdings. The women are the backbone of agricultural workforce, but worldwide her hard work has mostly been unpaid. This paper brings out that mass media is main role play to participation of women in agriculture sectors and allied services and mass media is communicating from a rural population to global population about rural agricultural products.

Gender Perspective of Political Leadership in Kerala is discussed by Hiranniya Kalesh and argues that the omission of women in politics of power seriously affects the ability to change the standardization of women in all its manifestations. This study critic that women in political parties is determinant of their political empowerment in national level, which influencing in shaping women's political prospects. This study suggests that provide gender-sensitive coverage of elections, avoiding negative stereotypes and presenting positive images of women as leaders.

Jitendra Wasnik's works on Women and panchayati raj in India: Present Scenario. The study discusses about the participation of women in Panchayat raj and what are the problems faced by them. The paper reveals that neither the reservation for women or their actual presence in the PRIs have become any more sensitive to the problems related to them. The study, rightly pointed out that the elected women not always treated with due respect and most of the elected women's suggestions were not considered seriously nor were they consulted while decisions were being made. This paper illustrates that the participation of women in local government is key role play to promoting just social order and they have to be included in the decision making process which helps to upward mobilization of communities.

Rural Women have been negated from mainstream development of the country. The problem of rural women do not addresses in a proper manner. Hence Asha Begum tries to understand the problem of rural women and the relations between women empowerment and Entrepreneurship Development in the rural scenario in Andhra Pradesh. The study aims at importance of entrepreneurial development among rural women and also to analyze the socio-economic framework, problems and prospects of women entrepreneurs in Guntur District, Andhra Pradesh with special reference to rural women. The study concludes that self- confidence, self-reliance have been increased among rural women.

Sreevidya's paper entitled 'skill development programmes to women SHGs: a study in Krishna district of Andhra Pradesh'. This paper deals with the abilities improvement through professional preparing alongside different measures such as Pradhan Mantri Kaushal Vikas Yojna, National Skills Development Corporation, National Skills Development Mission. Service of Labor and Employment has taken various activities in the field of aptitude advancement and business. The study concludes that women in the district are to be given more exposure in social, cultural, economic, political, educational, technical aspects and so on. Training and development programmes offered through SHG operations in Krishna district play a vital role in the economic and personality development leads to income-generating activities of women in the district. This paper states that the gender justice and social justice shall be achieved through skill development programmes.

Southern states of India are the role model of agitations to non-southern states for fighting political reservation, rights to access public places and right to access commons. As a result, most marginalized communities demand separate reservation, in this circumstance Arunthathiyars has come up to fighting inner reservation and political demand for upward mobilization. Pragati analyses an anthropological approach of inter - generational change in education, occupation and income of Arundhathiyar in Puducherry union territorial. This study finds that Arundhathiyar is traditionally involved in clearing the animal carcasses, using the animal skins for tanning, stitching, and mending footwear. The practice of this occupation has determined their local social hierarchical position. She pointed out that Arundhathiyar were untouchable among the untouchables and they are humiliated by the

Scheduled Castes and the higher castes. She founds that policy of educations have not been benefited by the Arunthathiyar communities and occupation and income is not significant for them. Jayapradaban's paper deals with migration issues and Scheduled caste. This paper revivals that how migration affects to social justice among SCs in Puducherry UT. He raises research questions are; 1. Can we forcefully change a Scheduled Caste candidate to a general category who seeks job and higher education under all circumstances? 2. Is there any law that forbids SC people of Pondicherry seeking matrimonial alliance of neighbouring states like Tamil Nadu within the SC community? Based on these questions, the study is moving towards the social justice.

Devi Prasad and Savita Yadav try to look out Caste, Ritual and Politics among Yadav Community in UP. This paper makes an attempt to map out the various strategies which are applied for getting the dominant position by Yadav leaders from local to the provincial level. Authors fix two major objectives, namely to study the social life of Yadav community, To understand the socio economic problems of Yadav community. This study is observed that the provision of reservation in education has given a chance to enter into the governmental institution. This paper found that Yadav communities have been adapted the Dr. B. R. Ambedkar's principles of educate, agitate and organize. Based on these principles Yadav communities captured educational mobilization and political power. Yadav communities felt that Ambedkar's principles only way to achieve the political power and social justice.

Recently honour killings have been practiced in Tamil Nadu, which is major threatening of social justice. Genani is trying to address these issues and she writes social roots of honour based violence (Honour Killing) in Tamil Nadu. This study looks at women's perspectives and her articles rightly highlights that India has registered a nearly 251 cases of honour killings in 2015 and Now Tamil Nadu witnessed 81 incidents of honour killings and notorious for many deaths of honour killings go unreported as passed off as suicides. Paper tries to analyses certain major honour killings occurred between caste groups in Tamil Nadu and discuss some ameliorative solutions and strategies in policy level. She demands separate laws which deal with this gruesome act of honour killings and any punishments regarding the same.

A paper on plagued with prejudice: subjugation of Dalit women in Rajasthan is written by Sunita Meena and her paper explores the dynamics of discrimination which has subjugated the Dalit Women of Rajasthan and it also examines the issues education among Dalit women and Political Participation with a comparison of upper caste women in Rajasthan. This study finds that government of Rajasthan made many provisions for upliftment of SCs but they are unable to enjoy such privileges due to the lack of education and also they are unable to understand policies. Thus, education is the main input to escape all this violence and discriminations.

Balraju Rajaram's paper on educational status of Lambada Tribes in Andhra Pradesh. The major discussion of this paper deals with the literacy status of Lambada tribes and how they benefit from educational policy. The study finds that Lambada Tribe is in developing stage in terms of education. At the same time they are facing a lot of exploitation from the society and they could not able to get the proper infrastructure facility to earn a proper formal education. The study observed that school gets funding, but not expensed to target groups. Vedapurieswaran's discussion is on Socio- economic conditions of women tea plantation workers in the Nilgiris district in Tamil Nadu which is based on sociological study. The study critically discusses the issues of tea plantation worker among women's communities. The present study deals with socio-economic conditions of Tea plantation workers and living condition of the women workers. The study also concentrates employment pattern of women workers in a tea plantation.

Final chapter deals with women workers in tea industry of Dibrugarh in Assam. Himadri Dutta and Mipun's study deals with Tea plantation labour market and work participation for women. The present research, analyses the contribution of tea gardens in uplifting the socio-economic status of women workers in tea industry of Dibrugarh district, which has the highest number of tea garden in Assam. The study observed that the tea plantation workers are found to be paid wages much below the minimum wages for agricultural workers so they cannot afford the minimum need of livelihood. They get an amount of Rs. 100 irrespective of permanent or casual and male or female labours.

Thus, we strongly believe that social justice can be achieved through literacy on government policies and education without any discrimination of gender and caste. Education is the only way to eliminate of atrocity and discrimination against SCs, STs, women, and transgender which can implement through legal ways. Acts like atrocities shall be strengthened which provides just social order among the society. We strongly convey the reservation policy should be extended into private sectors which help income generation occupational mobilization of the vulnerable communities

1

SOCIAL JUSTICE:

A CRITICS

— *B. P. PEREIRA*

Abstract

Social growth is vital in living society. Justice is a great virtue which we all should have. It is pertinent to record here that combination of these two as "Social Justice" is a blessing to the mankind. Constitutionally, ethically, legally and spiritually it is said to reach all the citizens without hurting or harming anyone instead of making the clear way to live in this universe with peace and principle. Sociality or Society is essentially a mental phenomenon. Ethics is concerned with the moral rightness or depravity of human actions. No ethical action is possible unless it is social. Social justice, the term and its modern concept were coined by the Sicilian Priest Luigi Taparelli d'Azeglio in 1840 based on the teaching of St. Thomas Aquinas and given further exposure in 1848 by Antonio Rosmini-Serbati. Social Justice generally refers to the idea of creating a society or institution that is based on the principles of equality and solidarity, that understands and values human rights, and that recognizes the dignity of every human rights and equality and involves a greater degree of economic egalitarianism through progressive taxation, income redistribution or even property redistribution. To reach the benefit of social justice to all of the citizens of our nation, constitutional guidelines through The Preamble promises Justice to all citizens, justice harmonization of interests between the individuals, between groups and even between individuals and groups on the one hand and interests of the community on the other. But in spite of having all these possibilities, feasibilities and viabilities, the question evolves from and within the portal, whether all the citizens of this holy land are subjected to avail the possible benefit of social justice or simply dreaming as a mirage with the mythical clouds. Franz Alexander said that the sense of justice must be recognized as one of the foundations of social life.

Key words: *Social Justice, Citizens, Injustice, Constitutional Justice, Human Rights.*

Introduction

To construe on application of a figure of speech in which the two words society, as well as justice, are compared or balanced, it will point its needle in the centre as two sides of a coin or two poles which/ support the essentialities for a peaceful life of all living things especially the human beings in this universe without a second option or skip to other choice practically. There is no correlation between these two words as it differs semantically and elaborately sprawls with multifaceted boundaries constitutionally and judicially. If we crawl into the concept of the two through the peep-hole to realize the philosophical needs and potency of ethics,

Meaning and Definition

F.H.Giddings (1927) defines society as "a number of like-minded individuals, who know and enjoy their like-mindedness, and are therefore able to work together for common ends", against the views of St.Thomas Aquinas "a stable moral union of rational beings co-operating to a common end". The Great Dictionary of the English Language (2005) explains Society as 'the aggregate of people living together to a more or less ordered community" as its Origin –Latin Societies, from Socius 'companion'. In short, a society is formed by a group of individuals irrespective of gender values. Social realities and social values interact. Society must be made to rest upon justice and love, without which it is but organizing wrong. The strongest urge in the world today is that of social justice and equality. Digging the facts and needs of Justice, Linda B. Ford opines "Justice is a concept", whereas A. De Tocqueville defines 'there is one universal law... that is Justice. Justice forms the cornerstone of each nation's Law'.

Conceptualization

The administration of law or some other authority according to the principles of just behaviour and treat, preferably on constitutional/

judicial provisions; derived from Latin Justilia, law or right. The above facts imply that Justice in the society is one of the prime factors and needs for the peaceful life of its individual. Social justice generally refers to the idea of creating society or institution that is based on the principles of equality and solidarity, that understands and values human rights, and the recognizes the dignity of every human being. Social Justice is based on the concepts of Human Right and equality and involves a greater degree of economic egalitarianism through progressive taxation, income redistribution, or even property redistribution. These policies aim to achieve what developmental economists refer to as more equality of opportunity than may currently exist in some societies and to manufacture equality of outcome in cases where incidental inequalities appear in a procedurally just system.

The Constitution of the International Labour Organization (ILO) affirms that "universal and lasting peace can be established only if it is based upon social Justice" Furthermore, the Vienna Declaration and Program of Action treats Social Justice as a purpose of the human rights education. All societies have a basic structure of social, economic and political institutions, both formal and informal, as Social Justice refers to conceptions of justice applied to an entire society. It is based on the idea of a just society, which gives individuals and groups fair treatment and a just share of the benefits of society. Hence, ethics has many spheres of ethics. According to Aristotle, Economics is a practical expression of ethics, the abased virtue rooted in justice. This concept of justice has been variously described as distributive justice or a fair share for all. In other words, the concept of social justice was accepted as being rooted in an ethical base or simply common sense and economics cannot be divorced from this. Similarly, economics and politics are inseparable. Social Justice is both a philosophical problem and an important issue in political economy.

Social Justice is also a concept that some use to describe the movement towards a socially just world. This context, Social Justice is based on the concepts of human rights and equality. So a very broad definition of social justice is that "Social Justice reflects the way in which human rights are manifested in the everyday lives of people at every level of society". It can be further defined as working towards the realization of a world where all members of a society, regardless of background, have basic human rights and an equal opportunity to access the benefits of their society.

Constitutionality

Looking on Constitutional Provisions, the Preamble promises justice to all Citizens. Justice means harmonization of interests between the individuals, between groups and between groups & individuals on the one hand and interests of the community on the other. Most significantly, the Preamble places Justice higher than the other principles of Liberty, Equality and Fraternity. The concept of Justice in the Preamble is indeed very wide. It is not confined to the narrow legal justice as administered by the courts. Our courts are, after all, only courts of Law. Justice is defined or elaborated as social and economic over political Justice. The Preamble is designed to realize socio-economic justice to all people including workmen (All India Statutory Corporation v. United Labour Union, AIR 1977 SC).

Social Justice implies that all citizens are treated equally irrespective of their status in society as a result of the birth, race, caste, religion, sex, title etc. Article 15 prohibits discrimination or disability in the matter of access to public places. Article 38 enjoins the State to strive to promote the welfare of the people "by securing and protecting as effectively as it may a social order in which justice social, economic and political shall inform all the institutions of the nation life". In the words of Pandit Jawaharlal Nehru: "Social Justice has always exercised as the appeal to sensitive persons. The basic attraction of Marxism for millions of people was not, I think, its attempt at scientific theory but its passion for social justice" Provisions for humane conditions of work, maternity relief, leisure, reduction of wide disparities, promoting of economic interests an a decent standard of living for the workers, weaker sections and backward classes, minimum wage, banning of forced labour (Article 23 and 43) were all directed towards Social Justice (Sadasivam v, Polin, AIR 1984 SC 1417; Lingappa v. State of Maharashtra, AIR 1985 SC 389).

Observation and Conclusion

The legally enforceable fundamental rights that the Indian

Constitution guarantees to every citizen will remain empty words unless these rights are recognized as human rights. It is the human rights content that gives meaning to fundamental rights. But unfortunately, for most of the lawyers and judges, fundamental rights are no more than legal concepts. The preamble to our Constitution, as adopted by the Constituent Assembly, spoke of "We, the People of India", makes a solemn resolve to constitute India into a "Sovereign Democratic Republic" securing for all its citizens Justice, Liberty and Equality, and promoting among them all Fraternity. Justice is further defined as social, economic and Political. Liberty includes liberty of through, expression, belief, faith, and worship, and Equality means equality of status and of opportunity. Even though The Constitution of India has solemnly promised to all its justices- social, economic and political; liberty of thought expression, belief, faith and worship; equality of status and of opportunity; and to promote among the all fraternity assuring and reiterating the dignity of the individual and the unity of nation; reaching them in action to the common men to be benefitted is in dreams and availing its full impact under Social Justice is felt to be a mirage due to improper governance and delay in considering the needs on time by the competent authorities and also so called rulers. Vladimir Putin rightly pointed out that the society which cannot defend its children has no future. The Justice which cannot defend its people has no forward justification.

References

1. Gisbert, Pascual.S.J(1959): Fundamentals of Sociology, Orient Longmans. Calcutta.
2. Kashyap, Subhash.C (1994): Our Constitution, National Book Trust, New Delhi.
3. Mohan, Venkata (2008): Sociological Thought Jawahar Publishers and Distributors, New Delhi.
4. Murali. R, (2013): Knowledge and Justice Vergal Publication, Madurai.
5. Samantroy D.K (2013): Handbook of Human Rights and Social Justice, Astha Publishers, New Delhi.
6. Suresh, Justice Hosbet (2003): Fundamental Rights as Human Rights, Sabrang Communication & Publishing Pvt. Ltd, Mumbai.

2

Democratic Justice through Electoral Reforms

— *Anandakumar. S*

Abstract

Effective electoral reforms in India are an age-old saying. We have Election Commission, Legislature, Executive, Judiciary, Political Parties, Media, Civil society to bring in major reforms. But who will take the initiative? India is the largest democracy in the world and Indian electoral system is largest system but lot of defects and it will invariably affect the basic democratic values like one man one vote one value and whereby undermining the people's choice. In another way, this is the open violation of the democratic justice of the citizens. This paper highlights that the need for mobilization in bringing back the democratic justice in the country.

Key Words: *Election Commission, Electoral System, Model Code, Political Parties, Criminalization, Electronic Voting Machine.*

Introduction

One of the most important features of democratic principles is to conduct elections at regular intervals. Elections constitute the signpost of democracy. These are the medium through which the attitudes, values and beliefs of the people towards their political environment are reflected. Elections grant people a government and the government has constitutional right to govern those who elect it. Elections are the central democratic procedure for selecting and controlling leaders. Elections provide an opportunity to the people to express their faith in the government from time to time and change it when the need arises. Elections symbolize the sovereignty of the people and provide legitimacy to the authority of the government. Thus, free and fair elections are indispensable for the success of democracy. The Objectives of this paper are to understand justice through electoral reforms and to study the role of electoral reforms to build just social order among Indian societies. The paper revolves round the political scenario. The problems of election and need for reformation have been described with examples. This paper is based on analytical method.

Brief History and Development

In continuance of the British legacy, India has opted for parliamentary democracy. Since 1952, the country has witnessed elections to the legislative bodies at both the national as well as State levels. The electoral system in India is hamstrung by so many snags and stultifying factors. Such maladies encourage the anti-social elements to jump into the electoral fray. Our system was largely free from any major flaw until the fourth general elections (1967). The distortions in its working appeared, for the first time, in the fifth general elections (1971) and these got multiplied in the successive elections, especially in those held in the eighties and thereafter. Many a time, the Election Commission has expressed its concern and anxiety for removing obstacles in the way of free and fair polls. It has had made a number of recommendations and repeatedly reminded the government the necessity of changing the existing laws to check the electoral malpractices. The Tarkunde Committee Report of 19751, the Goswami Committee Report of 19902, the Election Commission's recommendations in 1998 and the Indrajit Gupta Committee Report of 1998 produced a comprehensive set of proposals regarding electoral reforms. A number of new initiatives have been taken by the Election Commission to cleanse the electoral process in India. The important among these are being discussed here.

Model Code of Conduct

The Election Commission of India is regarded as a guardian of free and fair elections. In every election, the EC issues a Model Code of Conduct for political parties and candidates to conduct elections in a free and fair manner. The Commission circulated its first Code at the time of the fifth general elections, held in 1971. Since then, the Code has been revised from time to time. The Code of Conduct lays down guidelines as to how political parties and candidates should conduct themselves during elections. A provision was made under the Code that from the time the elections are announced by the Commission, Ministers and other authorities cannot announce any financial grant, lay foundation stones of projects of schemes of any kind, make promises of construction of roads, carry out any appointments in government and public undertakings which may have the effect of influencing the voters in favour of the ruling party. Recently, the Punjab Government, which announced the budget for 2008-2009, did not propose any new concessions, because the Code of Conduct was in force for the May 2008 Panchayat elections. However, the Punjab Congress levelled serious allegations against the ruling SAD-BJP alliance for misusing government vehicles and making certain announcements, thereby violating the Model Code of Conduct.

Despite the acceptance of the Code of Conduct by political parties, cases of its violation have been on the rise. It is a general complaint that the party in power at the time of elections misuses the official machinery to further the electoral prospects of its candidates. The misuse of official machinery takes different forms, such as an issue of advertisements at the cost of public exchequer, misuse of official mass media during the election period for partisan coverage of political news and publicity regarding their achievements, misuse of government transport including aircraft/helicopter, vehicles. For example, during the 2003 Himachal Pradesh Assembly elections, the Commission had issued strict instructions to the political parties to abstain from the use of plastic and polythene for the preparation of posters and publicity material. But the political parties, particularly the Bharatiya Janata Party and the BahujanSamaj Party, put up a large number of saffron and green publicity flags made of polythene. During the 2002 Punjab Assembly elections, an aggressive advertisement campaign was launched by the Congress against Chief Minister Parkash Singh Badal and his son, accusing them of corruption and bartering away the interests of Punjab. The Akali Dal hit back with its own set of equally aggressive advertisements against the Congress leaders. The Election Commission of India had to intervene to clarify that under the Model Code of Conduct, personal allegations against individual leaders were not allowed, though criticisms of policy decisions and performance were permitted. Similarly, the EC also held Narendra Modi and Sonia Gandhi responsible for violation of the Model Code of Conduct by making controversial remarks during an election campaign in the 2007 Gujarat Assembly polls. The EC expressed its severe displeasure over its violation by the two leaders and expected that both of them in future would adhere to the salutary provisions of the Code in letter and spirit. Despite sincere efforts on the part of the EC to check malpractices, in each and every election India witnesses violation of the Model Code of Conduct.

Disclosure of Antecedents by Candidates

In June 2002, the EC on the direction of the Supreme Court, issued an order under Article 324 that each candidate must submit an affidavit regarding the information of his/her criminal antecedents; assets (both movable and immovable) of self and those of spouses and dependents as well; and qualifications at the time of filing his/her nomination papers for election to the LokSabha, the RajyaSabha and the State Legislative Assemblies. But political parties believed that the Election Commission and the judiciary were overstepping their powers. At the all-party meeting, held on July 8, 2002, representatives of 21 political parties decided that the Election Commission's order should not be allowed to be implemented. The Supreme Court again came out as a guardian of the citizen's right to information. The Apex Court gave its judgment on March 13, 2003, basically asserting its previous June 2002 decision, which required full disclosure by all candidates. The order made it clear that failing to furnish the relevant affidavit shall be considered as a violation of the Supreme Court's order and as such the nomination papers shall be liable to be rejected by the Returning Officer. Furnishing of wrong or incomplete information shall result in the rejection of nomination papers, apart from inviting penal consequences under the Indian Penal Code. The 2004 General Elections were conducted under these rules.

The above order is an effective step to make democracy healthy and unpolluted. Citizens have every right to know about the persons whom they prefer as their representatives. The EC has directed all Returning Officers to display the copies of nomination papers and affidavits filed by candidates to the general public and representatives of print and electronic media, free of cost.

Registration of Political Parties

The party system is an essential feature of parliamentary democracy. However, there is no direct reference to political parties in the Constitution of India. The statutory law relating to registration of political parties was enacted in 1989 which was quite liberal. As a result, a large number of non-serious parties mushroomed and got registered with the Commission. Many of them did not contest elections at all after their registration. It led to confusion among electors as to whom to vote. To eliminate the mushrooming of parties, the EC had to take some rigorous steps. The Commission now registers a party which has at least 100 registered electors as its members and is also charging a nominal processing fee of Rs 10,000 to cover the administration expenses which it will have to incur on correspondence with the parties after their registration.

In order to ensure that the registered political parties practice democracy in their internal functioning, the Commission requires them to hold their organisational elections regularly in accordance with their constitutions. The measures taken by the Election Commission to streamline the registration of political parties have shown effective results. These have lessened the headache of the administrative machinery, as well as the confusion of the electorate.

Checking Criminalization of Politics

The criminalization of politics is a grave problem in India. This menace began in Bihar and gradually spread to every nook and corner of the nation. In 2003, a law was introduced to prohibit the election of criminals to the legislative bodies. However, persons with criminal background continue to hold seats in Parliament and State Assemblies. This leads to a very undesirable and embarrassing situation when lawbreakers become law-makers and move around under police protection. During the 13th LokSabha elections candidates having criminal cases against them numbered 12 in Bihar and 17 in Uttar Pradesh. It has been rightly observed by J.P.Naik: "Power is the spoiler of men and it is more so in a country like India, where the hungry stomachs produce power hungry politicians."

The EC has expressed its serious concern over the entry of anti-social and criminal persons into the electoral arena. From time to time, it has set down norms and made recommendations to the government to curb the menace of criminalization of politics. The Commission has urged all political parties to reach a consensus that no person with a criminal background will be given the party ticket. The candidates for an election are also obliged to submit an affidavit in a prescribed form declaring their criminal records, including convictions, charges pending and cases initiated against them. The information so furnished by the candidates shall be disseminated to the public, and to the print and electronic media.

Limits on Poll Expenses

To get rid of the growing influence and vulgar show of money during elections, the EC has made many suggestions in this regard. The Commission has fixed legal limits on the amount of money which a candidate can spend during the election campaign. These limits have been revised from time to time. During 2004 elections, the ceiling limits for LokSabha seats varied between Rs 10,00,000 to Rs 25,00,000. For Assembly seats, the highest limit was Rs 10,00,000 and the lowest limit was Rs 5,00,000. The EC, by appointing expenditure observers keeps an eye on the individual accounts of election expenditure made by a candidate during an election campaign. The contestants are also required to give details of expenditure within 30 days of the declaration of the election results. However, political parties do not adhere to the financial Lakshman Rekha (limits) as huge amounts are spent by parties under the garb of their supporters.

Apart from this, the EC is also in favour of holding the LokSabha and the Assembly elections simultaneously, and to reduce the campaign period from 21 to 14 days. This, they feel, will lead to trim down the election expenditure. The Election Commission's attempt to impose these measures has been a move in the right direction.

Multi-Member Election Commission

There was a longstanding demand to make the EC a multi-member body. The Supreme Court in the S.S.Dhanoa versus Union of India case had observed: "When an institution like the Election Commission is entrusted with vital functions and is armed with exclusive and uncontrolled powers to execute them, it is both necessary and desirable that the powers are not exercised by one individual, however wise he may be. It also conforms to the tenets of democratic rule." With the 1993 Constitution Amendment Act, the Election Commission was made a multi-member body. The EC was made a multi-member body by the government in the wake of certain controversial decisions taken by the Chief Election Commissioner, T.N.Seshan3. The Act provided that the decision of three members 'shall, as far as possible, be unanimous'. In case of difference of opinion among three members, the matter shall be decided according to the opinion of the majority'. It was a significant step to remove a one-man show in such an important function as that of conducting elections. A single member of EC would have no longer 'unbridled' powers. In view of the large size of the country and the huge electors, the Election Commission also made a proposal for the appointment of Regional Commissions to different zones to reduce its burden.

Use of Scientific and Technological Advancements

The Election Commission of India has been trying to bring improvements in election procedures by taking advantage of scientific and technological advancements. The introduction of 'electronic voting machines' (EVM) is one of the steps in that direction. The Election Commission has recommended the introduction of electronic voting machines with a view to reducing malpractices and also improving the efficiency of the voting process. On an experimental basis, the EVMs were first tried in the State of Kerala during the 1982 Legislative Assembly Elections. After the successful testing and long legal enquiries of the technological aspects of the machines, the EC took a historic decision to go ahead and start the use of EVMs for certain Assembly elections in November 1998. The Commission selected 16 Assembly constituencies in the States of Madhya Pradesh, Rajasthan and Union Territory of Delhi. Later, in the June 1999 Assembly elections, Goa became the first State to successfully use EVMs in all its Assembly constituencies. In the 2004 Lok Sabha elections, the machines were used all over the country. It is a major initiative taken by the EC to make the electoral process simple, quick and trouble-free. It has saved money, solved several logistical issues and also contributed to the conservation of the environment through saving of paper. Another major advantage of these machines is that the counting of votes becomes more fast and accurate. Now there are no invalid and wasted votes at all, as every vote recorded in the machine is accounted for in favour of the candidate for whom it was cast.

The Election Commission has not lagged behind in making use of Information Technology for efficient electoral management and administration. It launched a website of its own on February 28, 1998. This is now a good source to have accurate information about elections, election laws, manuals and handbooks published by the Election Commission. During the 1999 LokSabha elections, the Commission's Secretariat was directly connected with nearly 1500 counting centres across the country. The round-wise counting results were fed into the Commission's website from those counting centres. These results were instantly available throughout the world.

In order to bring as much transparency as possible to the electoral process, the media—both electronic and print—were encouraged and provided with facilities to report on the actual conduct of the poll and counting. The Commission had, in co-operation with the State-owned media (Doordarshan and All India Radio) taken several innovative and effective steps to create awareness among voters. All recognised national, as well as State parties, were allowed free access to the state-owned media on an extensive scale for their election campaign. During the 2004 general elections, the total free time allocated to political parties was 122 hours.

With a view to prevent impersonation of electors at the time of voting and to eliminate bogus and fictitious entries into electoral rolls, the Election Commission took a bold step. In 1998, it decided to take a nationwide programme for the 'computerisation' of electoral rolls. The printed electoral rolls, as well as CDs containing these rolls, are available to the general public for sale national and State parties are provided with these free of cost after every revision of electoral rolls. The entire country's electoral rolls are available on its website. Karnataka became the first State to prepare electoral rolls with the photographs of voters in the 2008 elections. The State EC developed the electoral roll management software called 'SEERS'4 (State Enhanced Electoral Roll System) to prevent duplication of voters lists and to eliminate wrong addresses. The EC has decided to introduce photo electoral rolls for proper verification of voters across the country by the 2009 general elections.

In an attempt to improve the accuracy of the electoral rolls and prevent electoral fraud, the Election Commission in August 1993 ordered the issuance of Electors' Photo Identity cards (EPICs) for all voters. A modest attempt to introduce the photo identity cards was made for the first time in 1978 at the instance of the then Chief Election Commissioner, S.L. Shakdher, in the case of elections to the Legislative Assembly of Sikkim. During the 2004 Assembly elections, it was mandatory for people possessing EPICs to furnish it at the time of voting. People who did not possess EPICs had to bring the proofs of identity as prescribed by the EC at the time of voting. During the 2007 Punjab Assembly elections, Parneet Kaur (MP from Patiala), could not cast her vote until late afternoon as she had misplaced her voter card. [The Tribune: 2007] The distribution of EPICs, on the part of Election Commission, was a major step to reduce electoral malpractices. Only genuine voters were listed in the rolls with the assurance of voter identity cards.

Observation and conclusion

Over the years, the Election Commission has conducted a number of laudable electoral reforms to strengthen democracy and enhance the fairness of elections. These reforms are quite adequate and admirable. Undoubtedly, the election machinery, under the aegis of the EC, deserves credit for conducting elections in a free and fair manner. However, our system is still plagued by many vices. To win votes, political parties resort to foul methods and corrupt practices.

Such maladies encourage the anti-social elements to enter the electoral fray. The problem is not lack of laws, but lack of their strict implementation. In order to stamp out these unfair tendencies, there is a need to strengthen the hands of the EC and to give it more legal and institutional powers. The EC must be entrusted with powers to punish the errant politicians who transgress and violate the electoral laws.

Our Election Commission tries its best to weed out the virus of malpractices. It is optimistic about strengthening and improving the working of democracy through free and fair elections. It has always devised better systems and is using advanced scientific technologies for maintaining the high reputation of the Indian elections. However, the success of reforms will largely depend upon the will of the political parties to adhere to and implement such reforms. An independent media and an enlightened public opinion have no substitute in pushing through reforms. If people vote according to their convictions and punish those who infract the rules, corrupt practices will automatically disappear. And this will go a long way towards enabling democracy to flourish and grow to its full capacity.

Notes

Jayapraksh Narayanan on behalf of the Citizen for Democracy had appointed a committee to study and report on schemes for electoral reforms in 1974. The members of the committee were V. M. Tarkunde, M. R. Masai, etc. and it is known as J. P. Committee or Tarkunde Committee.

In accordance with the Janata Dal's election commitment, the National Front government announced the appointment of Goswami Committee in the LokSabha on May 4, 1990.

Tirunellai Narayana Iyer Seshan known as T.N. Seshan is best remembered as the man who cleaned up elections in India. He was the Chief Election Commissioner of India, who reformed elections by largely ending its malpractices in the country.

Since 2008, the Election Commission has started implementing SEERS at the national level. One of the features of this is that data entry should be done for all claims regardless of the ultimate fate of application. It has, therefore, become imperative to put in place some system and device a mechanism to provide for continuous operation round the year and handle the RTI applications more effectively.

Reference

1. Alam, Javeed (2004), Who Wants Democracy, New Delhi: Orient Longman Private Ltd.
2. Axtman, Ronald (ed.) (2003), Understanding Democratic Politics, New Delhi: Sage Publications.
3. Bray, Daniel, Steven Slaughter (2015), Global Democratic Theory- A Critical Introduction, Cambridge: Polity Press.
4. Coppedge, Michael (2012), Democratisation and Research Methods, New York: Cambridge University Press.
5. Fadia, B. L. (2002), Indian Polity, New Delhi: Paper Back Publishers.
6. Hasan, Zoya (2002), Parties and Party Politics in India, New Delhi: Oxford University Press.
7. Kothari, Rajni (2005), Rethinking Democracy, New Delhi: Orient Blackswan.
8. Kumar, Venkatesh. B. (2009), Electoral Reforms in India: Current Discourses, New Delhi: Rawat Publications.
9. Nabatchi, Tina, Matt Leighninger (2015), Public Participation in 21st Century Democracy, New Jersey: John Wiley & Sons Inc.
10. Norris, Pippa (2004), Electoral Engineering- Voting Rules and Political Behaviour, Cambridge: Cambridge University Press.
11. Pillai, Raman. K. (2010), Facets of Indian Politics, New Delhi: APH Publishing Corporation.
12. Pinkney, Robert (2014), Democracy in the Third World, New Delhi: Viva Book Private Ltd.
13. Shah, A. M. (ed.) (2007), The Grassroots of Democracy- Field Studies of Indian Elections, New Delhi: Orient Longman Private Ltd.
14. Shapiro, Ian, Casiano Hacker-Cordon (ed.) (1999), Democracy's Edges, Cambridge: Cambridge University Press.
15. Swamy, Ratna. P. (2014), Handbook of Election Law, Noida: Saurabh Printers.
16. Vinaik, Achin, Rajeev Bhargava (ed.) (2010), Understanding Contemporary India- Critical Perspectives, New Delhi: Orient Blackswan.
17. Vora, Rajendra, Suhas Palshikkar (ed.) (2004), Indian Democracy – Meaning and Practices, New Delhi: Sage Publications.
18. Wallace, Paul (ed.) (2015), India's 2014 Elections- A Modi Led BJP Sweep, New Delhi: Sage Publishers.

19. Wallace, Paul, Ramashray Roy (ed.) (2003), India's 1999 Elections and 20th Century politics, New Delhi: Sage Publishers.
20. Wallace, Paul, Ramashray Roy (ed.) (2011), India's 2009 Elections-Coalition Politics, Party Competition and Congress Continuity, New Delhi: Sage Publishers.

3

Socio-cultural Mobilization through Welfare Programme: A Case of Indira Awaas Yojana Scheme (IAY) in Kashmir valley

— *Dr Manzoor Hussain, Gousia Yaseen*

Abstract

This study is carried out in order to note the social implications at the ground level that have taken place in the study area as a result of the implementation of this scheme. Four blocks from District Anantnag were selected as a universe of the study. Later on, required data was collected from beneficiary respondents through simple random sampling technique. An interview schedule was used as a research tool. As per findings of the study, the houses sanctioned under the scheme provided ownership and identity to the beneficiaries and affords psychological satisfaction and provided self-worth and confidence. Further, the houses supported livelihood and allowed social integration, enhanced social status and brought partial social mobility among the beneficiaries. The paper provides insight into the criteria of IAY Scheme and enables us to assess the socio-cultural impact of IAY Scheme on the beneficiary respondents. This study was conducted in a single district; therefore the findings may not be applicable to all the districts of Kashmir valley. However, the paper provides insight into the criteria of IAY Scheme and enables us to assess the socio-cultural impact of IAY Scheme on the beneficiary respondents.

Keywords: *Socio-cultural Mobalization, Public Policy, Indira Awaas Yojana, Social status, Anantnag district.*

Introduction

The term 'housing' embodies the whole network of services and amenities available to make a reasonable and comfortable living. It is one of the basic needs for the survival of human beings in a society and is not just a roof over the four walls but an extension of human personality and an abode where children take birth grow and acquire the decency and morality. Thus, housing satisfies a basic need next to food and clothing and provides social status, economic security and status for every normal person. For those who do not have it, its ownership brings in a profound social change in the existence endowed with an identity integrating the person with the immediate social milieu (Singh, H. et.al. 2004). Generally, the problem of housing is everywhere. However, it becomes acuter for those fighting with poverty. A large segment of the population lives in kutcha houses made of mud with a roof of grass and tree leaves, lacking all the basic amenities. So, those poor persons, especially from Scheduled Castes, Scheduled Tribes, economically weaker sections and victims of natural calamities, need special attention of the government in this regard.

The provision of shelter to all the needy poor is a basic need and has become a big challenge for ensuring dignified living. Adequate housing is not just the mere provision of four walls and a roof but implies access to basic services such as water, electricity, sanitation, healthcare, education, livelihood and security of tenure, all of which are essential for dignified living, personal growth and social wellbeing in a productive society. Making these services available as a part of habitat development can be ensured through the convergence of schemes and mutual efforts of the government, the private sector and the people themselves (Reddy, G.Y. et al. 2014). Housing is one of the basic requirements for the survival of human beings. The identity and social recognition associated with ownership of a house provide an individual with immense confidence to get involved in many social activities. Stable, affordable and accessible housing is directly and indirectly linked to human well-being. One can easily understand the socio-economic status of a family just by watching physical attributes of their housing.

Good housing and its surroundings indicate the standard of living of the family; it provides facilities for education, recreation and many other facets of life. A person deprived of this basic need faces all odds of life and remains discriminated and marginalized in the society. Housing contributes significantly towards the configuration of cultured human existence.

Around one-third of the human populations in urban as well as rural areas in the country are deprived of adequate housing facilities. Out of the estimated 200 million families in India, approximately 65 to 70 million families do not have adequate housing facilities. They are not able to procure a house for want of financial resources. The situation of the Scheduled Tribes, Scheduled Castes and the other socially and economically backward class families is worst affected by poor housing conditions (Indian Planning Commission, 2013). Hence, fulfilling the need for rural housing and tackling housing shortage particularly for the poorest is an important task to be undertaken as part of the poverty alleviation efforts of the government. Considering the need and importance, Government of India and various state governments are implementing several programmes to meet the housing needs of rural poor (Indian Planning Commission, 2013). Indira Awaas Yojana is one of an important programme of housing primarily for the members of Below Poverty Line (BPL) population.

Nature and Scope of Indira Awaas Yojana (IAY)

Initially, the scheme of Indira Awaas Yojana (IAY) was meant for providing dwelling units free of cost to the rural poor, i.e. Freed Bonded Labourers (FBLs) living below poverty line, members of Scheduled Caste (SC), Scheduled Tribe (ST) households, SC and ST households headed by widow and unmarried women, SC and ST households affected by flood, fire, earthquake, cyclone and similar natural calamities but from 1993-94 its scope has been extended to cover Non Scheduled Castes (NSCs) and Non Scheduled Tribe (NST) rural poor. The benefits of the scheme have also been extended to families of servicemen of the armed and paramilitary forces killed in action subject to the condition that:

(i) They reside in rural areas,

(ii) They have not been covered under any other scheme of shelter rehabilitation, and

(iii) They are houseless or in need of shelter or shelter up gradation.

Since, three per cent of the houses under the scheme are reserved for Below Poverty Line (BPL) disabled persons in rural areas and (Choudhury, R.C. et al. 1999). Thus, its scope has been extended to cover almost all strata of the rural poor population. IAY is centrally sponsored scheme with the resources being shared on 75:25 per cent bases between Centre and State respectively (Prashar, S.B. 2010). The IAY has proved to be a popular scheme and its targets have been exceeded in almost every year since its inception. The IAY is being implemented by State Governments through District Rural Development Agency (DRDA) specially set up in each district in each state of the country. At the district level, Deputy Commissioner (DC) is responsible for implementing the scheme, Block Development Officer (BDO) is responsible for implementing the scheme at the block level and Panchayat/ Gram Sabah is responsible for selection of beneficiaries at the village level (Prashar, S.B. 2010).

Literature Review

Selvarajan, E.et.al. (2004) in this work has talked that improvements in housing conditions in the villages have manifold significance. Housing encourages economic activities, generates employment opportunities and creates a solid base for healthy and hygienic living. It was revealed by Selvarajan that the houses constructed under the IAY Scheme have created four positive externalities to the beneficiaries. They were employments in construction, an increase in social status, trees and plants are grown and income from construction work. The first externality was that construction of houses generates employment opportunities. The Government has insisted that the beneficiary has to involve in the construction activities to ensure the quality of construction and also they can get some additional employment. The second positive externality was the increase in social status. The beneficiaries of the houses earlier lived in the huts or thatched roof houses. The provision of concrete house in the structured area would have witnessed the social status of the community. The third externality was trees and plants grown in their houses offered by the Government at free of cost which may help them to meet their needs. Another externality was income from the construction work.

Parvathamma, C.et.al. (1987) in this work has highlighted housing conditions faced by people of India and Karnataka and has also mentioned the socio-economic conditions of rural poor and houseless. It was discussed by him that men live in a world which poses many threats to their security. The cultures that men create represent ways of adapting to these threats to security. Housing, as an element of material culture, was one such device to overcome threats against physical security to life and serves an important purpose by making the provisions of shelter. The house serves the common purposes of feeding the members, working, sleeping, child rearing, entertaining leisure and many more activities. It helps people to interact with the family and with the outside world. Almost every person was affected in his day to day living with the kind of house in which he lives. Many people, particularly housewives, children and elders spend most of the time in the home than in any other single place. Therefore, a house becomes the place where individuals can exercise maximum autonomy. Housing conditions design the individual's place in the society and the country's progress at large. In this senses, the housing conditions should consist of both the physical and social contexts which would naturally reflect the living conditions of the people.

According to Rao, M.V. (2012) to man, a house is a physical, social, economic and psychological security. A house to a man was a symbol of prestige and identity. Creating this identity for the rural poor was a necessary step in improving their life. Rural housing increases economic activities, raises the quality of life and creates substantial employment opportunities for the rural poor. A government in order to promote the socio-economic development of the weaker sections has launched various housing schemes for scheduled castes, scheduled tribes and various other economically poor sections of the society. It was discussed by the Rao that the rural housing was one of the ambitious projects which have been implemented in India since 1957 under the community development movement. Under this movement, a loan of Rs 5000 was given to individuals and cooperatives for each house but due to inadequate coverage and non-fulfilment of the needs of rural poor, another scheme housing site-cum construction assistance was launched in the fourth five-year plan. This scheme was later transferred to the states by the recommendations of the national development council. From the beginning of the year 1980, the most popular scheme Indira Awaas Yojana (IAY) Scheme was implemented under the National Rural Employment Programmes (NREP) which became part of rural landless employment guarantee programme. Later, both of these programmes were merged with the Jawahar Rozgar Yojana (JRY) in April 1989. During 1985-86 IAY was implemented which was fully Subsidized Centrally Sponsored Scheme shared on 80:20 basis by the Centre and the State. In the year 1993-94, a new Rural Housing Scheme (RHS) was launched by the Central Government under which funds were provided by the Ministry of Rural Areas and Employment (MRAE) to the State Government. This scheme was later on merged with IAY with effect from January 1996. Thus IAY was the only Central Scheme for housing in rural areas.

Mohapatra, A. K. (2012) has discussed "basic need" approach which involves six strategy areas at a global level. These are health, basic education, nutrition, water supply, sanitation and housing. The degree of deprivation and socio-economic exclusion in the society can be measured by using all these strategic areas. Out of these housing is the most important basic need of mankind in terms of safety, security, self-esteem, social status, self-satisfaction and for sustainable development. A good house not only supports health, environment and quality of life but is also considered as an indicator of prosperity and growth of an individual and the country. The housing sector has multiple effects on economic growth and employment. It generates large-scale employment directly and indirectly to a cross-section of people. It also creates avenues and opportunities for dwelling based activities too. Miloon Kothari has rightly said that the human right to adequate housing is the right of every woman, man, youth and child to gain and sustain a secure home and community in which to live in peace and dignity. It was revealed by Mohapatra that the emphasis on rural housing should be more and more on inclusiveness and on quality improvement. When a poor man owns a house, it helps in giving him a self-identity. The housing sector has a positive impact on the overall standard of living of the rural people. Micro-housing financial institutions should be promoted and to be supported by the Government at the rural level so as to provide various types of credit to the rural poor either for construction purposes or for repairing of houses. Rural shelterless people need to be encouraged for their saving habit by offering the higher rate of interest. The reasonable rate of interest should be charged by banks on loans for credit cum subsidy scheme for rural housing and it has to be regulated by the Government from time to time. The Government should support various schemes of rural housing and ensure quality improvement in rural housing from time to time. Hence deliberate efforts have to be taken by the Government in rural areas for the betterment of deprived segments of the society in the planning process.

Mahadeva, M. (2004) in this work has analysed the condition of housing in India. He has discussed that there has been an increasing emphasis on the development of housing with important basic amenities on the integrated basis. This is because the housing unit as a physical structure provides security, protection and privacy to mankind, and amenities help to fulfil the human needs of the society. In fact, it has been argued that the quality of life is obviously determined by the availability and quality of housing and amenities. Also, social justice is one of the national goals of every country could also be ensured with a proper and equitable distribution of these facilities among the population. Providing integrated development of housing and other basic amenities to the people has various advantages. The most advantage would be that if all these facilities were planned simultaneously they would be less costly and more appropriate in terms of time. Otherwise, if they were planned in isolation not only will the cost of individual shoot up, but also it will take its own time to develop them. This uncertainty would only lead to non-fulfilment of basic human needs and increased deprivation. Therefore the objectives of human settlement policies should be to make the shelter as well amenities available to those who need them at a given social cost. It was also discussed by Mahadeva that if the goal of development was to bring about quality in the living standard, acceptable standard of the housing along with the provision of housing amenities like electricity, drinking water, toilet facilities was a precondition. Non-supply of any of these services or even their deficiency would lead to substandard quality of living. India was a typical example of substandard quality and habitation because neither in the case of development of standard housing nor in the supply of housing amenities, Indian strategies have covered the total population. Only 42 per cent of the total households have standard housing, the rest of the families have either constructed semi-standard or substandard housing units for their dwelling purposes and eventually these units would not have been provided with either of the facilities on the basis of which, states and union territories have been categorized as highly performed, moderately performed and low performed.

Butt, R. (2014) in this article has laid much emphasis on utilization, protection, enhancement of the natural, physical and human resources needed to make long-term improvement in rural living conditions. The author has revealed that rural development planning has become a concern as it was clear that the strategies adopted in developing countries has remained largely ineffective in alleviating poverty and inequalities in rural areas. There was a widely shared view that the essence of the rural development should be poverty alleviation and distributive justice oriented economic transformation. But speaking from the Kashmir centric viewpoint, we find none of these objectives getting realized. We find urbanization rampant and rural people disenchanted with their living conditions and always worrying about moving up the ladder of social development at the cost of traditional rural centric economy or value system. Panchayats have not been perceived as really empowering or contributing to the comprehensive concept of development.

Research Methodology

The Universe of the Study: The universe of the present study constitutes district Anantnag. It comprises of 8 community development blocks, 140 Panchayats and 645 villages. The blocks constitute; Shahabad, Achabal, Shangas, Qoimoh, Bring, Qazigund, Hoverport and Dachnipora

Sampling Plan and Design of the Study: The present study is based on a sample of 250 respondents selected from only 4 blocks (Achabal, Shangus, Shahabad, and Kohvirepora) out of 8 blocks of the district Anantnag. A list of Indira Awaas Yojana (IAY) beneficiary of these selected blocks was taken from Department of Rural Development (DRD). Later, on a simple random sampling technique was used to collect information from IAY beneficiaries. Besides, village community members and socially notable persons were approached to identify the respondents. For the present study, an 'evaluative research design' was used. The reasons for such a type of design were mainly methodological since the problem under investigation demands to critically examine the social implications of IAY Scheme and its impact on the beneficiaries.

Techniques and Sources of Data Collection:To carry out this study, the techniques of interview schedule and observation were used to get objective and reliable findings. The reasons for such kind of choice were mainly sociological and methodological, since the majority of our beneficiaries in the district were illiterate. The present study involved both primary and secondary sources of data collection. For primary sources, first-hand information was collected through interview schedule and observation in the field. The secondary source of information is based on books, journal papers, unpublished thesis, etc. available on the topic.

The Objectives of the Study:

1. to explain the implications of IAY scheme on social mobility among beneficiary respondents in the study area,
2. to evaluate the impact of IAY Scheme on the social status of the beneficiary respondents in the study area,
3. to trace the improvement brought by IAY scheme in the living standard of the beneficiary respondents in the study area.

Results and Discussions

This paper discuses with Enhancement of social status, Improvement in living standard, Social mobility experienced, Effect on dress pattern, Changes experienced in behaviour, and Respect gained in society.

Enhancement of social status to Indira Awaas Yojana (IAY) scheme

Housing is the most important basic need of mankind in terms of safety, security, self-esteem, social status and self-satisfaction. In the present study, the beneficiaries were asked to state whether the houses received by them under the Indira Awaas Yojana (IAY) Scheme has enabled them to experience enhancement in their status in the society. It can be observed from findings of the study shown in table 4.1 that out of the total sample of 250 beneficiary respondents, the majority of 239 beneficiary respondents (95.60 percent) agreed and only 11 beneficiary respondents (4.40 percent) strongly agreed that they have experienced an enhancement in their social status due to the benefits received by them under IAY scheme. It was because of the reason that the beneficiaries earlier lived in the thatched roof houses, the provision of concrete houses under IAY scheme has enabled them to witness the increase in their social status.

Table 1: Enhancement in social status due to IAY scheme

Sl. No.	*Enhancement in social status due to benefits of IAY scheme*	*Number*	*Percentage*
1.	Strongly Disagree	-	-
2.	Disagree	-	-
3.	Neither Disagree nor Agree	-	-
4.	Agree	239	95.60
5.	Strongly Agree	11	4.40
	Total	**250**	**100.00**

Improvement in living standard due to Indira Awaas Yojana (IAY) scheme

From the below table, it becomes clear that the majority of 146 beneficiary respondents (58.40 percent) agreed and 62 beneficiary respondents (24.80 percent) strongly agreed that their living standard has improved due to the benefits received under IAY scheme. The beneficiaries responded that the IAY scheme has provided us concrete houses; sanitary latrines thus raised the quality of life, created better conditions for life in terms of health, hygiene, and better environmental conditions. Providing a house to a beneficiary has a positive impact on beneficiaries' physical and mental health. By fulfilling this basic need of life, beneficiaries develop a sense of opportunity for livelihood, for improving living conditions. Thus, there is a direct link between a safe and secure housing to better standards of living. It was also found that 42 beneficiary respondents (16.80 percent) disagreed that there has been no improvement in their living standard due to IAY scheme because they felt that the houses provided to them under the scheme were not able to maintain privacy of their family members due to inadequate number of rooms and also the houses were not having good and quality kitchen.

Table 2: Improvement in living standard due to IAY scheme

Sl. Nol	*Improvement in living standard due to IAY scheme*	*Number*	*Percentage*
1.	Strongly Disagree	-	-
2.	Disagree	42	16.80
3.	Neither Disagree nor Agree	-	-
4.	Agree	146	58.40
5.	Strongly Agree	62	24.80
	Total	**250**	**100.00**

Social mobility experienced by Indira Awaas Yojana (IAY) scheme

Individuals are normally recognized in society through the status they occupy and the roles they enact. Not only the society is dynamic but also individuals are dynamic. Thus people in society continue to move up and down the status scale. This movement of an individual or group from one social class or social stratum to another is called social mobility. The beneficiary respondents have been asked to mention whether they have experienced social mobility by Indira Awaas Yojana (IAY) Scheme. It was found (see table 4.3 below) that out of 250 beneficiary respondents, the majority of 162 beneficiary respondents (64.80 percent) agreed that they have experienced partial social mobility and 88 beneficiary respondents (35.20 percent) strongly disagreed that they do not have experienced social mobility by IAY scheme. By fulfilling the housing need of the beneficiaries, the IAY scheme has definitely enabled them to pay their attention to other needs of life and helped them to bring improvement in their living standards. The provision of concrete houses under the scheme has provided more respect to the beneficiaries in the society and has enabled them to achieve self-respect, self-esteem and enhancement in their social status. But the scheme has not enabled the beneficiaries to experience change in their social class.

Table 3: Social mobility experienced by IAY scheme

Sl. No.	*Partial social mobility experienced by IAY scheme*	*Number*	*Percentage*
1.	Strongly Disagree	88	35.20
2.	Disagree	-	-
3.	Neither Disagree nor Agree	-	-
4.	Agree	162	64.80
5.	Strongly Agree	-	-
	Total	**250**	**100.00**

Effect on dress pattern due to Indira Awaas Yojana (IAY) scheme

An attempt was made in the study to explore the impact of IAY scheme on the dress pattern of the beneficiaries. Enquiring into this aspect, the beneficiaries have been asked to express their views. It was found (see table 4.4 below) that out of 250 beneficiary respondents, the majority of 152 beneficiary respondents (60.80 percent) disagreed

Table 4: Effect on dress pattern due to IAY scheme

Sl. No.	*Effect on dress pattern due to IAY scheme*	*Number*	*Percentage*
1.	Strongly Disagree	152	60.80
2.	Disagree	94	37.60
3.	Neither Disagree nor Agree	-	-
4.	Agree	-	-
5.	Strongly Agree	4	1.60
	Total	**250**	**100.00**

and 94 beneficiary respondents (37.60 percent) strongly disagreed that IAY scheme has brought changes in their dress pattern and only a minority of 4 beneficiary respondents (1.60 percent) agreed that they have experienced change in their dress pattern due to IAY scheme. Thus from the above findings of the study, it becomes evident that the IAY scheme has not laid any direct impact in changing the dress pattern of the beneficiaries.

Changes experienced in behaviour due to Indira Awaas Yojana (IAY) scheme

Table 4.5 below shows that out of 250 beneficiary respondents, the majority of 217 beneficiary respondents (86.80 percent) agreed and 27 beneficiary respondents (10.80 percent) strongly agreed that they have experienced changes in their behaviour due to IAY scheme and only a minority of 6 beneficiary respondents (2.40 percent) disagreed that they do not have experienced any change in their behaviour due to this scheme. The beneficiaries responded that earlier they lived in thatched and unserviceable houses; the provision of concrete houses under the scheme has enhanced their social status, improved their living standard and has helped them to acquire more respect in the society. They further responded that earlier the open fields around their houses were used as open air lavatories but the provision of sanitary latrines under the IAY scheme has enabled them in stopping this unhygienic practice, provided them self-respect and thus brought changes in their habits. Thus the findings of the study clearly reveal that the IAY scheme has brought changes in the behaviour of the beneficiaries.

Table 5: Changes experienced in behaviour due to IAY scheme

Sl. No.	*Changes experienced in behaviour due to IAY scheme*	*Number*	*Percentage*
1.	Strongly Disagree	-	-
2.	Disagree	6	2.40
3.	Neither Disagree nor Agree	-	-
4.	Agree	217	86.80
5.	Strongly Agree	27	10.80
	Total	**250**	**100.00**

Respect gained in society due to Indira Awaas Yojana (IAY) scheme

It was found that out of 250 beneficiary respondents, the majority of 192 beneficiary respondents (76.80 percent) agreed and 56 beneficiary respondents (22.40 percent) strongly agreed that they have gained more respect in the society by IAY scheme. These beneficiaries have realized that they are given more respect in society now than they were given before receiving the comfortable house under IAY scheme and only a minority of 2 beneficiary respondents (0.80 percent) disagreed that this scheme has not helped them to gain respect in society in any way.

Table 6: Respect gained in society due to IAY scheme

Sl. No	*Respect gained in society due to IAY scheme*	*Number*	*Percentage*
1.	Strongly Disagree	-	-
2.	Disagree	2	0.80
3.	Neither Disagree nor Agree	-	-
4.	Agree	192	76.80
5.	Strongly Agree	56	22.40
	Total	**250**	**100.00**

The provision of concrete houses under the scheme has helped them to experience enhancement in their status, improvement in their living standard, and has helped them to achieve dignity in the society. The identity and social recognition associated with ownership of a house provided the beneficiaries self-identity and immense confidence to get involved into many social activities. Housing is one of the basic needs of life and a person deprived of this basic need faces all odds of life and remains discriminated and marginalized in the society. Thus the above findings reveal that the IAY scheme has fulfilled this basic need of beneficiaries and has enabled them to receive respect in the society.

Observation and conclusion

The findings of the study depict that almost all the beneficiary respondents agreed that they have experienced enhancement in their social status, because the beneficiaries earlier lived in Thatched and

Kutcha houses, the provision of concrete houses under the IAY Scheme has enabled them to witness increase in their social status; 83.20 per cent of beneficiary respondents have realised that the IAY Scheme has improved their living standards in terms of health, hygiene and better environmental conditions and has laid a positive impact on the beneficiaries physical and mental health; 64.80 per cent beneficiary respondents agreed that they have experienced partial social mobility by acquiring new houses under the IAY Scheme. About 98.40 per cent beneficiary respondents have responded that the scheme has not brought direct change in their dress pattern and eating habits but the findings of the study also indicate that 97.60 per cent beneficiary respondents agreed that the scheme has brought change in their behaviour. They have responded that earlier they used to pass their urine in the open fields but the provision of sanitary latrines under the scheme has helped them in stopping this unhygienic practice, the provision of concrete houses has improved their living standard, helped them to acquire more respect in the society and thus brought changes in their behaviour.

Indira Awaas Yojana (IAY) Scheme is the very beneficial scheme and has many advantages for an uplift of people living in the society especially poor. The main focus of the scheme has been to raise the poor families Above Poverty Line (APL) by fulfilling one of the basic needs of their life. As per findings of the study, the scheme has laid a positive impact on the accommodation, health, hygiene and environment of the beneficiaries by providing them with a house, sanitary latrine and drinking water facility and thus it has been a means for a better life. Besides, the houses sanctioned under the scheme provided ownership and identity to the beneficiaries and affords psychological satisfaction and provided self-worth and confidence. Further, the houses supported livelihood and allowed social integration, enhanced social status and brought partial social mobility among the beneficiaries. In other words, the scheme has laid a positive impact on the beneficiaries' physical and mental wellbeing and brought a profound improvement in the overall quality of life of rural people. Thus, it can be said that there is a direct link between a safe and secure housing to better standards of living and reduction in vulnerability. However, the study has identified several problems associated with the selection and implementation of IAY Scheme. Selection rules of the scheme are clearly stated in the programme guidelines of Ministry of Rural Development, however, the implementing agencies were not able to strictly follow the guidelines in the selection process of the scheme due to which there remains loopholes which need to be reduced for its effective implementation.

References

1. Singh, H. et.al. (2004). Social Housing Programmes for the Ruralities: A Case of Indian Punjab. *International Conference, Centre for Urban and Community Studies, University of Toronto*. p. 1.
2. Reddy, G.Y. et al. (2014). Transparent Selection: A Case of IAY Programme. *International Multidisciplinary Research Journal*, 3(12), pp.1-7. Retrieved on 17.8.2014 from http: www.isrj.net.
3. Indian Planning Commission, Evaluation Study of IAY. 2013. p. 1.
4. Choudhury, R.C. et al. (1999). *Basic Rural Infrastructure and Services for Improved Quality of Life*. Hyderabad: NIRD Publication, p.632.
5. Prashar, S.B. (2010). Policy Environment, Performance and Efficacy of Indira Awaas Yojana in Haryana. *Political Economy Journal of India* 19(2) p. 89.
6. Selvarajan, E. *et al.* (2004). *Rural Development Programmes and Externalities*. New Delhi: Serials publication, pp. 628.
7. Parvathamma, C. et al. (1987). *Housing Rural Poor and Their Living Conditions*. New Delhi: Gian Publication, pp.136.
8. Rao, M.V, Rural Housing in India: Lessons Learnt and Challenges to be Met. In Choudhury, R.C. et al. (1999). *Basic Rural Infrastructure and Services for Improved Quality of Life*. Hyderabad: NIRD Publication, pp. 659-673.
9. Mohapatra, A.K. (2012). Rural Housing: The Core of Rural Infrastructure. *Kurukshetra*, 60 (12), pp. 36-41.
10. Mahadeva, M. (2004). Housing and Amenities in India: An Explanation Towards Development and Deprivation. *Man and Development*, XXVI (2), pp. 25-39.
11. Butt, R. (2014). Rural Development: Ideal and Reality. *Greater Kashmir*, Srinagar.

4

Socio-Economic Status of Transgender: A study with Special Reference to Dharwad District in Karnataka

— *Dr Anji. A, Dr A.Ranjithkumar*

Abstract

The term of transgender was created in the 1990's by epidemiologists to study the spread of disease among men who have sex with men, regardless of identity. The term MSM is often used in medical literature and social research to describe such men as a group for research studies without considering issues of self-identification. The contemporary term "transgender" arose in the mid-1990 from the grassroots community of gender-different peoples. They are facing problem in a different manner across the world. Hence, this research paper deals with the current situation of the Transgender's Community of Hubli-Dharwad district of North Karnataka. This study focus on Socio-Cultural, Economical, Political, Psychological, Biological, Educational, unemployment and Health problems of Transgender community and to analyses the various Government Policies and Schemes for Transgender Community. In this paper, we have used case study method.

Key words: *Transgender, Socio-Cultural Status, Economical, Psychological, Unemployment, Health.*

Introduction

The term of transgender was created in the 1990's by epidemiologists to study the spread of disease among men who have sex with men, regardless of identity. The term MSM is often used in medical literature and social research to describe such men as a group for research studies without considering issues of self-identification. The contemporary term "transgender" arose in the mid-1990 from the grassroots community of gender-different people. In contemporary usage, transgender has become an "umbrella" term that is used to describe a wide range of identities and experiences, including but not limited to transsexual people; male and female cross-dressers, intersexes individuals; and men and women. In its broadest sense, transgender encompasses anyone whose identity or behaviour falls outside of stereotypical gender norms. These people are sometimes called transsexual if they desire medical assistance to transition from one sex to another. Transgender is also an umbrella term: in addition to including people whose gender identity is the opposite of their assigned sex, it may include people who are not exclusively masculine or feminine. Other definitions of transgender also include people who belong to a third gender or conceptualize transgender people as a third gender. The objectives of the study are: To find out Socio-cultural Problems of Transgenders in Dharwad District, To find out the psychological Problems of Transgenders in Dharwad District, and 3. To analyze the Government Policies and Schemes for Transgender

Sampling

Structured self-reporting technique will be used to collect the data. Permission will be taken from samples and an informed consent will be obtained from the samples. In Hubli-Dharwad district according to Government institute RUDA Rural and Urban Development Association, there are 1057 MSM, out of which 32 are transgenders registered and many are migrated to Bangalore, Hyderabad, Puna and to some other places. So because of lack of availability of many respondents, a researcher has taken Case study i.e 5 respondents. The respondents were of different age groups, caste groups, religion, Kothi, Panthi, Transgenders and differentiated in their geographical areas.

Study Area

Hubli-Dharwad is a twin city in the Indian state of Karnataka. Hubli-Dharwad is the second-largest conurbation in Karnataka after

Bengaluru. While Dharwad is the administrative headquarters and the city of Hubli, situated about 20 km south-east of Dharwad, is the commercial centre and business hub of North Karnataka. The cities have a single municipal corporation called Hubli-Dharwad Municipal Corporation (HDMC). Hubli-Dharwad Municipal Corporation is the municipal corporation for twin cities of Hubli and Dharwad in Karnataka state in India. It was constituted in 1962 by combining two cities separated by a distance of 20 kilometres. The area covered by the corporation is 181.66 km^2. spread over 45 revenue villages. The population of the twin cities as per the 2011 census is 943,857 of which 475,980 are males and 467,877 are female. Total literates are 736,506 of which 389,290 are males while 347,216 are female. The average literacy rate of Hubli and Dharwad city is 87.28 per cent of which male and female literacy was 91.67 and 82.83.In Hubli-Dharwad, there are 1057 MSM's and out of which 32 are Transgenders registered. The population of Hubli-Dharwad, as per provisional census 2011 figures, is 1,349,563. Hubli-Dharwad's population increased 22.99% between 1981 and 1991, from 527,108 to 648,298; and by 21.2% between 1991 and 2001. The corporation covers 202 km2. The primary data was collected from the transgender in selected areas of Dharwad old bus stand, Azad Park and R .N Shetty ground and from other geographical areas. The primary data were collected from various individual respondents in the month of June 2017 in Hubli- Dharwad district through RUDA- Rural and Urban Development Association, Dharwad. The Sampling Criteria is People who are willing to participate in this study, People who know Kannada and English, People present at the time of data collection.

Transgender Terminology In India

Hijra –biologically, male who rejects his 'masculine' identity to identify either as woman, or"not-man",or "in-between man and woman", or "neither man nor woman". They have a long-standing tradition/culture in Indian society and have strong social ties formalized through a ritual called "reet" (becoming a member of Hijra community). There are regional variations in the use of terms referred to Hijras. For example, Kinnars (Delhi) and Aravanis (Tamil Nadu). Eunuch – a person who is born male but is castrated or emasculated. The term

Eunuch is commonly used interchangeably with the term Hijra in India. However many transgender persons consider the term 'eunuch' to be derogatory. This was confirmed by the group in Bhubaneswar, who did not care for this term. Kinnar– regional variation of Hijra used in in Delhi/ the North and other parts of India such as Maharashtra. Aravani – regional variation of Hijra used in Tamil Nadu. Some Aravani activists want the public and media to use the term 'Thirunangi' to refer to Aravanis. Kothi - biological male who shows varying degrees of 'femininity.' Some proportion of Hijras may also identify themselves as 'Kothis,' but not all Kothis identify themselves as transgender or Hijras. Shiv-Shakthi - males who are possessed by or particularly close to a Goddess and who have feminine expression, typically located in Andhra Pradesh. Jogtas/Jogappas-are those persons who are dedicated to and serve as the servant of Goddess Renuka Devi (Yellamma) whose temples are present in Maharashtra and Karnataka.'Jogti Hijras' is used to describe male-to-female transgender persons who are devotees/ servants of Goddess Renuka Devi. This differs from 'Jogtas' who are usually heterosexuals and who may or may not dress in woman's attire when they worship the Goddess. Guru/Chela-While some transgender Indians voluntarily leave home to join transgender communities, many of them are abandoned by their families, who are not accepting of their child's transgender status. It is for this reason that they form their own close-knit family-like units, led by a 'guru,' - an older leader that acts as a mentor to their younger disciples or 'chela.'It is often the case in these communities that the guru takes payment from her chela, in exchange for providing her with her material subsistence. This has led to concerns that some chela may be at risk of exploitation by their gurus.

Review Of Literature

Subramanium (2011) Social Welfare Report of Ministry of social welfare. A government of India. His revival of the term transgender (TG) which was popularized in the 1970's (but implied in the 1960) describing people who wanted to live cross-gender without sex reassignment surgery. In the 1980's the term was expanded to an umbrella term and became popular as a means of uniting all those whose gender identity did not mesh with their gender assigned at birth.

In the 1990's, the term took on a political dimension as an alliance covering all who have at some point not conformed to gender norms, and the term became used to question the validity of those norms or pursue equal rights and anti-discrimination legislation, leading to its widespread usage in the media, academic world and law. The term continues to evolve. The population of hijras in India is estimated to be between 50,000 and 1.2 million. There is a huge disparity in the numbers because population censuses only give space to define either males or females. There are no reliable statistics. Tamil Nadu in a path-breaking move has come to recognize transgenders – (the term itself is no monolith as transgender is more of an umbrella term). Most hijras live at the margins of society with very low status; the very word "hijra" is sometimes used in a derogatory manner. Few employment opportunities are available to hijras. Many get their income from performing at ceremonies, begging, or sex work—an occupation of eunuchs also recorded in premodern times. Violence against hijras, especially hijra sex workers, is often brutal and occurs in public spaces, police stations, prisons, and their homes. As with transgender people in most of the world, they face extreme discrimination in health, housing, education, employment, immigration, law, and any bureaucracy that is unable to place them into male or female gender categories.

Thilakaravi (2011) "Mental Health Concerns of Transgender Population Living in Chennai, South India – A Study" A research study has documented the link between mental health disorders and discrimination. The coming-out process for an older LGBT person, who has lived most of his or her life in a hostile or intolerant environment, can induce significant stress and contribute to lower life satisfaction and self-esteem. Managing social stressors such as prejudice, stigmatization, violence, and internalized homophobia over long periods of time results in higher risks of depression, suicide, risky behaviour, and substance abuse. LGBT populations, therefore, may be at increased risk for these and other mental disorders. There may be a higher lifetime prevalence of affective disorders in LGBT persons, but no difference in current prevalence of such disorders. However, while little is known about the actual prevalence of mental health disorders in LGBT adults, even less is known about the prevalence of mental health disorders in older LGBT adults.

Mark J Simone, ed al., (2011) "Clinical paediatrics. Addressing the Needs of Older Lesbian, Gay, Bisexual, and Transgender Adults" A study examined the relationship between psychological well-being variables (i.e., depression, anxiety, and self-esteem) and level of outness in male-to-female (M t F) transsexuals. Participants were 105 M t F transsexual attendees at an annual transgender conference held in Atlanta, Georgia. Participants completed seven questionnaires, including the Demographics Questionnaire, the Outness Demographics Questionnaire, the Outness Attitude Scale, the Openness Scale, the Beck Depression Inventory-II, the Beck Anxiety Inventory, and the Rosenberg Self-Esteem Scale. A canonical correlation was conducted with psychological well-being variables as the predictor and the outness variables as the criterion. Results indicated that psychological well-being variables are related to outness. Treatment implications, limitations, and suggestions for future research are discussed.

Arnold H.G, Anthony R. D.(2010) "Transgender Youth. Life-Threatening Behaviours" A recent study was undertaken to understand the level of General wellbeing of Male-to-female (MTF) Transgender population living in Chennai shed light on the mental health concerns of the transgender population in Chennai. The study consisted of transgender (n=33), and that had been selected for the study by using Purposive sampling technique because it was a challenge to collect data from the population, given their obscurity. A standardized Tamil version of the Wellbeing Questionnaire-12 was used. As for the results of the quantitative data, 75.76 per cent of the samples fell under Average Wellbeing Category, 24.24 per cent of samples fell under Better Wellbeing Category and 0 per cent fell under Poor Wellbeing Category. From the In-Depth Interviews, it is inferred that the socio-economic status of Transgender is very poor, they feel inferior to others and are constantly humiliated and ill-treated by the society at large. However, support within the community is strong.

Jeffrey D Strain and I Michael Shuff (2010) " Psychological Well-Being and Level of Outness in a Population of Male-to-Female Transsexual Women" A study conducted on the fear of experiencing discrimination often provoke symptoms of psychological distress. One coping resource is positive identification with one's social group—known as collective self-esteem. This preliminary study investigated whether collective self-esteem was related to fears regarding a transsexual identity and psychological distress among 53 self-identified male-to-female transsexuals (mean age = 50.79 years). Participants were recruited from transgender events held in Arizona and California. The majority (81 percent) reported living full-time as women (mean length of time living as a woman = 6.33 years). Negative feelings about the transsexual community and fears regarding the impact of a transsexual identity were positively related to psychological distress. A regression model revealed that the fear of how a transsexual identity would affect one's life was the best predictor of the severity of psychological distress. These results are consistent with findings from other historically marginalized groups, whereby the stress of being stigmatized by society adversely affects mental health.

Case: 1

The name of a respondent is Roshini of 35 years old; her name was changed from Abdul to Roshini at the age of 16. Her parents are Akbar Soudagar and Raziya Begum, she was transited from a male to female (MTF), Belongs to Muslim religion and belongs to Belgaum Bendi Bazaar Gharana. She has completed her 7th std at Dharwad Government school, her hobbies are playing badminton, cooking, riding etc. She has a brother and a sister, now she is staying with her community at Hubli, she is suffering from back pain and cold cough frequently and undergoing ICTS HIV/AIDS test once in a month, she is a sex worker and a leader of her community attending in various fights for rights. She is single and offers prayer at Masjid, the respondent said that, she was discriminated by her family and always by the society and they saw her with suspicious attitude, she likes to dress up like a Women and wear satla (local word used for women dress), she takes Part in NGO and CBO's. She is getting 500/- pension from the government under "Mytri Yojane" scheme. She doesn't do any physical exercises or meditation. She has not undergone any SRS surgery.She has fear in meeting new people. She is not ashamed of anything or depressed; she likes to stay alone when depressed or hurt by any other persons. Sometimes she feels loneliness. Her main work is Prostitution, she earns 20,000 -24,000/- per month. She has the problem in a shelter she has a rented home and often migrating to different cities. She has the bank account at State Bank of India. She has no land property; she has the Ration card and gets sugar, wheat, rice and kerosene from State Government for subsidised rates. She has a facility of safe drinking water and toilet at her home. She uses mobile phone, TV, refrigerator and a two-wheeler vehicle. She has no election card but she has applied in Corporation Dharwad and she has no Aadhar card and she is interested to work in Politics in local body elections and she is a well-known leader of her community of Hubli-Dharwad district, and her only single demand from government is loan for construction of new house and she uses condoms given free of cost by Rural and Urban Development Association (RUDA).

Case: 2

The name of a respondent is Arun Mahadevappa Patil, He was born on 3/5/1995 at Dharwad, His father's name is Mahadevappa Patil and his mother's name is Laxmibai. He was transited from male to female (MTF) at the age of 19.He is Hindu, Marata completed his 4th std and left school. His hobbies are cooking, reading a newspaper, watching television, listening to music etc. He stays with his family.He has no major health problems. He is single often visits a temple, said he was discriminated at school, people look at him with suspicious attitude, likes to dress up like the man and likes to do makeup like the woman. He often visits counselling centres and participates in community programmes. He is not getting any pension from Karnataka Government not got any loan still now. He is getting the free medical facility and he didn't undergo SRS surgery. He uses mobile phone, TV, refrigerator and a two-wheeler vehicle. He doesn't know any exercise or yoga, and as well as he said, this kind of practice is no use at all. In future, he wants to adopt children from Orphanage. He has fear in going to public places and him ashamed of being in MTF condition, he is not depressed, and he likes to meet his friends whenever he feels loneliness. He works as the call boy at Gurukrupa Lodge earns 8000/- per month, having saving bank account in Mysore bank. He is not having his own house. He is not having the Ration card, has a good facility of safe drinking water and toilet facility at home. He has an election card and voted many times before and in future, he wants to participate in local body elections. He attends various Transgender development programmes undertaken by RUDA-Rural and Urban Development Association. He has plans of starting his own business if he gets the loan from Government and his demand to Government is the loan for constructing his own house.

Case: 3

The name of a respondent is Heena, She changed her name from Hazrat to Heena, She was transited from male to female (MTF)at the age of 15. She was born at Dharwad on 6/8/ 1975, Her father's name is Maulana and Mother's name Ruksar. She belongs to Muslim religion and studied still 7th class, left school later. She belongs to Hyderabad Gharana. Her hobbies are cooking, dancing, riding etc. She is the single child of her parents, stays away from her parents, recently married to Shaukat and since marriage, she has stopped working as the sex worker. She has skin problems and often gets cold, cough. She is getting the free medical facility. She offers prayers or performs Namaz at her home.She was discriminated at her home and often called "Curse" by their parents. She likes to dress up like a woman called "Satla" in a local language. She is getting 500/- rupees from Karnataka Government under "Mythri Yojane". She got the non refundable loan of 20,000/- from Karnataka Government. She has not undergone any SRS Surgery, she is undergoing ICTS HIV/AIDS test once in a month from the Civil hospital through RUDA and aware of all allied disease occurring from Sexually Transmitted Diseases and uses condoms given free of cost from RUDA. Often undergoes counselling programmes and participates in CBO's development programmes. She is willing to adopt children in future. Initially, she has fear of meeting people and travelling and now she has overcome it. She likes to stay alone when stressed or depressed. Likes to spend time with friends. She worked as a prostitute, she left after getting married to Shaukat and living happily with him she said. She has bank savings account at State bank of India. She has no land property. She has a facility of safe drinking and toilet facility and has the Ration card. She has an election card and voted many times before. She is also having Aadhar card and willing to take part in local body elections.She likes to grow and come up in life and also wants her community to develop in all aspects. The demand for Karnataka Government is compulsory free education still 10th so that they go to college to study degree course.

Discussions

The fact that HIV prevalence among MSM is so high in many countries means that members of this group have an increased chance of being exposed to the virus, due to mainly having sexual relations only within this group. However, there are also other factors that put MSM at heightened risk of HIV. So NACO sponsored RUDA (Rural and Urban Development Association), are located at Hubli- Dharwad city,there are total 2 such centres present one is at Dharwad and another one at Hubli, these are counseling centres and also dropping centres, which spreads awareness about HIV /AIDS and makes these people undergo ICTC test once in a month at Civil hospital Dharwad.

HIV counselling and testing services were started in India in 1997. There are now more than 4000 Counselling and Testing Centres, mainly located in government hospitals. Under National Aids Control Programme NACP-III, Voluntary Counselling and Testing Centres (VCTC) and facilities providing Prevention of Parent to Child Transmission of HIV/AIDS (PPTCT) services are remodelled as a hub or 'Integrated Counselling and Testing Centre' (ICTC) to provide services to all clients under one roof. An ICTC is a place where a person is counselled and tested for HIV, of his own free will or as advised by a medical provider. As of today, only 13 per cent of HIV positive people in the country are aware of their HIV status. The challenge before NACO is to make all HIV infected people in the country aware of their status so that they adopt a healthy lifestyle; access life-saving care and treatment and help prevent further transmission of HIV. Thus, counselling and testing services are important components of prevention and control of HIV/AIDS in the country.

Biological Factors

According to this study, the observations made are: One major reason for high vulnerability to HIV among this group is that unprotected anal sex which carries a higher risk of transmission than vaginal sex. This is because the walls of the anus are thin and more easily torn, creating an entry point for HIV into the bloodstream. Having a sexually transmitted infection (STI) also makes a person more susceptible to HIV infection. Among MSM, HIV testing and sexual health check-up frequency are low (less than 55% across all regions), so many are living with an undiagnosed STI that may put them at higher risk of HIV/ AIDS.MSM are often not aware of the particularly high risk of having unprotected sex with a person who has recently become infected.

Behavioural Factors

Having multiple sexual partners is more common in this community and many do not use condoms consistently. In fact, MSM reporting easy access to condoms in 2012 varied from 29% in upper-middle income MSM's, to 45% in high-income MSM's, meaning that access to condoms remains inadequate for this group. Like condom access, HIV testing access is equally low, ranging between 25% and 54% in them. By not testing for HIV, many MSM is unaware of their HIV status which can mean they are unaware of the need to take protective measures to prevent onward transmission to others. Alcohol and drugs are a common part of socialising in some communities of men who have sex with men. Whenever drink and drugs are taken, it can make it more likely that people will have unprotected sex and a higher number of sexual partners, elevating vulnerability to HIV and they are the victims of Anxiety and Depression in personal life.

Social and cultural factors

Many men who have sex with men have experienced homophobic stigma, discrimination and violence. This drives MSM to hide their identity and sexual orientation, and many fear a negative reaction from healthcare workers. As a result, MSM is less likely to access HIV services.MSM are more likely to experience depression due to social isolation and disconnectedness from health institutes, which can make it harder to cope with aspects of HIV such as adherence to medication. Their main work is begging and it's called "Basti". The tool, Implementing Comprehensive HIV and STI Programmes with Men Who Have Sex with Men, provides recommendations for HIV prevention, testing and treatment for MSM and is based on successful community-led approaches.

They usually hide their residential addresses, according to the records available at RUDA. Their dwelling places at Dharwad are only 3, they are Dharwad old bus stand, Azad park and R.N Shetty ground.99% are involved in sex work and begging at bus stand, railway stations etc, only 1% do business e.g a Transgender named Shivu, got 20,000 amount as non refundable amount from Karnataka Government for self employment scheme and he now owns his garment shop at Ram Nagar Dharwad. All transgenders are getting 500/- amount as pension per month under Karnataka Government's "Mythri Yojane". After leaving their homes, they go and join community, there are 9 such communities they are called Gharana system or gharana Padathi, some of them are Pune gharana, Mumbai gharana, Belgum bendi bazaar gharana, Hyderabad gharana etc, They never say their family name, they identify themselves under these gharanas, if any person wants to undergo SRS (Sex Reassignment Surgery), the amount required for this surgey will be given by these communities or gharanas under Guru chela system and the elderly MSM 's will be getting financial assistance from these gharanas.Men who want to dress as women are called "Satlas".

Conclusion

The Government of Karnataka has various schemes and policies for them they are: The Hon'ble Supreme Court vide judgment dated 15th April 2014 has recognized transgender as the third gender apart from the existing binary genders for the purpose of safeguarding their constitutional rights as well as the right to self-identify as male, female or third gender. Centre and State Governments have also been directed to operate separate HIV Sero-surveillance Centres since Transgenders face several sexual health issues. The problems being faced by Transgenders such as fear, shame, gender dysphoria, social discrimination, depression, suicidal tendencies, social stigma, etc. and any insistence for SRS for declaring one's gender is immoral and illegal should be taken up seriously. Proper measures should be taken up to provide medical care to TGs in the hospitals and also provide those separate public toilets and other facilities. Steps to create public awareness should be taken so that TG's feel that they are also part of the society, regain their respect and are not to be treated as untouchables. The solution to their problems requires concerted efforts to mainstream them and adoption of an inclusive approach in all spheres of life. Taking into account the judgement it is necessary for the State Government to frame a Policy for the transgenders covering the areas of health, education, employment, housing, protection from harassment and abuse. The solution to their problems would require concerted efforts to mainstream them by adopting an inclusive approach in all spheres of life. The Government has launched a lot of Schemes and programme for their welfare; Schemes for Housing/Shelter - Santhwana Centres, Schemes for Education, and Schemes for Healthcare – Transgenders should be included in the Rashtriya Swasthya Bhima Yojana and all other health insurance schemes of the State. Scheme on a provision of food, the Monthly pension scheme for destitute transgenders, Other programmes like Awareness among the young generation, programmes for providing job opportunities in areas where they have been trained on the contract basis and also in MGNREGA, generation of livelihood opportunities and higher education. Organising events regularly with NGO's working for the welfare of Transgenders and other Transgender Associations to discuss all issues and solutions for transgenders to enable finalise future strategies for their welfare.

The Committee would comprise of Chief Secretary as the Chairperson, the official members would be Principal Secretaries/ Secretaries of Departments of Social Welfare, Law, Education, Health and Family Welfare, Employment and Training, Rural Development and Panchayat Raj. The only motto of their lives is earning money, live for today, don't think of saving money for tomorrow since they don't have children. "Today, there are so many positive developments in terms of LGBT rights. The ridicule has lessened; doctors, policemen and government officials sit up and listen to us," says Gauri Sawant, the founder of the transgender rights group Sakhi Charchowghi Trust. Pune-based Sawant, along with fellow activist Meera Gauri, had filed the PIL that led to the landmark judgment. The recent positive developments includes: These are some of the recent positive developments in Transgender community, but if these people try to utilize the Government schemes and policies effectively, they will definitely develop in coming years in India and the spirit of the Indian Constitution is to provide equal opportunity to every citizen to grow and attain their potential, irrespective of caste, religion or gender," the court said in its order, which is expected to alleviate the conditions of transgender people in India, through access to welfare programs, employment opportunities and education. So that they will also be empowered socially, economically, psychologically and politically.

References

1. Dr. Subramanium. Social Welfare Report. Ministry of social welfare. Government of India.
2. Chakrapani. V Newman, Mhaprolkar, H Kavi AR: Sexual and Social Networks of MSM and Hijras in India. Mumbai: 2007.
3. Denise F. Polit and Bhernadette .P. Hungler: Nursing Research Principles and Methods, 5th edition, vol. I, J.B. Lippincott Company Philadelphia.2003.
4. Dr R.F. Fleming J S: Measures of transgender behavior. California state university Northridge. USA. Jun 2001.
5. Bauer G R, Hammond R, Travers R, Kaay M: How erasure impacts health care for transgender people. The University of Western Ontario. London, Ontario, Canada.
6. Seil, D. (2004). The diagnosis and treatment of transgendered patients. *Journal of Gay & Lesbian Psychotherapy, 8*(1/2), 99-116.
7. Docter, R. F. & Fleming, J. S. (2001). Measures of transgender behavior. *Archives of Sexual Behavior 20*(2), 255-271.
8. Lawrence, A. A. (2004). Autogynephilia: A paraphilic model of gender identity disorder. *Journal of Gay & Lesbian Psychotherapy, 8*(1/2). 69-87.
9. Schaefer, L. C. & Wheeler, C. C. (2004). Guilt in cross gender identity conditions: Presentations and treatment. *Journal of Gay & Lesbian Psychotherapy, 8*(1/2), 117-127.
10. Carroll, L. & Gilroy, P. J. (2002). Transgender issues in counselor preparation. *Counselor Education & Supervision, 41*(3), 233-242.
11. Lev, A. I. (2004). *Transgender emergence" Therapeutic guidelines for working with gender variant people and their families*. Binghamton, NY: Hawthorn Clinical Practice Press.
12. Devor, A. H. (2004). Witnessing and mirroring: A fourteen stage model of transsexual identity formation. *Journal of Gay & Lesbian Psychotherapy, 8*(3/4), 41-67.
13. Sanchez, Francisco J, Vilain, Eric. Journal of Counseling Psychology. Collective self-esteem as a coping resource for male-to-female transsexuals 2009 Jan; 56(1): 202-9.

14. Arnold H. G, Anthony R. D. Transgender Youth. Journal of Homosexuality (serial online) 2006 (cited 2008 oct 17); 51(1): (2y screens).
15. Arnold H. G, Anthony R. D. Transgender Youth. Life-Threatening Behaviors. 2010 Dec
16. Thilakaravi. Mental Health Concerns of Transgender Population Living in Chennai, South India – A Study. MeD INDIA Networking for health January 2011.
17. Mark J Simone, Jonathan. Appelbaum. Clinical Gediatrics. Addressing the Needs of Older Lesbian, Gay, Bisexual, and Transgender Adults: 2011; 19(2) p.38-45.
18. Jeffrey D Strain, I Michael Shuff. Psychological Well-Being and Level of Outness in a Population of Male-to-Female Transsexual Women Attending a National Transgender Conference. International Journal of Transgenderis: 2010 Oct-Dec p. 230-240.

5

PLIGHTS OF OLD AGE WOMEN:
INCLUSIVE PERSPECTIVES

— *DR. P. DHANALAKSHMI*

Abstract

Since there is no beam of expectation in their present life and a long life ahead, they get themselves totally lost. At this point, they have no alternative yet to modify themselves in whatever conditions. In these unfriendly conditions, more established ladies need to stay helpful inside the four dividers of their own families till the final gasp. For a tranquil and deferential life, they need to trade off with every single odd circumstance and never protestation about anything.

Key Words: *Aged women, Medical Problems of Aging, Inclusive policy, Socio-Psychological Problems.*

Introduction

The human body is the most wonderful machine which nature has ever produced but it also wears down has time. The term old/Aged willingly, there is no clear delineation which implies the aged as old. Owing to the physical features, one looked young at 53 or other may not. In the cultural aspect if one fulfils all responsibility or he/she has grandchildren considered as old. Old age is usually regarded as synonyms with pensionable age or age at retirement. The word old literally means long-standing alternatively, having existed for a considerable period of time. Thus, old age is a phase of the life cycle where people reach after having lived a considerable number of years. The following objectives have been formulated for the present study; To understand the socio-economic conditions of aged women. To analyze the mental trauma experienced by aged women. To expose the nature of old age care and support provide to elderly women. To understand the aspiration and expectation of old age women and the reality. To suggest the solution to their problem in order to make them read aged women.

Problems of Aged women

Problems faced by aged women such as economic, psychological, familial and health. A miserable state of deprivation, dependence, desertion, depression etc. Most illness in the aged women present as multiple problems than as a single disease. For eg., A person suffering from arthritis may also have diabetes, asthma, paralytic, stroke, a silent heart outlet etc. Ageing effects are not only evident in the biological sphere but also in the psychological realm of aged women. Physical appearances of ageing like greying of hair telling tale signs of advancing age. And also most of the aged ones are retired persons and they feel lonely and insecure. Majority of the aged women have financial problems. Because most of the aged women are retired one and they are in the condition of unemployment. It increases economic dependency. Even those who are having retirement benefits find difficult to meet basic requirements.

The physiological decline in ageing refers to the physical changes an individual experience because of the decline in the normal functioning of the body resulting in poor mobility, vision, hearing, inability to eat and digest food properly, a decline in memory, the inability to control certain physiological functions, and various chronic conditions. Change in socio-economic status adversely affects the individual's way of life after retirement. The economic loss is due to a change from salary to pension or unemployment leading to economic dependency on children or relatives. A feeling of low self-worth may be felt due to the loss of earning power and social recognition. This state of mind is harmful. With the prospect of this situation worsening in the coming decades, ways and means of managing the stress effectively need to be examined.

Old Age

Aging is a natural and universal phenomenon and human concern about it is old age. It is an inescapable part of human destiny and comes to every one of us. Aging is a process which takes place during the entire lifespan of the organism and is the final phase of human development (Gumming & Henry, 1961) it must be seen as part of a continual process of change.

Old age means different things in different cultures. Seniority may bring high status and in some societies old age has traditionally been a time of relative relaxation and freedom from worry. In others old age is linked to life stage or generation and may or may not be something to look forward to. However, for the purposes of this discussion, old age is defined as a period in the life course when the collective social support of some kind becomes essential because of advancing years.

Problems Associated With Old Aged Women

Old age comes to every one of us. For many people, it comes as a phase of tranquillity and serenity, as a phase of life in which a human being can still grow towards completion of his personality and inner values. But it can also be a phase of life which is marked by physical and mental instability, by proneness to disease and by a steady escalation of misery and suffering. The problems of old age have gained importance in the contemporary society due to the rapid increase in the number of aged people in the society.

Old age is often viewed as a problematic period of one's life which brings numerous problems. The problems of aged are manifold. Moreover, these problems vary from individual to individual and culture to culture but there are certain common problems experienced by most of the aged person across culture and geographical location. These have been categorized as biological, social, economic and psychological problems. These problems are interdependent and interactive in nature (Kapoor & Kapoor, 2000; Kumar, 1999). Therefore, ageing needs to be studied with a holistic approach combining not only the biological and demographical viewpoints but also the psychological, economic, emotional, spiritual, social, political as well as cultural viewpoints.

Physiological Problems

The process of life is consists of physical and mental changes characterized by growth and decline. It is during this period in life (i. e. old age) where individual begins to experience cumulative effect of such gradual alterations in physical status that have taken place throughout the adult years. These changes are associated with a number of diseases. Due to changes, such as loss of elasticity in muscle tissue, the ability to move about freely and comfortably becomes more restricted, the elderly people tire more easily, participate less in physical activities and cannot endure stress. Tooth loss is most common change, due to tooth loss the aged have dietary inadequacy which leads to nutritional deficiencies (Kapoor & Kapoor, 2000). Respiratory conditions affect the health and well being of elderly persons due to decreased lung efficiency. Circulatory problems include accumulation of faulty tissues in heart muscle. The most commonly reported disorder of digestive system in old age includes peptic ulcer and frequent constipation (Hamilton, 1994). The biologically ageing process is characterized by the gradual decline in the functioning of all the body's systems.

Social Problems

Every human being is a part of society and interacts with other members of society in a number of ways. At the time of birth, the social network is very limited and in adulthood, the social network is at its peak. When old age sets in, this network starts shrinking. Though, there are different kinds of explanations for this shrinkage. Modernization and urbanization have resulted in a decline of the status enjoyed by the ignored, stressful, and economically dependent and out thrown. A breaking of a joint family, as well as decreased cohesiveness of family and social bonds with the change in values and norms, is also visible. The stress and strains of these changes have made the position of elderly vulnerable especially for sick and infirm, resulting in loneliness and increased death anxiety (Desetty & Patnam, 2000).

With advancing age, there is the decline in health and individual can lose their independence become isolated and change their self-perception. Social disengagement or withdrawal process may be initiated by the individual, which is often associated with decreased emotional involvement in the social network, lack of belongingness, lack of communication and mutual delegation in turn negatively affect their well being.

Psychological Problems

Old age is also associated with a number of psychological problems. These problems are either due to old age or as a result of an interactive effect of social and economic problems. Affective disorders such as alterations in normal mood states, depressive reactions, elation and bodily preoccupation are the most common psychogenic illness found in old age. Certain psychosomatic symptoms, such as loss of appetite, sleeping difficulties and fatigue usually accompany affective disorders. Many people fear that senility is an inevitable curse of old age. Such persons have a limited ability to grasp abstractions, lack of ideas, think more slowly, unable to pay attention to them. Because of such mental deterioration, the aged may be unable to cope with such routine tasks as keeping clean and well groomed (Hamilton, 1994).

Intellectual ability has also been reported to decline to some degree in old age distinguishing between fluid intelligence and crystallized intelligence. Psychologists have observed that fluid intelligence is "culture free" based on the psychological structure of the organism, while crystallized intelligence is acquired in the course of social experience. Traditionally, the elderly have been seen as retaining their wisdom (crystallized intelligence) whilst losing their wits (fluid intelligence). One aspect of cognitive functioning which is quite commonly observed in old person is memory loss. Memory loss among the elderly has many causes. Some of them are related to the retention of knowledge and still others to the retrieval of knowledge. Older people, for instance, tend to organize new knowledge less well and less completely than they did when they were young. They are not so effective in carrying out the elaborate encoding of information which is essential for long-term retention. At present two theories: interference and neurochemical change in combination appear to be the best explanation for short-term memory loss in older people (Kimmel, 1980). Some psychologists have suggested a 'decay' theory that forgetting is due to deterioration in the memory traces in the brain. Others have advanced on 'interference' theory that a retrieval cue becomes less effective as more and new items come to be categorized. Faulty retrieval information is also a major cause of memory loss. With age, there is a decline in speed in both mental and physical performance. Reading skills also decline with age. Sensory changes also occur resulting in decreased vision and impaired hearing. Forgetfulness is also the earliest manifestation of brain dysfunctioning (Bagchi, 2000).

Economic Problems

The economic position of the aged is closely associated with the socio-economic environment in which they live. In general, the economic status of a person is a function of his/her past work status, level of education as well as the present activity status. It is found that with the increase in age the level of work participation among the elderly declines. This may probably be attributed to their competence and restricts their activity. Consequently, they may not be able to perform certain role and work, such disability decreases their earning capacity and forces them to depend on the family. Hence, the financial dependency is a predominant characteristic of the elderly. This feeling of dependency further complicates the attitude of the aged making them feel helpless, unwanted and segregated from the family. Due to the economic hardship, they may not be able to maintain their optimum standard of food, clothing and housing amenities. Depletion of purchasing power affects their health and nutrition and makes the aged susceptible to accelerated ageing (Puri and Khanna, 1999).

Under usual circumstances most of the elderly are supposed to be out of labor force in old age, depending on their past income (in the form of rent, pension etc.), but some of them, however, continue to be in the workforce because of financial necessity even as their physical strength gradually decreases with the increasing age. When the elderly person became dependent upon theire grown up children, who are by then having their own families, the later spend more money on their growing children by decreasing the expenditure on their aged parents. Added to the physical disability, economic disability also leads to a serious depression among elderly persons. As, they use to take all the major economic decisions for the family, but now not even consulted by their wards or children. The old age people living in rural and isolated areas and women may be more vulnerable to these.

Medical Problems of Aging

Aging is neither a disease nor an illness. To be old does not mean to be sick or senile. As we age, we change and sometimes that change is a slow decline in life function. Too many times, the elderly themselves and their loved ones feel that aches and pains, as well as more serious medical problems, are part of being old. If an elderly person has a health problem, appropriate medical attention should be given, as with any other age group.

When an elderly person is sick, more serious future problems can be avoided with prompt medical care. Most so-called age-related bodily changes are affected by lifestyle factors, such as poor diet, smoking and environmental factors, such as pollution and chemical exposure. No two individuals are the same way and not all elderly individuals experience similar health problems.

Considerable research has shown that older adults vary tremendously in their health status and the problems they suffer. Above all, it is important to keep in mind that the elderly can do something about their health in later life. For example, a small change in lifestyle, such as exercising more or quitting smoking, may lead to a significant change in health status.

The aged women can have special problems that require equally special understanding for diagnosis and help. There are many underlying psychological changes. Although these changes are normal, they may alter the way an elderly person responds to disease and is able to cope with physical problems. Understanding is important, but surprisingly, medical schools have only recently begun to educate their students about normal ageing. Physical disease in the elderly may be more difficult to detect. Signs or symptoms may be diminished or absent. They also may be delayed at onset or not characteristic of the same disease in a younger person. For example, an elderly heart attack victim may have no chest pain because of age-related nerve changes. An elderly person with a severe infection may not be able to produce white blood cells to fight the infection or even produce a fever.

A physical disease may show a mental change. The same elderly heart attack victim with no pain may have symptoms only of confusion because of an insufficient blood supply to the brain. The patient with pneumonia may be called senile because a lack of oxygen slows brain functioning. It takes a sharp mind to notice changes in an elderly person's thinking and recognize physical disease as one the culprits. All too often, people with new thinking problems will be called senile, and ignored or put in an institution. They're underlying, often treatable, illness will go undetected.

Drugs in the elderly may act differently, interact frequently, and be harder to control. Since elderly persons tend to have many medical problems, they often take many medications and the risk of drug toxicity and drugs' interacting with other drugs rises enormously. In addition, some elderly patients take drugs for problems that they or their physician have long forgotten, or for problems that have been long resolved. They may also be taking over-the-counter medications without the physician's knowledge. Because of the changes that come with ageing, the older body and brain handle drugs somewhat differently. A good health care professional is aware of this and adjusts drug doses appropriately for the patient's age, kidney, liver, and brain functions. Drug dosages and use must be monitored regularly and carefully.

Medical problems of the elderly are frequently multiple. As we age, we can develop new and complicate health problems. The geriatric healthcare worker has to keep in mind these multiple ailments and treat them as carefully as possible without jeopardizing the "whole" patient. This can be complicated, especially when the treatment for one problem condition may exacerbate another. Along with multiplicity, health problems in the elderly are frequently chronic. This is an enormous burden for the aged patient in terms of physical health, life satisfaction, and finances. Remember, about half the medical expenses of this country are for treating chronic problems. Most of this expense is borne by the 10-15% of the elderly population. In fact, older adults visit their physicians six times for every five visits by the general population. They are hospitalized twice as often, have longer hospital stays, and use twice as many prescription drugs as younger persons. Obviously, the medical problems of the elderly are special and often complex.

Although ageing is not itself a disease, geriatric health care workers must be knowledgeable of this normal life process and the many special problems that accompany ageing. A good rule is to find a physician who is interested in the healthcare of elderly patients. Many doctors display little interest in geriatric health care. Their interests may lie elsewhere. You do yourself and those physicians a favour by seeking a competent clinician concerned with the special problems of ageing. There are many clinicians who find this work rewarding and those who are genuinely interested will generally give the best care

Observation and conclusion

Most of the family members treated old age woman as problematic because they are not earning and they are not helping the family, so they perceive aged people as a problematic. The old woman mostly depends on their family members. They are expecting monitory help and benefits from the aged woman. So they are maintaining the relationship with old age woman from economic aspects. Most of the family members, neighbours, and community people are did not give respect to the old age person. It is found that 60% of the aged women are suffered from the psychological conditions like frustration, health problems and mental illness. Majority of the respondents are suffered from the psychological problems like stress and tension, frustration and health problems. Government plans and policies do not properly reach the senior citizens and they are not enjoying their old age peacefully. We must diagnose the elder's problems and we have to take care of the aged woman in all the ways and dimensions. The family members and societal members are forgotten to give care and supports. The mind setup should be changed and shaped to safeguard the rights, feelings of the elderly women.

Based on study the researcher suggests that (a) Guidance and counselling should be given to the family members, neighbours and youngsters to protect the elder's women, (b) Economic illnesses should be cured by providing employment opportunities to the elder's women,

(c) Health care must be given to the old age people in the hospitals free of cost and hospital should maintain a homely atmosphere in giving treatment and care, (d) A government should develop separate counselling centres for the aged ones and counselling must be given to the family members, especially to their children and in-laws, (e) GOs and NGOs should create plans and policies to take care of elders and they should look out whether their policies and programmes will reach the elders and they are benefited are not, and (f) Each and every one should take care of their own elders and don't leave them as orphans. They are the roots of our family, community and society and we are just the branches and keep this in mind. Without root, there is no identification for branches.

References

1. Burchardt, T., Le Grand, J. and Piachaud, D. (1999) 'Social exclusion in Britain 1991-1995', Social Policy and Administration 33, 3: 227-244.
2. Byrne, D. (1999) Social Exclusion, Open University Press, Buckingham.
3. European Commission, Combating poverty and social exclusion. A statistical portrait of the European Union 2010, Luxembourg, Publications Office of the European Union, 2010.
4. European Commission, Joint report on social inclusion 2004, Luxembourg, Publications Office of the European Union, 2004.
5. Gurusamy.S (2011), "Social Exclusion and Inclusion", APH Publisher, New Delhi (2011).
6. Hills, J. (2001) 'Inclusion or exclusion? The role of housing subsidies and benefits', Urban Studies 38, 11: 1887-1902.
7. Hills, J. et al. (2001) Understanding Social Exclusion. Oxford: Oxford University Press.
8. Scharf, T. and Smith, A.E. (2004) 'Older people in urban neighbourhoods: addressing the risk of social exclusion in later life', in C. Phillipson, G. Allan and D. Morgan (eds) Social Networks and Social Exclusion, Ashgate, Aldershot, 162-179.

6

Child Rearing Practices among the Mahar Community: A Case of Karnataka

— *Dr Prabudha S. Kamble*

Abstract

Child Rearing practices are a major determinant of morbidity status of infants. Most important of these are the feeding practices. Breastfeeding during infancy is of particular importance because it is fundamental for survival, growth and development, health and nutrition of infants. Breast feed is the first fundamental right of the child.

Keywords: *Child rearing practices, Infants, Breast Feeding, Mahar Community.*

Introduction

Child is the future of family community as well as the nation in which he is born. A child's mind is just like a mud. He /she can be shaped in any way whatever the parents/caretakers want like a potter makes a pot in different shape using mud. As John Locke suggested that the child's mind is like an empty slate/white sheet of paper that can be filled up by the parents/caretakers/adults advice. So, the main focus for the good mindset and good thinking process lies in the hands of the child rearing practices who are taking such main role for the development of one's mind at the early stages. If you observe the child rearing practices in the Indian scenario, you can find many differences among north-eastern part, northern part, and western part n southern part. Inside one part also you find differences in terms of the ethnic level, cultural level etc. inside the ethnic level you find differences from one family to another family.

In the study it is encountered and observed that the child rearing practices are in different ways. In one context it is observed that how the child is exploited for their daily two square meal in very poor family especially male and parents use girls for nurturing their young ones.

Child Rearing practices are a major determinant of morbidity status of infants. Most important of these are the feeding practices. Breastfeeding during infancy is of particular importance because it is fundamental for survival, growth and development, health and nutrition of infants. Breast feed is the first fundamental right of the child. World Health Organization recommends exclusive breastfeeding of all infants until 6 months of age. In spite of all the efforts deployed as information, education or training campaigns to promote mother's milk as the best food for the infant, the prevalence of exclusive breastfeeding remains low. This is because psychosocial and cultural barriers still exists to early breastfeeding. Non-exclusive breastfeeding which includes prelacteal feeding is an important cause of infant morbidities. The other contributory factors for infection are improper and inadequate weaning foods and unhygienic feeding practices like bottle feeding found in the study area.

According to an analysis, breastfeeding was identified as the single most effective preventive intervention, which could prevent 13-16% of all childhood deaths in India. Adequate complementary feeding between the age of 6 and 24 months could prevent an additional 6% of all such deaths. Inadequate and faulty practices of feeding newborns and children also have resulted in under nutrition. Under nutrition has lead to poorly body functioning and immunity and hence infections. This in the study area has also coupled with exposure to contaminated environment. Therefore poor complimentary feeding practices mean that many children continue to be vulnerable to irreversible outcomes of stunting, poor cognitive development and significantly increased risk of infectious diseases such as diarrhea and acute respiratory infection. Apart from the feeding practices, there are certain other rearing practices which also influence the health of infants and are widely prevalent among families or communities in the study area.

These are oil massaging the baby before giving a bath, application of oil into eyes and ears of infants, burping the baby, application of black carbon into the eye, trimming of nails, etc. Familiarity with these rearing practices is of considerable significance to a health worker serving the community as well as the mother of the child. For promotion of infant health, the health care provider must identify the beneficial, innocuous and harmful rearing practices. she has to be tactful in persuading the people to abandon the harmful ones such as oil application into the eyes or ears of the baby.

Overall, a good number of infant morbidity and mortality is attributed to improper new born care practices which depend on the knowledge, attitude and practice of the community in addition to other factors like availability and accessibility of medical services including the medicines, Doctors and trained Ayas, (health worker). Hence the social pattern and customs influencing the feeding pattern and rearing practices in a community needs to be understood in order to improve the nutritional and health status of infants at the primary care level. With this background, this longitudinal study was conducted to find out the rearing practices among infants in a rural area of south India.

Objectives

To find out infant /child rearing practices in the study area.

Materials and Methods

Observation, Interview, Questionnaire and Group Discussion , methods were used to know the child rearing practices in the study area.

Study settings

This longitudinal study was done in Peeranwadi, Macche and Hunchanatti villages of Belgaum city outskirts. Ethical clearance for conducting this study was obtained from the local leaders both elected as well as traditional leaders.

Sample size

The sample size for the study was all the pregnant mothers and all the mothers who had children less than five years of age. Based on the birth rate of 21 per 1000 population, 420 births were expected over a period of 1 year or 210 over 6 months period. Over the enrollment period, i.e. first 6 months of study period.

Study period

All new born during the first 6 months of study period, i.e. from November 2014 to April 2015 formed the birth cohort who was followed up for 1year. Therefore, the study period was of one a year from November 2014 to October 2015.

Inclusion criteria

All newborns of mothers who were permanent residents of the study area and who were available for follow-up for 1 year and single on pregnancies were included in this study.

Exclusion criteria

Babies born to mothers who had come to parental house for delivery were excluded. It is a common cultural practice in India for pregnant women to come to their parental house few months before delivery and stay there till few months after. This is to obtain better care and support during these vital periods. When the baby is a few months old they go back to their place of residence. That would make them unavailable for a full-year of follow up.

Data collection

During the initial phase, the investigator visited houses of mothers within 10 days of childbirth and collected baseline data on a pretested Performa after obtaining their informed consent. Thereafter, monthly follow-up visits were done for 1 year to enquire about their feeding and rearing practices during the period of infancy. Anthropometric measurements like weight, height, head circumference, chest circumference and mid-arm circumference were also recorded during each of these visits.

Background

The way your children are brought up can influence how fruitful they will be sometime down the way. In view of analyst Nancy Darling, in the article "Parenting Style and Its Correlates," child brain research scientists distinguish four unique sorts of child rearing practices that influence children's life results. Contrasts among the four parenting styles lie predominantly in whether a parent makes numerous or few tenets for his child and whether a parent is sincerely responsive or careless. Rearing practices are a major determinant of nutritional and health status of infants. Therefore these practices need to be better understood.

Observations

It was observed that the mothers received prelacteal feeds (PLF) the common given to newborns was sugar water. The mothers were known about the breast feeding to baby but very few were feeding within half an hour of delivery. The feeding varied from two hours to twenty four hours.

Later on the time interval of feeding to child was practiced on demand feeding. The other mothers gave at fixed gap of time and the remaining gave when time permitted.

The period of breast feeding was observed in all cases for at least six months and few for the period of one year and few for complete two years.

Type of weaning foods given to infants were semi-solid and solid diet in majority cases; animal milk, semi-solids, and solids in remaining half cases; formula powder milk, semi-solids and solids in very few cases and a combination of all the above in rare cases. Bottle feeding was seen in few countable cases.

The weight gain in infants was found to be significantly more when the infants were fed on breast milk along with semi-solids and solids followed by animal and formula powder milk along with semi-solids and solids.

Oil massage was done using coconut oil and it was given before bathing the infant. Oil application into the eyes and ears of infants was practiced by majority mothers respectively. This was seen significantly more among infants of illiterate mothers compared to literate mothers.

Conclusion

Faulty rearing practices such as pre-lacteal feeding, not practicing exclusive breast feeding and on demand, early discontinuation of breast feeding, application of oil into the eyes and ears of infant, delay in giving bath to infant, application of black carbon into the eyes of infants, ignorance of correct burping method and not trimming the nails of infant were very much prevalent in this study area. Illiteracy and low socioeconomic status were found to be the influencing factors behind these faulty practices. This magnifies the importance of health education which is the best cost-effective intervention in a rural set up. Gain in all anthropometric measurements was more in the initial 6 months of infancy compared to latter. Weight gain was found to be maximum among infants EBF for 6 months and weaned with semi-solid and solid diet. Overall, the present study identified several deficiencies in new born and infant care practices in the study area. From these observations it appears that traditional and customary child rearing practices are still prevalent in rural areas and certainly not to the advantage of the growth and development of children. Only education on infant health and nutrition imparted to young mothers would correct such age-old infant feeding and rearing practices. The present scenario can be improved through enhancing information education communication (IEC) activities, distribution and display of locally developed IEC material and training of health staff with emphasis on preventive and primitive health-care practices. By these means we can ensure a healthy childhood and stronger India.

References

1. Garg R, Deepti S, Padda A, Singh T. Breastfeeding knowledge and practices among rural women of Punjab, India: A community-based study. Breastfeed Med. 2010; 5:303–7.

2. Geneva: World Health Organization; 1998. Complementary feeding of young children in developing countries: A review of current scientific knowledge; p. 237. (WHO/NUT/98.1)
3. New Delhi: National Institute of Health and Family Welfare; 2000. Reproductive and Child Health Module for Health Worker Female.
4. Kulkarni RN, Anjenaya S, Gujar R. Breast feeding practices in an urban community of Kalamboli, Navi Mumbai. Indian J Community Med. 2004; 29:179–80.
5. Chaturvedi M, Nandan D, Gupta SC. Rapid assessment of infant-feeding practices in Agra district. Indian J Community Med. 2007; 32:227.
6. Raval D, Jankar DV, Singh MP. A study of breast feeding practices among infants living in slums of Bhavnagar city, Gujarat, India. Healthline. 2011; 2:78–83.
7. Das P, Ghosh S, Ghosh M, Mandal A. A study on delivery and newborn care practices in a rural block of West Bengal. Indian J Public Health. 2008; 52:159–60.
8. Srivastava SP, Sharma VK, Kumar V. Breast feeding pattern in neonates. Indian Pediatr. 1994; 31:1079–82.
9. Sinhababu A, Mukhopadhyay DK, Panja TK, Saren AB, Mandal NK, Biswas AB. Infant- and young child-feeding practices in Bankura district, West Bengal, India. J Health Popul Nutr. 2010; 28:294–9.
10. Awasthi NN, Kaushik A, Mathur BD. Feeding and rearing practices in rural area of Jhansi-Bundelkhand. Indian J Pediatr. 1983; 50:33–7.
11. Bhosale NA, Deshpande SG, Zodpey SP, Jog SN, Vasudeo ND. Infant feeding practices in urban population–a clinic based study. Indian J Med Sci. 1997; 51:396–9.
12. Bandyopadhyay SK, Chaudhury N, Mukhopadhyaya BB. Breast feeding practices in rural areas of West Bengal. Indian J Public Health. 2000; 44:137–8.

7

WOMEN'S REPRODUCTIVE HEALTH: A CONCEPTUAL STUDY

— *DR. SHILPA M. SANGAM*

Abstract

It is shown that such a conceptualization is defective, as conduct is molded by social relations and foundations. Utilizing ethnographic proof, the estimation of a social investigation of the neighborhood settings of reproductive health is featured. A structure is set out for directing such a social investigation, which is fit for producing information important to permit health projects to evaluate the suitable methods for enhancing the responsiveness of service-conveyance structures to the necessities of the most powerless. Six key issues are distinguished in the structure for the examination of social defenselessness to poor reproductive health results. The key issues are: destitution and vocation procedures, sexual orientation, health-chasing conduct, reproductive conduct, and access to services. The article finishes up by quickly recognizing the key intercessions and procedures demonstrated by such an investigation.

Introduction

Health is an important aspect of the survival of human. It is a very broad concept. It is the general condition of a person's mind and body usually meaning to be free from illness, injury or pains. The World Health Organization (WHO) has defined health in 1946 as "a state of complete physical, mental and social well-being and not merely the absence of disease or infirmity." Provision of health should be considered a fundamental human right. Health is the multidimensional phenomenon.

Women's health has long been a concern for WHO but today it has become an urgent priority. It involves their emotional, social and physical well-being. It is determined by the social, political and economic context of their lives as well as by biology. Women's reproductive health is an indispensable ingredient of health. It is a crucial component of a women's general health which encompasses health and well-being of women particularly during the reproductive years (15-49yrs). It also refers to health issues i.e., the diseases and disorders specific to their reproductive systems and sexual lives during all stages of life which will affect not only her lives directly before, during and beyond child bearing age but also her environment from her families to her economic and vice versa.

Objectives

(a) To know the problems of women in respect of their reproductive system

(b) To assess the reproductive behavior of women

Method

Comparative and descriptive methods are used for the study

Scope

The paper covers poverty and livelihood strategies, gender, health-seeking behaviour, reproductive behaviour, and access to service

Theoretical Frame work

The reproductive period is the most important period in the women's life. It extends from menarche to menopause and the intervening periods are marriage, pregnancy, childbirth and contraception. The pregnant women have been widely recognized as a vulnerable group from the health point of view. They need more care for the proper nourishment of the growing foetus. The healthy reproductive status of women is extremely important to give a healthy baby as well as her healthy life. However, the poor reproductive health becomes a significant cause of disease and death.

The subject of reproductive health can be studied from reproductive mortality and morbidity rate. According to the World Bank, about one-third of the total disease burden among women aged 15 to 44 years in the developing countries and is associated with pregnancy, childbirth, abortion, HIV and reproductive tract infections. The high mortality rates among sepsis, anaemia, toxaemia, haemorrhage, abortion, STIs including STDs etc indicate that women's health in general and reproductive health, in particular, remains low.

Health status of women in rural outset is being infinitely a broad topic. India, as a country with more than 70% of its population residing in rural areas, it is worthwhile to know the health condition of women in villages. The 2/3rd of the population in the country consists of women of child bearing age and children under the age of fifteen years. In India, women of the reproductive age between 15-49 years and children below five years of age comprise 62% of the total population.

In a developing country like India, the reproductive health status of women in the rural area is low and has been largely and sadly neglected. The reproductive health status of rural women presents a sobering picture. The maternal mortality ratio ranges from between 448 and 397 per 100,000 births in rural and urban areas respectively, in 1992-93. It is also estimated that 4,00,000 maternal deaths occur every year in the world and out of these 1,00,000 deaths occur in India. Community-based assessments have addressed all three natal periods indicate 41% of maternal morbidity in Karnataka.

More than 90% of the estimated 5,36,000 maternal deaths occur in the world and out of them 1,00,000 deaths occur in India (NFHS 1992-93).When maternal morbidity is often overlooked; the little evidence is available on women's health. For every maternal death, it is estimated that 15-20 mothers suffer from impaired health during the antenatal, natal and post natal period.

A significant proportion of maternal deaths and illness among women are the combined effects of poor health, poor nutrition, early marriages, early pregnancies, lack of health education, less of an opportunity to learn about their sexual and reproductive health and rights, culture and communities more rigorously to customary laws and norms of social stratification, discrimination, inadequate maternity services and the poor quality of health care received during pregnancy which is responsible for both high levels of neonatal and maternal morbidities and mortalities. Therefore, rural women in India are among the most disadvantaged people in terms of their health status particularly when Sexual and Reproductive Health (SRH) is concerned. This might be one of the reasons why reproductive health could not be successful in India particular in rural areas.

Though the State's Health Department does not maintain district-wise statistics on MMR, it has classified districts of Yadgiri, Gulbarga, Bidar, Raichur, Koppal, Bijapur and Bagalkot under 'C' category as the maternal mortality rate is bad here based on the education and health indicators.

Reproductive health of women has recently become the focus of attention due to its implications for women's own health, the health of their children, family members, socio-economic development of society and population programmes. The reproductive health status of women, especially in the developing world including India, requires urgent attention. Over one-third of all healthy lives lost among adult women are due to reproductive health problems (WHO, 1995).

At the International Conference on Population and Development in Cairo (ICPD) in 1994, a programme of action shifts the focus away from demography and targets towards reproductive health, empowering women, education and choice. It must be viewed as three interconnected domains that include universal rights, women's empowerment and health service provision. These three concepts must work in unison in order to achieve healthy reproductive and sexual lives. (ICPD; Programme of Action, 7.3).

Reproductive Health

Within the framework of WHO's definition of health, the ICPD Cairo in 1994 has defined the term reproductive health. It outlines the sexual and reproductive health (SRH) is not merely about reproduction. It must be viewed as three interconnected domains that include universal rights, women's empowerment and health service provision. These three concepts must work in unison in order for individuals to achieve healthy reproductive and sexual lives

Reproductive Health was first defined in the Programme of Action of the 1994 United Nations International Conference on Population and Development (ICPD). Within the framework of WHO, the ICPD at Cairo defines Reproductive health as – "a state of complete physical, mental and social well-being and not merely the absence of disease or infirmity, in all mat-ters relating to the reproductive system and to its functions and process. Reproductive health, therefore, implies that people are able to have a satisfying and safe sex life and that they have the capability to reproduce and the freedom to decide if, when and how often to do so." Implicit in this last condition are the right of men and women to be informed (about) and to have access to safe, effective, affordable and acceptable methods of family planning of their choice, as well as other methods of birth control which are not against the law, and the right of access to appropriate health-care services that will enable women to go safely through pregnancy and childbirth and provide couples with the best chance of having a healthy infant.

Hence, reproductive health means a total well-being in all aspects of reproduction, i.e., physical, emotional, behavioural and social. A society with people having physically and functionally normal reproductive organs and normal emotional and behavioural interactions among themselves in all sex-related aspects might be called reproductively healthy.

Sexual Health

Above comprehensive definition of reproductive health (ICPD 1994) includes sexual health which is defined by the WHO website as "a state of physical, mental and social well-being in relation to sexuality. It requires a positive and respectful approach to sexuality and sexual relationships as well as the possibility of having pleasurable and safe sexual experiences, free of coercion, discrimination and violence."

Sexual and Reproductive Health (SRH) is the concept of human rights which is applied to sexuality and reproduction. It is a combination of four fields which are more or less distinct from each other in some contexts, but less so or not at all in other contexts. These four fields are sexual health, sexual rights, reproductive health and reproductive rights. In the concept of Sexual and Reproductive Health and Rights (SRHR) these four fields are treated as separate but inherently intertwined. The distinctions between these four fields are not always made. Sexual health and reproductive health are sometimes treated as synonymous with each other as are sexual rights and reproductive rights. In some cases, sexual rights are included in the term sexual health or vice versa.

Sexual Health does not matter who we are, men and women, boys and girls, gays, lesbians, transgender and intersex. They all have an equal right to well-being and sexual well beings. Sexual health is women's and men's ability to enjoy and express their sexuality and to do so free from the risk of sexually transmitted disease, unwanted pregnancy, coercion, violence and discrimination. Sexual health also means being able to have an informed, enjoyable and safe sex life, based on self-esteem, a positive approach to human sexuality and mutual respect in sexual relations. Sexual health enhances life, personal relations and the expression of one's sexual identity.

The WHO's definition of reproductive health specifically highlights the importance of an individual's right to maintain their own sexual health status. The proponents of reproductive health framework believe that reproductive health is inextricably linked to the subject of reproductive rights and freedom. These rights rest on the recognition of the basic right of all couples and individuals to decide freely and help to attain the highest possible standard of SRH. They also include their right to make decisions concerning reproduction free of discrimination, coercion and violence.

Hence the concept of reproductive health addresses: The reproductive processes, functions and system at all stages of life, Freedom to make decisions regarding a healthy sex life. Access to appropriate reproductive health care services.

Reproductive Health Care

In line with the ICPD at Cairo definition of reproductive health, the reproductive health care is defined as "the constellation of methods, techniques and services that contribute to reproductive health and well-being by preventing and solving reproductive health problems. It also includes sexual health, the purpose of which is the enhancement of life and personal relations and not merely counselling and care related to reproduction and sexually transmitted diseases".

Hence, the concept of reproductive health can be understood, maintained and achieved through the proper reproductive health care techniques or methods which would include certain fundamental and basic components of Reproductive Health Care.

Safe Motherhood is the ability of a mother to have safe & healthy pregnancy & child birth. It begins at conception with proper nutrition and a healthy lifestyle and continues with appropriate prenatal care, prevention of complications when possible and the early and effective treatment of complications. Safe motherhood is designed to reduce the high numbers of deaths and illnesses resulting from complications of pregnancy and childbirth. In many countries, the most maternal deaths result from haemorrhage, complications of unsafe abortion, pregnancy-induced hypertension, sepsis and obstructed labour (WHO 1991)1. Safe motherhood seeks to address these direct medical causes and undertake related activities to ensure women have access to comprehensive reproductive health services and help to improve maternal health. WHO has recommended four strategic interventions for making Safe motherhood. They are: Family Planning, Antenatal Care, Clean & Safe Delivery and Essential Obstetric Care.

Family Planning and Contraceptive Methods

It plays a crucial role in helping the women to remain healthy by preventing unwanted or untimely pregnancies. Accesses to quality family planning services that provide women with a range of contraceptive options and informed choice can help to reduce the maternal mortality and morbidity by reducing high-risk pregnancies associated with multiple pregnancies. It also helps women to avoid undesired and unsafe abortions. Family planning indirectly contributes to children's health, development and survival by reducing the risk of maternal mortality and morbidity.

Low female literacy levels and the lack of widespread availability of birth-control methods are hampering the use of contraception in India. Awareness of contraception is near-universal among married women in India. However, the vast majority of married Indians (76% as per 2009 study) reported significant problems in accessing a choice of contraceptive methods.

Safe Abortion Facilities

Safe Abortion is one of the important components of Reproductive Health. It addresses in brief, the clinical care for women undergoing an abortion. Safe abortion services are provided by trained health workers. It includes termination of an unwanted pregnancy safely, legally and affordably which includes the services such as pre-abortive care (before the abortion), abortion methods (during the abortion) and post-abortive care (after abortion & follow up). They also contribute development and survival by reducing the risk of maternal mortality and morbidity due to unsafe abortion.

Unsafe abortion is a global problem. Millions of women around the world risk their lives and health to end an unwanted pregnancy. Every day 55, 000 unsafe abortions take place, 95 % of them in developing countries and lead to the deaths of more than 200 women daily. Globally, one unsafe abortion takes place for every seven births. In India, the problem of unsafe abortions is especially acute. There were 620,472 reported abortions in 2012; experts say the true number of abortions performed in the country could be as high as 7 million with two-thirds of them taking place outside authorized health facilities. A woman in India dies every two hours because an abortion goes wrong.

Male Participation and Responsible Behaviour

The men must adopt a positive behaviour responsibility and participate and actively involved in all the activities of Reproductive and Sexual Health. There was an agreement in Cairo ICPD Programme of Action (1994) that special efforts should be made to promote men's active involvement in such areas. It said, "special efforts should be made to emphasize men's shared responsibility and promote their active involvement in responsible parenthood, sexual and reproductive behaviour including family planning; prenatal, maternal child health; prevention of STDs, including HIV; prevention of unwanted and high-risk pregnancies; shared control and contribution to family income, children's education, health and nutrition; recognition and promotion of the equal value of children of both sexes. Male responsibilities in family life must be included in the education of children from the earliest ages. Special emphasis should be placed on the prevention of violence against women and children". Hence, the men's positive behaviour responsibility and active involvement as participation in activities of RSH can help and facilitate to prevent many reproductive and sexual issues.

Adolescent Reproductive and Sexual Health (ARSH)

Adolescent is a period of transition from childhood to adulthood (between the ages 10-19 years). It is a vital stage of growth and development which results in sexual, psychological and behavioural maturation. ARSH is a healthy condition concerning the system, function and reproductive processes of adolescents. It is affected by pregnancy, unwanted pregnancy, abortion, unsafe abortion, STI including HIV/AIDS, all forms of sexual violence and coercion and by the systems that limit access to information and clinical services.

The ARSH reports that the sexual activity, early pregnancies and STI including HIV infection rates are increasing at unprecedented rates among adolescents. Approximately 15 million young females ages 15-19 give birth each year, accounting for more than 10 per cent of all babies born worldwide. Only about 17 % of them use contraception. Young mothers, especially those under 16, have increased likelihood of serious health risks. The risk of death in childbirth is five times higher among 10-14 year olds than among 15-19 year-olds and, in turn, twice as high among 15-19 year-olds as among 20-24 year-olds. The incidence of STDs is also disproportionately high among young people; 1 in 20 adolescents contracts a STDs each year, and half of all cases of HIV infection take place among people under age 25 years. Youth are vulnerable to sexually transmitted infections, including HIV, and account for 31% of AIDS burden in the country (NACO, 2007).11

ARSH needs to know in order to have correct information about the reproductive process and the various factors that are nearby. With the right information and service programmes for adolescents are expected to have the attitude and responsible behavior on the reproductive process which results in improved health of young people. Since the 1994 ICPD in Cairo, Egypt, Youth Friendly Reproductive Health Services (IFRS) have been recognized as an appropriate and effective strategy to address the SRH needs of adolescents. The YFRHS focused on improving the availability, accessibility and quality of SRH services in an efficient, effective and equitable manner to young people.

Women's Reproductive Health Issues and Prevention

Reproductive health issues remain the leading cause of ill health and death for women of childbearing age worldwide. Most of the reproductive health problems arise during the reproductive years. A reproductive health issue of the women encompasses obstetric and gynaecological morbidity. Obstetric issues include diseases related to during pregnancy, delivery and post-partum period. Gynaecological issues include diseases related to menstruation, RTIs/STIs, HIV/AIDS, breast problems, infertility and cancers. In addition, there is related morbidity like urinary tract infections (UTIs), anaemia, high blood pressure etc.

However poor reproductive health becomes a significant cause of disease and death. The prevalence of dysmenorrhea is estimated to be approximately 25% of women. Reports of dysmenorrhea are greatest among individuals in their late teens and 20s, with reports usually declining with age. Poly Cystic Ovarian Syndrome produces symptoms in approximately 5% to 10% of women of reproductive age (12–45 years old). It is thought to be one of the leading causes of female infertility. Globally approximately 235 million people are affected with uterine fibroids as of 2010 (6.6% of females).14 STIs cause the second highest burden of disease for women aged 15-44 years in developing countries, after maternal mortality and morbidity. Each day 500 000 young people are infected with an STI. The WHO estimates that each year, there are over 333 million new cases of curable STIs. In addition, UNAIDS calculates that in 2000 alone, 5.3 million people became infected with HIV. Endometrial cancers are the most common gynecologic cancers in developed countries with over 142,200 women diagnosed each year. It appears most frequently between ages of 55 – 65 years and uncommon below 40 years of age. Worldwide, breast cancer accounts for 22.9% of all cancers (excluding non-melanoma skin cancers) in women. In 2008, breast cancer caused 458,503 deaths worldwide (13.7% of cancer deaths in women). Some estimates suggest that worldwide "between three and seven per cent of all couples or women have an unresolved problem of infertility. Many more couples, however, experience involuntary childlessness for at least one year: estimates range from 12% to 28%."

Protection from Sexual and Gender-Based Violence

Gender-based violence (GBV) is the fate of millions of women all over the world and these are affecting their productivity both in the homes, communities and places of work. There are different types of gender-based violence which occur at different levels like within the family, community and state. The WHO estimates that at least one in every five of the world's female population has been physically or sexually abused at some time (Population Reference Bureau, 2001). It can affect the female psychologically, cognitively and inter-personally. There can be fatal results of SGBV. More common are non-fatal consequences including reproductive ill-health, physical disabilities, emotional and psychosocial disorders and negative social outcomes. Hence, freedom from unwanted sexual relations and harmful or unwanted sexual practices, including violence & coercion within sexual relationships can help and facilitate to prevent many reproductive and sexual issues.

Reproductive Rights

Reproductive rights are the rights relating to sexual and reproductive health. These are understood as rights of both men and women but are most frequently advanced as women's rights. The UNFPA and the WHO advocate for reproductive rights with a primary emphasis on women's rights. WHO defines Reproductive Rights as: "Reproductive rights rest on the recognition of the basic right of all couples and individuals to decide freely and responsibly the number, spacing and timing of their children and to have the information and to do so and the right to attain the highest standard of sexual and reproductive health. They also include the right of all to make the decision concerning reproduction, coercion and violence".

Control over reproduction is a basic need and a basic right for all women. Reproductive rights include the basic rights of all couples and individuals regardless of age, gender and other characteristics to make choices regarding their own sexuality and reproduction, provided that they respect the rights of others. It includes the rights to: Reproductive health as a component of overall health throughout the life cycles for both men and women i.e. the right to life. Reproductive decision-making, including Voluntary choice in marriage, Right to equality in divorce, Right to family formation and determination of the number, timing and spacing of one's children (family planning), Right to have access to the information and means needed to exercise voluntary choice. Equality and equity for men and women to enable individuals to make free and informed choices in all spheres of life i.e. the right to Non-discrimination based on gender. Seek, receive and impart information. Education (to allow full development of sexuality and the self) Sexual and reproductive security, including Freedom from sexual violence and coercion and the right to privacy. The right to the benefits of scientific progress (e.g. control of reproduction).

Sexual Rights

The Platform for Action from the 1995 Beijing Conference on Women established that human rights include the right of women freely and without coercion, violence or discrimination to have control over and make decisions concerning their own sexuality including their own sexual and reproductive health.

Unlike the other three aspects of SRHR, the struggle for sexual rights includes and focuses on sexual pleasure and emotional sexual expression. One platform for this struggle is the WAS Declaration of Sexual Rights which was adopted the Universal Declaration of Sexual Rights at the 14th World Congress of Sexology. The WAS adopted eleven sexual rights as follow:

1. The right to sexual freedom.

2. The right to sexual autonomy, sexual integrity and safety of the sexual body.
3. The right to sexual privacy.
4. The right to sexual equity.
5. The right to sexual pleasure.
6. The right to emotional sexual expression.
7. The right to sexually associate freely.
8. The right to make free and responsible reproductive choices.
9. The right to sexual information based upon scientific inquiry.
10. The right to comprehensive sexuality education.
11. The right to sexual health care.

Reproductive Rights and Women's Empowerment

The reproductive rights are the important means of women's empowerment. The sexual and reproductive rights will provide education and create awareness among the women so that they will handle their own problems in living and use their rights in attaining the highest possible standard of life in general, sexual and reproductive health in particular. Hence the Sexual and Reproductive Rights are essential for the empowerment of women and to all quality of life issues concerning social, economic, political and cultural participation by women. The neglect or inadequate use of these rights will results in many issues concern to sexual and reproductive health which will be going to increase the maternal mortality and morbidity rate which further have direct impact on the economy of a country.

Reproductive Health & Rights and Feminism

Feminist theorists present several diverse perspectives on how best to increase and protect women's rights. They mainly focus on women's liberation through the woman's movement which aspires to the right to control their own bodies, control and reproductive freedom, safe and better motherhood, provision for day-care of children, the right to decide whether a pregnancy should or should not be terminated. All these movements help to maintain the healthy reproductive state of women and promote women's empowerment in the field of health.

Conclusion

Women's health is made complex by the fact that, apart from the general health needs, women have special health needs related to their reproductive health. The good and healthy reproductive status of an individual is extremely important to give a healthy baby as well as healthy life. The poor reproductive health is frequently associated with disease and death. The reproductive health can be maintained and achieved through the proper usage of reproductive health care methods and reproductive rights. They promote and to attain the highest possible standard of Sexual and Reproductive Health and are the important means of women's empowerment. Feminist theorists help to maintain the healthy reproductive state of women and promote women's empowerment in the field of health.

References

1. http://en.wikipedia.org/wiki/Breast_cancer; 3/12/2011
2. http://en.wikipedia.org/wiki/Dysmenorrheaý; 3/12/2011
3. http://en.wikipedia.org/wiki/Endometrial_cancer;3/12/2011
4. http://en.wikipedia.org/wiki/Infertility; 3/12/2011
5. http://en.wikipedia.org/wiki/Polycystic_ovary_syndrome;3/12/2011
6. http://en.wikipedia.org/wiki/Sexual_and_reproductive_rights 30/12/2011
7. http://en.wikipedia.org/wiki/Uterine_fibroidý-Epidemiology;3/12/2011
8. K.P.Neeraja:"Rural Women"; Published by Discovery Publication House; 2003, PP-1
9. N.K. Behura & R.P. Mohanty : Family Welfare in India – A Cross Cultural Study; Published by Discovery House, New Delhi, 2005; Page 66-77
10. Neeta Tapan: Need for Women Empowerment; Published by Rawat Publication, Jaipur and New Delhi; Page – 91, 92; 2000; (Bhatia, S.C. (Ed), Social Justice in Health, IUACE, New Delhi, 1988, P-26 & 114.)
11. Neeta Tapan: Need for Women Empowerment; Published by Rawat Publication, Jaipur and New Delhi; 2000; Page – 114. ; Reproductive Health Outlook (RHO): Men and Reproductive Health Section - http://www.rho.org/html/menrh.htm#; 2/11/2011
12. Radhika Ramasubban & Shireen J Jejeebhoy - Women's Reproductive Health In India; Rawat Publications Jaipur& New Delhi.2000. PP- 134-145 & 205-210
13. Safe Motherhood - www.unfpa.org/emergencies/manual/3.htmý 20/07/2011

14. Sushma Srivatsav: "Women and Family Welfare"; Published by common wealth, 2008; Page – 112
15. The Hindu - News Paper: Maternal mortality rate in two districts 'alarming'; Bangalore, dated 4/8/2012 Hence, there is need to understand the concept of women's reproductive health.
16. The Hindu News Paper dated 6th May 2103 Topic - Unsafe Abortions Killing A Woman Every Two Hours: Ipas India
17. web.unfpa.org/about/report/report97/adolesce.htm; 16/11/2011; Dr. K Saroja; Mahile Arogya – Ondu Maruchintane, Published by Prasaranga, Kannada Vishwa Vidyalaya Hampi, Vidyaranya, 2008, pp. 23, 24
18. www.popcouncil.org/pdfs/RTIFacsheetsRev.pdf; 3/12/2011
19. www.unfpa.org/swp/1997/box19.htm;(18/07/2011); http://www.cdc.gov/reproductivehealth/Refugee/PDF/Appendix.pdf(18/07/2011)

8

The impact of Mass Media and Role and Participation of Women in Agriculture

— *Raju Kamble, Dr S.M. Malagatti*

Abstract

Women have an important role to play in all economic and productive activities. Their contribution in the agriculture sector is very significant in farming activities on small and marginal land holdings. The women are the backbone of agricultural workforce but worldwide her hard work has mostly been unpaid. She does the most tedious and back-breaking tasks in agriculture, animal husbandry and homes. Agricultural extension is essentially a communication process. It coveys improved or recommended practices to farmers in a bid to improve their methods of production and marketing of their agricultural produce. Mass media are agents of information education, entertainment and motivation to farmers for accepting agricultural people. Mass media consist of both print and electronic media. Agriculture can be an important engine of growth and poverty reduction. But the sector is underperforming in many countries in part because women, who are often a crucial resource in agriculture and the rural economy, face constraints that reduce their productivity. In this paper we draw on the available empirical evidence to study in which areas and to what degree women participate in agriculture. Aggregate data shows that women comprise about 43 per cent of the agricultural labor force globally and in developing countries. But this figure masks considerable variation across regions and within countries according to age and social class. Women, despite having key role in advancing agricultural development and food security, their contribution is undervalued and they have been neglected in the making of agricultural policies. In this paper it has been tried to bring out the impact of Mass Media and Role and Participation of Women in Agriculture.

Keywords: *Mass Media, Women, Agriculture, Role, Participation.*

Introduction

Agriculture is the backbone of the Indian economy; it supports about 70% of the population directly and provides inputs for the secondary sectors of the economy. The success of agricultural development programmes in developing countries largely depends on the nature and extent of use of mass media in mobilization of people for development. The planners in developing countries realize that the development of agriculture could be hastened with the effective use of mass media. Most of Indian farm holdings are small and marginal i.e. less than 5 acres. On these holdings, the entire family is engaged in agricultural activities. The farming is integrated – often combining the varied natural resources of land, water and vegetation to support farming, animal husbandry, and horticulture, to provide a variety of products needed to support life. Agriculture sector is vital for the food and nutritional security of the nation. The sector remains the principal source of livelihood for more than 58% of the population though its contribution to the national GDP has declined to 14.2% due to high growth experienced in industries and services sectors. Compared to other countries, India faces a greater challenge, since with only 2.3% share in world's total land area; it has to ensure food security of its population which is about 17.5% of world population. This leads to excessive pressure on land and fragmentation of land holdings. The Objective of the study is to study about role and participation of women in agriculture and to examine impact of mass media on agriculture. The study proposes to test the following hypotheses; That, women's participation in agriculture is mainly due to low income, and That, women participate in various types of agricultural activities.

Review of literature

Doss (2011) in their working paper has observed that, the agriculture sector is underperforming in many countries because women, who are often a vital resource in agriculture and the rural economy, face constraints that reduce their productivity.

Lal and Khurana (2011) in their research article has tried to link with the important role played by the women in agriculture and the gender discrimination and its negative impact on socio-economic status of women. They have opined that there is under estimation and under valuation of rural women's work in the space of development.

Sharma (1984) in her article "Caste Class and Gender: Women's Role in Agricultural Production in North India" has mentioned that female participation in production activities mirrored caste and class position. She has viewed that the position of Indian women under capitalistic development policy has worsened

Rais (2013) in their research paper have tried to assess the economic status of rural women involved in agriculture and livestock forming activities in Pakistan. He has showed that majority of the respondents have income from agriculture but a very few of them are employed.

Mishra (2009) has found that it is the wage, which affects mostly the efficiency of women agricultural laborers. The other major factors affecting the efficiency were use of leisure time, family pressure, age, family support, distance, health, use of labor saving devices and inter-personal relationship

Ani (2002) to get the best from the mass media, it is imperative to identify and examine each type medium of mass communication, identify the strength of each and weakness as a precondition to determining when a particular medium is most desirable.

Development of Thought

Among the several mass media, newspaper and farm magazine are commonly used. They have a vital role to play in the communication of agricultural information among the literate farmers. Increasing rate of literacy in the country offers new promises and prospects for utilizing print medium as a means of mass communication. The print media widened the scope of communication. It is cheap and people can afford to buy and read them at their convenience. It is a permanent medium in that the message are imprinted permanently with high storage value which makes them suitable for reference and research. Agricultural journalism is of recent origin in India. It came into existence just five decades ago. It is now gaining importance, particularly after the establishment of agricultural university in India; technical information needs to be provided to the farmers at the right time and in the right way, so that the productivity can be increased. India has farm magazines in every state, published mostly in local languages. Agricultural department also encourages the publishing of such farm magazines particularly through farmers association. The coverage of different subject matter by radio, television, newspaper and farm magazine are almost similar with regard to agriculture, horticulture, animal husbandry, agricultural marketing, agricultural engineering and cooperatives.

Women in Agriculture at a Glance

Horticulture

The State Horticulture Missions have been directed to earmark at least 30% of the budget allocation for women beneficiaries in all ongoing programmes.

Macro Management

The States have been instructed to allocate funds for SC/ST women farmers proportionate to their population and utilize the 10%-20% provided under "New Initiatives" for implementing activities for gender empowerment, development and to include Schemes which encourage group formation among Women/ SC/ST farmers in the Work Plan. During the financial year 2010-11, 2014598 women farmers have benefited under the scheme.

Agricultural Extension

Minimum 30% resources meant for programmes and activities are allocated for women farmers and extension functionaries. Since inception of the scheme in 2005-06, total 26,73,772 farm women have participated in farmer oriented activities like exposure visit, training, Demonstrations, trainings & Kisan melas including 3,89,503 women farmers benefited during 2010-11 (up to January, 2011) i.e 55602 through Exposure Visits, 96268 through Trainings, 24855 through Demonstrations and 212778 through Kisan Melas.

Cooperation

National Cooperative Union of India (NCUI) is running four exclusive development projects for women viz., Shimoga (Karnataka); Berhampur (Orissa), Bhopal (MP) & Imphal (Manipur. 'Special Women Development component' – a part of each Field Project caters to the training and extension and marketing needs of women. One women educational and development project is running in North Eastern Region at East imphal, Manipur. About 71 women members are reported to on the Board of Directors of some of these Cooperatives and about 1354 members are expected to get employment through activities of the cooperatives.

Rain fed Farming System

Since 2007-08, 24348 Women Self Help Groups and 18075 User Groups of Women have been formed in the project areas covered under the programme.

Crops

States have been advised to set aside at least 33% of the total allocation for small and marginal farmers, including women farmers.

Mechanization & Technology

During 2010-11 (up to December, 10), around 2925 gender friendly tools /equipments have been distributed among farm women and 499 women have been imparted training at Farm Machinery Training and Testing Institutes.

Agricultural Marketing

Under institutional lending a back-ended subsidy as term loan is provided by the banks up to a minimum of 50% of the project cost (46.67% in case of NE States, hilly areas, Women Farmers / their self help groups / co-operatives and SC/ ST entrepreneurs & their self-help groups / Cooperatives). These are the projects belonging to women farmers.

Availability of mass media in the study area and respondents preference

The available mass media in the study area indicates; radio, television and newspaper and the respondents prefer radio. The respondent prefers radio to as available with them and most preferred television 10% and newspaper 4%. The availability of radio in the study area and preferred by respondents as their best source of information is because radio is portable, affordable and can be heard anywhere, while television is prestigious but not available with majority of the respondent. And, newspaper is not in used by the respondent because majority of the respondent in the study area are not educated and it is expensive for the respondent to buy newspaper for obtaining farm information.

Impact of mass media on respondent's agricultural production

The impact made by the respondent through the use of mass media as their sources for obtaining farm information include getting access to input supply, (65%), farm resources (38%), and market information (46%). Others are, on availability to technology and innovations as well as on general farm information, (23%) respectively. The respondents disclosed that they have access to tractor hiring, input supply such as fertilizer chemicals and insecticides and on general information on market and innovation. Hence, the availability of various farm information have impacted greatly on their production output and income because it has open up opportunities for them to trace where and how to acquire new technology and market information. The respondents disclosed that radio is effective because information pass across is easy to obtain through their friends, Relatives and Neighbors even if they missed the chance to hear direct at the right time of broadcast. While also, meetings with their colleague (farmers) and local leader are also influencing getting information and communication effectively because local leader are interacting with the extension workers and they serve as a source of information. Some of the respondents gave reasons that due to their illiteracy level for not reading and writing, they have no preference for the use of newspaper and printed materials as source of information.

Empowering Women through Agricultural Extension

A prerequisite for sustainable, effective and efficient development is the application of extension services; and consequently, educating professional women and performing developmental programs for female farmers is aimed at women gaining access to extensional services, communicating with women group and encouraging female farmers to participate at extensional activities' programs. The base of developing programs should be on special realities, conditions and recognizing women's need in agriculture.

Conclusion

Agriculture has been the main source of livelihood of the Women's community in the village. Agriculture being practiced by the Women farmers of the village is still rooted in traditional notions of divine blessings for a good crop and the practice of appeasing rituals is still continued. Agriculture is not just an enterprise for livelihood but a socio-economic and cultural activity. While agriculture revolves around seasons, the socio-cultural life of the tribal farmers in the region revolves around agriculture. However, many beliefs and religious rituals are now giving way to rational thinking in the cultivation of the crops. This approach was used for empowering women through financial services with education. In this approach, women were familiar with importance of credits through education and extension, and also they were familiar with ways to access credits through establishing different groups. Findings of this study indicate that participation of women farmers in various areas of extension programmes was very low in the study area. Agricultural extension services should no longer continue considering women as housewives and mothers only, focusing mainly on male farmers. Mass Media is acknowledged as the most important medium for communicating with the rural populations of developing countries. Farming systems thinking is presented with a continuing challenge to move beyond the "technology triangle" of research-extension-farmer linkages whereby information is selectively released and controlled towards a learning-centered approach for knowledge sharing. Improving participation of women farmers in various areas of extension programmes is the best option for empowering farm women for better networking of agricultural information.

References

1. Jana B L: (2014), *Agricultural Journalism*, ATPA Pub, New Delhi
2. Dr. Vir Singh & S K Kashyap: (2013), *Agricultural Communication: Opportunities for Sustainable Agriculture and Rural Development*, Biotech Pub, Delhi
3. N A Mujumdar & Uma Kapila: (2006), *Indian Agriculture in the New Millennium Vol.1*, Academic Foundations, Haryana
4. M S Swaminathan: (2007), *Agriculture Cannot Wait: New Horizons in Indian Agriculture*, Academic Foundations, Haryana
5. Marco Ferroni: (2012), *Transforming Indian Agriculture India 2040: Productivity, Markets and Institutions*, Sage India
6. Shakuntala Sridhara: (2009), *Women in Agriculture and Rural Development*, New India Publishing Agency, Delhi
7. Raj Mohini Sethi: (1992), Women in Agriculture, Rawat Pub, New Delhi

9

GENDER PERSPECTIVE OF POLITICAL LEADERSHIP IN KERALA

— *DR HIRANNIYA KALESH P*

Abstract

The number of leadership positions at the local, regional and national level do not commensurate with their numbers in society. The inferior status of women in political institutions also results from the underlying "biologism" (biologism means a prejudice based on sex which determined gender roles by biologically assigned characteristics.) Of male gendered policies for gender equality. The omission of women in politics of power seriously affects the ability to change the standardization of women in all its manifestations. Women have to be in power politics, to participate as women and to change the very nature of that power which serves to preclude women.Political parties are among the most important institutions affecting women's political participation. In most countries, parties determine which candidates are nominated and elected and which issues achieve national prominence. The role of women in political parties is therefore a key determinant of their prospects for political empowerment, particularly at the national level. Because political parties are so influential in shaping women's political prospects, Governments and international organizations seeking to advance the participation of women in elections justifiably tend to focus on the role of political parties.

Key words: *Women, Political Leadership, Participation, Gender Bias*

Introduction

In the progress of 20th century, the legality of gender as a political category was successively asserted, then denied and then asserted again. In between the negative discrimination of the 1920s and affirmative action of the 1990s, gender considered as largely irrelevant on the political stage. In the 1920s gender was a major political category, in all democracies, women were denied the right to vote because they were women. The liberal theory of Spheres was then dominating the western political thought.

Objective of the Study

Main objective of the study was to find out socio-cultural determinants of women political leadership in Kerala with special reference to Village Panchayat elected representatives. Further elaborating on the specific objective the study tried find out gender dimension of women's participation in grassroots level politics.

Methodology

We have selected 123 women as well male (60 Women/ 63 Men) Panchayat representatives from Palakkad and Alapuzha Districts of Kerala, by using systematic random sampling method. Primary source of information was interview schedule and observation notes made during participating in the Gram Saba meetings. In the study efforts have been made to analyze leadership positions of the respondents according to their gender. And tried to find out whether gender had any role in determining leadership positions in the party.

Scope of the study

In Kerala, which is boasted of being the state with highest women literacy, participation of women in public life is somewhat limited. Here also women from the political family back ground can assert their positions in power politics. They also do not represent the women folk; they do represent the agenda of their respective party. All the above factors makes it clear that political field is a gender biased one, in such a situation, study of political situation of women according to their gender is important. The study was conducted as part of training need assessment of women panchayat leaders in India during 2015-16.

Analysis

Political status can be assessed by individual's voluntary participation in political affairs through membership, voting and partaking in the activities of the political parties, legislative bodies and/or politically motivated movements. In our study it was found that among the 63 male panchayat representatives nearly half of them were enjoying taluk level as well as district level memberships in their respective political parties. While among the 60 female panchayat representatives less than one quarter of them have taluk or district level membership political parties. During the electoral campaign of 1996, the need to ensure a strong presence of women in elected assemblies was emphasized in the manifestoes of all major political parties, from the communist to the Hindu right Stephane, agrees that the present legitimacy of gender as a political category relies on two main founding principles;

(1) Indian state's mission of social justice and

(2) the dominant interpretation of electoral representation as "mirror-representation". The interpretation of political representation as mirror-representation has gained strength over the last two decades of India. New political parties have emerged, gathering people through discourse that appeals to collective identities – be they based on caste, religion, region or language. The fact that gender is now acknowledged, through Women's Reservation Bill, (WRB) as a major social division; Mirror-representation involves both identity politics and group representation which doubly problematic as far as women were concerned.

The second founding principle of the legitimacy of gender as a political category is the idea that elected assemblies must reflect the diversity of the population by whom they are elected. In other words, the conception of political representation as "mirror –representation" prevails over that of "mandate – representation".

A study conducted by Dr. Uma Joshi (1999) try to find out following reasons, which causes hindrance to women's leadership. She classified reasons in to three personal, social and political. Finding are;

Personal Reasons

At first women are ignorant about their rights and responsibilities. And secondly women do not visualize politics as a career for themselves. Generally women are not interested in politics. Fourthly women's reproductive role prevent her from political participations.

Social Reasons

(1) Women are unwilling to enter in to politics due to the prevalence of goondaism, corruption and communalism. Women are not allowed to use family wealth for political purposes. (2) men are unable to accept the political participation of women. (3) in adequate training opportunities for better participation of women in politics.

Political Reasons

Politically fund collections for election are a great problem for women. If she is not contesting under a recognized party, situations become worse. And it is difficult for women to establish contacts with party workers in male dominated party structures.

Women generally participate in large numbers in voting but in other activities, such as attendance of public rallies and membership of social and political organizations. But their leading roles in these organization is lacking. But the scenario changed very soon, today women taking part in the political affairs and holding high offices. Though their number is not very high, but their capacity in administrative and political matters has been well recognized. Gender equality is a pre requisite for effective participation of women in politically higher positions. This will strengthen the democratic process.

The number of leadership positions at the local, regional and national level does not commensurate with their numbers in society. The inferior status of women in political institutions also results from the underlying "biologism" (biologism means a prejudice based on sex which determined gender roles by biologically assigned characteristics.) Of male gendered policies for gender equality. The omission of women in politics of power seriously affects the ability to change the standardization of women in all its manifestations. Women have to be in power politics, to participate as women and to change the very nature of that power which serves to preclude women.

Women's participation in politics is very much related to certain important aspects of women's life, such as marriage, family and employment. Needless to say, that there is no country in the world today, where women have equal status with men in all walks of life, family, health, reproduction, education, work, government and cultural expression. Psychological, situational structural, socio-economic and political variables account for the low position of women in political sphere.

Linda K Ritcher(2008) underlines the highest form of women participation in politics ie. Female leadership in the south and East Asia, she states that the main factors which have affected the emergence of top women leaders in south and South – East Asia are patriarchy, family ties, martyrdom, social class, female life style, the independence movements, prison experience and electoral arrangements. But despite the prominence of several women leaders in the region, opportunities for female leadership have been rare. The percentage of women in elective politics is dropping in these countries. In many nations women became more detached from the politics also. And they are detached from the political socialization process also. Another point of view is that women as a group do little to broaden access to political positions. Although women elite have lower educational and professional achievements than men, they came from more urbanized, high socio-economic back grounds. There are four factors which deter them; lack of education, economic independence, social needs and legal questions.

In political scenario, women leadership is confined to those who have their relatives in politics. Another point is that they always failed to represent women as whole in political bodies, as men do. Tradition and role prejudice are two other factors which deter the women leadership in India. Even today girl child did not have equal voice in family matters as boys enjoy. Involvement of factors such as caste, religion, and regionalism also restricted emergence of women leadership in India.

Size and nature of family

The family structure and composition determines the political participation of women all societies. It was observed that, two-third of the female panchayat representatives were from nuclear family back ground but more than half of the male representatives have extended family back ground. In nuclear families women enjoys more freedom, than in joint and extended families. That may be one of the reasons behind fact that more women from nuclear families took part in politics. Similarly, decision making in the family help the person to enhance his/her confidence in making decisions in larger contexts. Among our respondents it was found that one-third of female respondents make decisions in their family and they agreed that most of the times it was spouses or the parents made decisions. Though the contribution of women in socio-cultural context of Kerala is greater but stragely they have not been given due credit in decision making roles, this in turn put the women always submissive position and restrict them from opinion making public.

In order to understand the gender dimension of political leadership, we looked into the political activeness of the family of the panchayat leaders and it was found that for more than half the panchayat representatives at least one of their family members were active in politics. Among the female representatives two-third of them has relatives (father, brother or spouse) in politics which helped them to contest the elections. Our study clearly establishes that family political background and participation of women in active politics are closely related. It is very difficult for women to establish her in the political world without the support. Earlier studies also proved that, relatives in politics as a most needed condition for women leaders.

Traditionally role of women is considered to be with in the family. Duality of role, as far as women leaders were concerned, create a lot of problem. We asked about the same, and found that half of the female respondents very successfully met the demands of the family and political life. Even though they are elected leaders, the role related behavior they internalized as a result of socialization, compel them to fulfill the family needs and this put them into stress. Apart from this among the married representative when half of the male representatives reported that their spouses make complaint about less participation in family affairs, but in the case of female representatives three-fourth of them face the issue.

Though more than half of the female representatives came in to politics as a result of their spouse's participation in politics, their husbands' demands more participation in family matters from their wives. This is hardly a new claim; there is a large stockpile of evidence and scholarship sizing up the "mommy penalty" (Lun-dberg and Rose 2000) shows that the gender gap persists principally in careers (like politics) that seem to require long and irregular hours.

Age of entry into politics is another factor need to be analyzed through gender dimension, the previous studies shows that the disproportionate burden of family work on women at younger age tend to pull back their career prospect as political leaders. Our study shows that the female representatives stated their career rather delayed. Only one –tenth of them began their career in below 20 years of age. Half of the female representatives entered in to politics at the beginning of 30 years and after that. As mentioned earlier most of the female respondents started their career after their marriage, and the average age of marriage of women in Kerala is higher than rest of the country. So naturally most of them entered in to politics at this particular age group. High Chi-square value suggests that age of entry in to politics and sex of the respondents were related.

From the local to the global level, women's leadership and political participation are restricted. Women are underrepresented as voters, as well as in leading positions, whether in elected office, the civil service, the private sector or academia. This occurs despite their proven abilities as leaders and agents of change, and their right to participate equally in democratic governance. Leadership position of women in the higher level political organizations in Kerala is rare. Our study shows that compared to female representatives men were enjoying more (58.14%) state level district/state level party positions. Only one –tenth of the female representatives have the same. Women require societal changes before they treated equally. However male representatives suggest that, the problem of women office holders stemmed from their own inadequacies, emotionalism and weakness, demand for extra privilege and interest in trivialities and minuet.

As the women respondents were came in to politics by their relative's presence in political parties, 60 per cent of the female respondents came in to leadership positions through consensus. But it was observed that kinsmen in bureaucracy and gender of the representatives were not related.

Kerala is a state where student politics is vibrant. Many of the current ministers and famous politicians are products of the vibrant School/college campuses where student politics was the 'call of the nation'. When we analyzed the participation in politics at school level on the basis of gender of the representatives it was observed that, regardless of gender two-third of our respondents never participated in political actives during their school days. Before becoming panchayat representatives 90 per cent of the female representative never cherished the idea of becoming political leader or getting into active politics. This may be due to the way in which a girl child is being socialized.

Compared to male representative, two-third of female representatives joined politics to serve the party. The study area covered were bastions of Communist Party of India(M) in Kerala, and were party has the priority over the individual. They also opined that at panchayat level the expenditure contest elections are less compared to larger contexts.

Table 1: Gender And Motivation to Join Politics

Sex	*Motivation to join politics*			
	Earning popularity	*Money and status*	*To service to party*	*Total*
Male	32 (50.79%)	15 (23.81)	16(25.40%)	63 (100%)
Female	9 (15%)	12(20%)	39 (65%)	60 (100%)
Total	41 (33.33%)	17 (13.82%)	55 (44.72%)	123 (100%)

Chi-square =9. 35 df=2

* Tabled value = 5.99

* 5% Level of significance

Table 1 shows that gender and motivation to join politics were related. 65 per cent of female respondents had a motivation of serving party. While 51.54 per cent of male respondents had the motivation to earn popularity. Identifying themselves with party gives more security to their positions. Only in the banner of a party they get recognition in larger context. Participation in politics also gives them social status and dignity. The high Chi-square value suggests that two factors were related.

Trade unions determine the political atmosphere of a particular area. In Kerala we know that trade unions are more active than in other parts of India. Besides that trade unions developed a new generation of leadership apart from the national movement leaders. These leadersbelongs various parties. Our study revealed thatonly one-fourth of the female representatives were started their career in trade unions. These were mainly in the cashew sector and coir sectors. Otherwise trade unions need aggressive leaders, that kind aggression is lacking in the women leaders, as far as Kerala is concerned.

In the case of caste organizations, also only one-third of women representatives participated in caste organizations. Generally caste organizations are dominated by males. But today all the caste organizations started their women wing to attract more women in to caste organizations.

It was observed that a gender bias was there in the hierarchy of political leadership, and lack of proper political socialization of women causes their backwardness in political leadership. Trade union participation, membership in caste organizations, working in women organizations are seemed to be essential for women leaders to attain their positions.

Findings & Conclusions

In the study it was observed that leadership hierarchy in the state was gender biased one. Most of the higher positions in the party were owned by male respondents. And the women came in to politics through their relative's presents in the party. And the participation in trade unions was also very low among the women. Less awareness about political happenings, lack of proper political socialization, attitude towards political developments, were deter the women leadership in Kerala. Local level leadership was more common among the women members.

And this was due to provision of reservation for women in local body elections. Male leaders blamed that women herself is behind her failure. And contact with party workers is less among the female members. Training of women is necessary for development of leadership qualities among them.

Conclusion

Politics has traditionally been a male domain that many women have found unwelcoming or even hostile. Societies in which traditional or patriarchal values remain strong may frown on women entering politics. In addition to dealing with unfavorable cultural predilections, women are often more likely than men to face practical barriers to entering politics, including a paucity of financial resources, lower levels of education, less access to information, greater family responsibilities, and a deprivation of rights that has left them with fewer opportunities to acquire political experience. The present study suggests that provide gender-sensitive coverage of elections, avoiding negative stereotypes and presenting positive images of women as leaders.Help establish and support cross-party cooperation among women; Provide support and training to women who have been elected to office to enable them to function more effectively in their new roles.Provide incentives for political parties to promote women candidates, including resources, training and increased access to broadcast time. Providing increased airtime for women in politics between elections could also advance women's participation by enabling voters to make informed assessments at election time of the overall performance of political parties, including their support of women who have been elected as representatives.

References

1. Ballington, Julie, and Muriel Kahane. 2014. "Women in Politics: Financing for Gender Equality," in International Institute for Democracy and Electoral Assistance (IDEA), ed., Funding of Political Parties and Election Campaigns: A Handbook on Political Finance.
2. Lawless, Jennifer, and Richard Fox. 2014. "The Ambition Gap." American Political Science Review.
3. Burns Nancy and Donald Kinder. 2011. "Categorical Politics: Gender, Race, and Public Opinion." in Adam Berinsky, ed., New Directions in Public Opinion, London: Routledge.

4. Kaul Shashi and Sahni, Shradha, 2009, 'Study on the participation of women in Panchayati Raj Institution', Stud Home CommSci, 3(1): 29-38
5. Linda K Ritcher in Women' Politcal Participation and Representation in Asia- Obstacles and Challenges (ed) by KazukiIwanga, Nias Press (Nordic Institute of Asian Studies), 2008.
6. Siva kumar Sowmya Kerbert & Madhuresh 2006: Study of 97 women elected chairpersons in Bihar's Panchayati Raj: Summary of findings, for The Hunger Project, March 2006.
7. Shvedova Nadezhda 2005: Obstacles to Women's Participation in Parliament, in Ballington, Julie &Karam, Azza 2005 (eds): Women in Parliament: Beyond numbers, revised edition, Stockholm: International IDEA, Publications office.
8. Ross Karen, 2002, (ed), Women, politics and change, Oxford University Press, p. 190.
9. Joshy Uma- Why do Women shun Politics? Social Welfare 1999, March, Vol. 45, No. 12. pp. 3-11. ISSN-0037-8033
10. Susan Gluck Mezey – Does sex make Difference? A case study of women in politics, Western Political Quarterly. Vol. 31, 1978, pp. 496-98.
11. Santha E.K. 1999, Political Participation in Panchayati Raj: Haryana, Kerala and Tamil Nadu, New Delhi: Institute of Social Sciences.
12. Srivastava Aparna- Reasons for low participation of Women in politics. Social Welfare, Vol. 45. No. 12 march-1999.
13. Hiermath Ujwala- Women in Grass root politics. Social Welfare. Vol. 44. No. 2 May -1997.

10

Women and Panchayati Raj in India: Present Scenario

— *Dr. Jitendra Wasnik*

Abstract

Panchayati Raj Institutions (PRIs) in India have always been considered as a means to good governance and 73rd Constitutional Amendment was effected in the hope that it would lead to better governance and provide political space to the disadvantage section of the society like Schedule Caste, Schedule Tribes and women. The paper is an effort to know the extent of participation of women elected representative in PRIs and the problems faced by them. The paper revealed that neither the reservation for women or their actual presence in the PRIs have become any more sensitive to the problems related to them. The women who are elected are not always treated with due respect. Many elected women complained that their suggestions were not considered seriously nor were they consulted while decisions were being made. Some felt that their views were ignored only because they are women. At times they were pressurized by their husbands to approve their decisions made by the male dominated PRIs.

Key words: *Panchayat Raj, Women Participation, 73rd Constitutional Amendment Act, Local Government*

Introduction

In the recent years, in the context of globalization, there has been a resurgence of the debate on empowerment of women within the new development paradigm. Women's issues are no longer looked at from merely the perspective of family and social welfare. In general, they have been socially segregated, economically deprived and politically disempowered. Many countries of the world acknowledged the importance of increasing the role of women in government. Many repots and action plan developed contains statements expressing the concern of women about their opportunities to participate meaningfully in government decisions that affect their lives. Although equal political opportunity for women is a goal shared by both men and women, but in reality it has been rarely practiced. This paper tries to study the role of woman in Panchayat administrative system, and to understand the extent to which the women are successful in giving satisfactory administration. Historical and descriptive methods are used for the study.

Women's participation in politics cannot be separated from other important aspects of women's lives such as marriage, family, and empowerment. When the confines of local beliefs are strong and difficult to overcome, there can be a steadfast refusal to see that a real inequity is involved in the way women are treated in their own society, and many women are themselves led to a belief about women's alleged intellectual inferiority based on the supposed 'evidence of the eyes', drawing on a faulty reading of local observations within a stratified society (Sen, 2009: 162).Thus, an understanding of the success of women in political participation as well as the barriers women face in reaching equal participation requires a discussion of the context within which women live. However, the women's movement succeeded to forward their problems as well as their dignity in society. Fifty per cent population of women gave them very prior role in politics of India. Because of the importance of women in voting, all political parties made forward women's problems in their party agenda. But these political parties gave tickets to very few women candidates in elections. In spite of this selfish politics, women are raising themselves.

In the previous two or three decade in India, all political parties insisted on the representation and participation of women in politics. In this concern various problems of women are discussed on every dice of politics. Many scholars noted that, the presence of women particularly in the Panchayati Raj Institutions (PRIs) is an indication of the collaboration that is desired of them in the rural development of the country. Women's presence in PRIs opens a new way for them to make their voice heard and thus bring to the forefront, the rich content of feminine thought and action in the development as well as it ensures their identity and empowerment.

Participation of Women in Panchayati Raj

There is no country in the world today where women have equal status with men in all of the major areas of life: family, health and reproduction, education, work, government, and cultural expression. It would be least incorrect to state that none of the successive governments at the Centre or at the State levels went beyond paying a ceremonial lip-service of promising empowerment to the Indian women and took no serious measures to alter the existing power relations to bridge the gender-gap. It took almost half a century for the Indian Parliament to understand the rationale behind providing reservations for women in Panchayati Raj.

The Maharashtra was the first state which introduced the provision for the nomination of one or two women to each of the three tiers PRI sunder its Zilla Parishad and Panchayati Act of 1961. Later Karnataka in 1983and Andhra Pradesh in 1986 introduced the policy of reservation of 25 seats for women in Gram Panchayats and Zilla Parishads. The state like West Bengal, Madhya Pradesh, Kerala, Himachal Pradesh, Haryana, and Orissa had also made the provision to reserve 20 per cent to 30 per cent of the total seats for women candidates in different tiers of local bodies in their respective states. However the provision of co-option could not bring a large number of women members to PRIs. The method of co-option was not made compulsory and therefore the women members could not get the benefit of it. The requirement of co-option was not followed uniformly for all PR bodies and in every state. Uttar Pradesh and Jammu and Kashmir for instance did not follow the scheme. Co-option was primarily used as patronage. Most of the women were from the politically connected families. The co-opted women hardly attended Panchayat meetings. They were called in only when quorum was the problem; otherwise their signatures were obtained from houses after the meetings(Lima, 1993:22-23).According to Rajput

(1993:39-41) most of the women members were neither ware of their role, rights or duties nor did they know much about the functioning of the Panchayats. They were just satisfied with the prestige and status symbol of being a member. They did not feel confident enough to discuss various issues relating to rural development or women's development. Women members consequently could not play an important role in the Panchayati Raj Process.

The realization that women always have been disadvantaged and marginalized from various development processes had led to a conscious effort among the development planners to provide equal space to women to participate in development process. Development planners had learned that without women's full and informed participation, development projects are unlikely to succeed and women's empowerment cannot be achieved. Attempts had been made at national level to bring equality and to provide equal opportunity to both men and women to participate in development programmes. Government started many development projects especially for women to help them overcome their inequalities. But unfortunately, the developments since independence have not produced the desired results in actual practice due to social inhibitions and organizational deficiencies. An enormous disparity still exists between formal political equality of women and their meaningful exercise of political power. Despite all the legislation, policies and programmes of the government, it has been realized that women still continue to be one of the most oppressed sections of society. Government sponsored development activities seem to have benefitted only a small section of women, mainly of the urban middle class. The large majority of women have not benefitted from development. Its reflection is found in a report titled "Towards Equality" published by the Committee on the Status of women in India (CSWI) in 1974.The Committee very strongly recommended that women should be provided with special opportunities for participation in the representative structure of Local Government. This committee also suggested for establishment of women's gram Panchayats to involve more women in the activities of Panchayats.

The National Perspective Plan (NPP) for women (1988) also highlighted that co-option of women in PRIs did not bring about any perceptible impact on women's participation in Panchayats. The NPP also asserted that special intervention was necessary to give more thrust and responsiveness to the policies and programmes related to empowerment of women in the participatory democracy. The final report of NPP therefore recommended for women the following policy perspectives. (a) 30 per cent reservation of total seats in local governments-both in panchayats and municipalities, (b) 30 per cent reservation of executive heads in all PR bodies,(c) reservation of certain percentage of constituencies in lower PR tiers as exclusively women constituencies and (d) 50 per cent of all grass-root functionaries would be women. Consequent upon the recommendations of the NPP regarding reservation of seat and post for women in local governments, the 64th Amendment Bill was introduced in Lok Sabha on 15th May 1989. The special feature of this Bill was 30 per cent reservation of seats for women in the three tier PRIs. Despite of putting so much effort on the Bill it was not passed. The bill was defeated in the upper house. Another Bill was introduced in September1990 but it could not be taken up because of the fall of the then government.

After the general elections of 1991, new government came to power and introduced the 73rd Constitutional Amendment Bill. The Bill was referred to the Joint Committee of Parliament and after incorporating suggestions of the joint committee the Bill was finally passed in Parliament on December 23, 1992 and came into force from April 24, 1993. The 73rd Amendment Act opened up a new vista in Indian politics as far as women's political participation is concerned. It reserved constitutionally 33% of seats for women in PRIs. This Amendment aimed at making rural women not only beneficiaries of development but more importantly contributors to it. Following this Amendment, states and Union Territories have modified their Panchayat Acts to conform to the new dispensation within the stipulated date of April 24, 1994. Panchayats Acts of the States and union territories have reserved not less than one third seats and posts for women, Till the end of 2000, elections were held in 20 states and 4 union territories reserving panchayat seats and posts for women. Some states have gone further to incorporate in the Panchayati Raj Acts the provision to enable women to assume the post of vice chairperson if the post of chairperson does not befall to them. In Maharashtra every chairperson is to hold office for one year instead of usual five years. In Karnataka, the tenure of chairperson is to rotate after 20 months so that majority of member including women, will get the chance to head the PR body. The reservation provision for women provided by the 73rd Amendment Act has been hailed as a bold, revolutionary and a right step. The reservation provided to women in PRIs created the 'necessary enabling conditions for women empowerment' their sustained interest and involvement in public affairs. It is presumed that gradually an environment would evolve which will deepen the concept of participatory democracy by providing gender equality, justice and equity in India. In the post 1993 phase women's participation seems to have improved in relative terms but still women members are to overcome a number of hindrances. The Act itself is considered as a significant step to make inroads to democratization process. It is a beginning which needs to be substantiated by changes in many other fields related to socio-economic, political and attitudinal values of our society. Various social restrictions still prevail in our society to lend support to the policy perspective provided by the 73rd Amendment Act. The changes in PRIs structures over the years have certainly ensured higher visibility of women in grass root level democracy but whether that translates to real empowerment of women is subjected to corresponding changes in many others fields.

In 1992, the government of India enacted the 73rd and 74th Constitutional Amendments to provide for one-third representation of women in local government. By 1993 all states except Bihar had ratified these amendments. Previously, Panchayats were governed by State Panchayat Acts, which allowed the nomination of only two or three women. As a consequence, in all the 223,000 Panchayats across India, only 13 per cent members were women. However, with the onset of the silent revolution in the form of these Constitutional Amendments, the numbers of women rose to 33 per cent or one million. Under the Constitutional Amendments, women can be members as well as Chairpersons of these local government institutions. Whatsoever might have been the logic behind zeroing in on not less than 33 per cent figure, the number was inadequate to represent women. Unfortunately, a 33 per cent only for all the states, on the one hand, and on the other, even this 33 per cent was not vertically maintained to the level of various quorums of Panchayat meetings where the most crucial decisions regarding Panchayats were taken.

Therefore, recently the cabinet (21st July 2011) approved the proposal for moving an official amendment made to article 243Dof the Constitution (One hundred and Tenth Amendment Bill, 2009) of India for enhancing reservation for women in PRIs at all tiers from 33% to at least 50%. Bihar, Madhya Pradesh, Chhattisgarh Rajasthan, Himachal Pradesh, Uttarakhandand, Maharashtra held their elections in recent past under the new arrangement and followed by the other state according to their due and terms(Tiwari, 2012: 37). A survey commissioned by the Ministry of Panchayati Raj in 2009 observed that reservation for women in PRIs has played a significant role as four-fifths of all the representatives got elected from reserved seats. The role of reservation was also evident from the fact it emerged as an important motivator for contesting the election. It will facilitate more women to enter the public sphere and this will lead to further empowerment of women and also make PRIs more inclusive institutions, thereby improving governance and public service delivery. At present, out of the total elected representatives of PRIs numbering approximately 28.18 lakh, 36.87% are women. With the proposed Constitutional amendment, the number of elected women representatives is expected to rise to more than 14 lakh. The increased in their proportion in PRIs could help them to maintain their social and political dignity in local politics, grassroots democracy and public life. Once women got opportunity to serve, they are doing well in social as well as in political life.

The issue is not the numbers of women alone, but their self-knowledge, confidence, clarity of purpose, priorities, commitment and ability to skillfully present their perspectives. Their multiple roles as wives, mothers, daughters, community workers and income-generators severely limit their time for community interaction and mobilization. In India, women have the right to vote, as well as other rights, but their low level of education has meant that woman may not be aware of their rights. Poverty and lower economic development have meant that woman have had to spend much of their time devoted to sustaining the family. This may mean full time involvement in child care or include generating income in agriculture. With so many different cultural and religious backgrounds, Indians do exhibit some differences in their inclusion of women in activities outside the home. Traditionally women are discouraged from mingling with men and therefore work or political activities generally are not acceptable additions or alternatives to family life. Women have specifically avoided those areas because the working conditions presuppose public contact with the opposite sex, a threat to morality taboos associated with principles of family honor and prestige. Another important fact is that many family members do not want that their women members to participate in the Panchayats meetings. They also do not allow their elected women representatives to interact with government officials and others in the matter of taking decisions. There are cases, where husband opposed their wife's active participation (Bhuyan, 2008: 36).The widely-held perception was that political activity is "dirty" and not for decent women.

Inside the PRIs, women have yet to make their presence felt. In spite of the increases in their numbers provided for by the Constitution, their performance has been muted. This has been attributed to lack of self-confidence, a limited capacity to communicate and a lack of understanding of working procedures. Other problems include being shouted at in council proceedings or being ignored by presiding members when women members want to make interventions. The short notices for meetings and transportation costs incurred during Panchayats work have also been indicated as constraints for them. Women members working in the agriculture or formal sector also identify difficulties in combining Panchayats responsibilities. Elected women also worry about being able to undertake development activities to justify their selection. Perhaps part of the difficulty of making women's presence felt at the Panchayat level is the general paucity of women in government and administration.

Barriers to Women's Participation in Panchayati Raj

The major obstacle to women's full participation in politics, education, employment and other important life activities is a nearly universal, societal attitude that has valued women principally as mothers and wives. Throughout history, there are many examples of women transferred like property from fathers to husbands to fulfil this role, and women often were not allowed to hold or inherit property. Within the household, the virtuous wife and mother might be rewarded and given latitude in household-related decisions. Where family honour has been tied to female chastity, however, the segregation of women from participation in the outside world has been deemed necessary to keep them from being tempted. When this has occurred, women have been restricted from equal opportunities.

The caste-based cleavages, social class configurations, patriarchal culture, poverty etc. are always did not appear as deterrents to political participation of women in both the tiers of PRIs. The psychological factors that inhibited women's active participation in PRIs were shyness and submissiveness and lack of understanding of their roles and responsibilities. As for as demographic factors are concerned, only one factor i.e. low level of education can be treated as most inhibitor of women's active participation in PRIs (Bhatt, 2011: 36). This societal attitude has been reinforced by most religious doctrines and structures. Doctrines often stress the importance of women's role as wife and mother and may also place women in a secondary position in relationship to men. Some religions require the separation of women from the outside world or physical separation of men and women at religious services. Religious structure reflects this view, too.

- In striving for participation in Panchayati Raj, women face several types of barriers which arise from the traditional societal attitude toward women.
- Men often have negative attitudes toward women in politics specifically and in activities outside the home in general.
- Many women may lack the skills and self-esteem necessary for effective participation Panchayati Raj. Women have been underrepresented in prestigious occupations that tend to produce leadership skills.
- Women have the double burden of Panchayati Raj commitment and major family responsibilities.
- Some women may find it difficult to appreciate and support women candidates and officials women in politics have selected a role different from the traditional one. In addition,

if women have self-esteem, they may not be able to put trust in the women.

These barriers impede women's gaining access to elective and appointed offices and make it more difficult for women to govern effectively when they hold office. Women tend to have education and job experience to prepare them for running or holding an office. This makes women appear less qualified than men. It also means that women may feel less confident to seek office themselves and be less receptive to accepting the responsibility of a government position if asked. Female personality traits as a barrier, because women have ordinarily been thought to be more passive and nurturing than men, it is harder for women to exert strong leadership. Lack of assertiveness may be the result of women's ambivalence about what their social role should be: family related or participant in the outside world. Women who' are assertive and behave more like men in leadership positions are sometimes thought to be bossy or strident because they are behaving in an unexpected way. Women in PRI generally do not begin their political careers with strong linkage with the male power structure and find it more difficult to build the links because it is less socially acceptable. For all of the above reasons, those women tend to hold a position in Panchayati Raj. Once in office they may find it difficult to advance or to be as effective as they would like to be. The obstacles to active participation can be reduced by appropriate actions of governments, political parties, and women themselves.

Increasing Women's Participation in Panchayati Raj

Although nations and individuals may agree with the objective of increasing female participation in politics, actions to promote this objective must be tailored to fit country's particular economic conditions, government structure, and cultural history. Thus, any list of recommendations must be viewed as suggestions to be considered when attempting to promote increased participation of women. There is no single blueprint for bringing about greater female participation. Many kinds of loosely interrelated activities can eventuality yield positive results. There are some policies which governments and political parties can undertake on behalf of women and there are some changes women will probably have to take responsibility for alone.

Change would come more easily if both men and women could be convinced that women are a large and underused resource, and that opening up all parts of society to women would add substantially to national talent and the quality of life for everyone. This is however, a difficult task in India.

There is plenty of evidence that women get the opportunities that are typically the preserve of men; they are no less successful in making use of these facilities that men have claimed to be their own over the centuries. The opportunities at the highest political levels happen to have come to women, only in rather special circumstances-often related to the demise of their more established husbands or fathers--but the chances have been invariably seized with much vigour (Sen, 2008: 199-200).On this background, in order to ensure women's active participation in Panchayati Raj, national governments must continue to guarantee women's rights in education, family life, employment, and political participation. History, however, shows that legislation alone is insufficient. Government commitment to making rights widely known and enforcing laws is essential.

National policy must encourage equal participation at all levels of education. Lack of education has often benefited as a reason why women do not feel confident about participation in politics. It also is used by political parties to explain why women are not as acceptable or as qualified as candidates compared to men. In the educational system, girls should not be programmed into traditional female studies that lead to low-paid occupations which already have a high concentration of women. Treatment of women in textbooks must reflect the many kinds of jobs and roles which women play. If women appear only as housewives, mothers, teachers, or nurses, children receive a limited vision of women's capabilities and acceptable societal roles.

At the national and local levels, the appointment of women to cabinets, ministries, boards and judicial posts also can serve to bring women into the political system. In the past, women have had every small percentage of appointments, and these have tended to be in areas seen as extensions of women's family role-particularly health, education and social services. More effort needs to be made to increase the number of women appointed and the types of areas in which they serve. Greater commitment to appointed women at every level of government is likely to increase women's political participation in general.

Government has encouraged the formation of national and grass roots women's groups that can lobby for change and give women's issues visibility. Among those at grass roots, Self-help groups and other groups can serve to develop women's political leadership and organizational skills. These skills are important to women's success in political parties and government. The organizations also develop linkages among women (networks), another critical element in political success.

Women's Role in Increasing Their Participation

Women will not gain equal participation in Panchayati Raj without undertaking major efforts themselves, the major source for change in the role and status of women has come in the past from women themselves. Future change will probably be the result of the efforts of women, too.

There are many activities which can help women in reaching more equal representation in Panchayati Raj and local decision making. Suggestions include the following:

- Obtaining better education.
- Training for jobs that provide more direct routes to politics.
- Building networks to increase access to information and reduce isolation.
- Improving the image of women by monitoring text books and media Portrayals.
- Working for more even distribution of household responsibilities.
- Forming women's groups for lobbying activities and skill development.
- Effectively working within political party structures for women candidates.
- Supporting women candidates and men who are sensitive to women's concerns.

Many additions could be made to this list, but the suggestions above address several critical areas in which women's participation is limited. Often women lack the confidence and self-esteem to pursue political office. Obtaining better education and wider job skills, especially beyond traditional women's training, can improve confidence. Sharing experience and discussing confidence building within small women's groups can reduce the sense of isolation women may have as they try new activities, and the groups can serve as a basis of support. Women can help each other in taking risks.

Working with other women in larger organizations can build networks for broader access to information and build the political skills important for holding public office. These larger organizations can effectively present women's issues to the entire population monitor how women are being depicted in society, develop strategies for changes necessary to increase women's participation, and identify and support women who could hold public office. A major problem women face is finding the time required for political participation. Activities essential to the survival of the household unit consume women's days. Economic development may begin to reduce the burden of women as would convince men to accept a larger share of family responsibility.

Panchayati Raj is probably the easiest level of government in which women can actively participate. Many of the problems that concern women about the quality of life such as schools, child care, and social services, are most affected by local decisions. Women are the first to take an interest in-and the first concerned by–the daily, practical problems of community living. Their views and suggestions weigh greatly in decision making. In addition, women are less likely to encounter resistance to participation in Panchayati Raj than in other levels because local governments appear to have concerns closer to family concerns. Women's connection to the local power structure maybe underdeveloped, but women can build coalitions with neighbors and friends.

Conclusion

The decisions of Panchayati Raj have a profound bearing and

motherhood years; women generally are the major consumers of Panchayati Raj services in health and family activities either directly for themselves or indirectly on behalf of their children. The issues that concern women are among the major concerns of Panchayati Raj. Therefore, the perspective of women and their experience in dealing with local concerns especially qualifies them to participate in Panchayati Raj. They can accomplish this in many ways: holding elective office or appointed positions; being officials and non-officials in Panchayati Raj; and indirectly influencing decision makers through grass roots and voluntary organizations or from their positions in society.

The Panchayati Raj system has facilitated the entry of all sections of the society including women, SCs and STs in the political domain; yet the issue of extent of their participation has not been fully resolved. Quite often the question raised is will mere inclusion and cheers over their growing numerical strength solve the problems associated with social and economic dependence or disempowerment. Available data show that they are increasing their participation in most of the ways mentioned. Inthe long run, if societies become less discriminatory in occupational stereotyping on the basis of sex, it would be expected that opportunities for men and womenwould become similar, as would their participation in PRIs. In the short run, however, because sex roles in society are still somewhat distinct, it is especially important that women be represented in positions of leadership and become more visible in PRIs, so that their interests and perspective can be reflected fully.

References

1. Bhatt, G. D. (2011): "Post 73rd Constitutional Amendment & Women Leadership in Sikkim", Kurukshetra, August.
2. Bhuyan, Dasarathi (2008): "Participation in Panchayati Raj", Yojana, October.
3. Lima, Hazel D. (1993): "Participation of Women in Local Self-Government" in Sushila Kaushik (ed.), Women's Participation in Politics, New Delhi: Vikas Publishing House Pvt. Ltd.
4. Rajput, Pam (1993)"Women Leadership at the Grass-root Level in Punjab", in Sushila Kaushik (ed.), Women's Participation in Politics, New Delhi: Vikas Publishing House Pvt. Ltd.

5. Sen, Amartya (2008): Development as Freedom, New Delhi: Oxford University Press.
6. ——————— (2009): The Idea of Justice, England: Allen Lanne.
7. Tiwari, Nupur (2013): "Women in Panchayati Raj", Yojana, June.

11

Rural Women Empowerment and Entrepreneurship Development: A case study of Andhra Pradesh

— *S. K. Asha Begum*

Abstract

Women's Empowerment has emerged as an important issue of recent times. The economic empowerment of women is being regarded in progress for a country; hence the issue of economic empowerment of women is of paramount importance to political thinkers, social scientist and reformers. The Self Help Groups (SHGs) have paved the way for the economic independence of rural women. The members of SHGs are involved in Micro Entrepreneurship. Through that, they are becoming economically independent of rural women through entrepreneurship and the advantage entrepreneurship among the rural women economic empowerment and the advantages entrepreneurship among the rural women. Women's entrepreneurship to the economic well-being of the family and communities and also reduce poverty. It ensures country's economic growth and development. The empowerment of women to a large extent depends on taking part in some development activities, Therefore the promotion of micro and small-scale entrepreneurs has been recognized as an important strategy for advancing the economic empowerment of women. At the household level, women's micro-entrepreneurs and small-scale business play an important role in ensuring the survival of poor household and in building up women's confidence, skills and socio-economic status. However, it is seen that women are the most deprived category in the society specifically in developing countries. In India also the economic status of women' is very low especially in rural areas and opportunities of earning are very less. Women are less encouraged to start business units due to the various issues like financial problems, lack of motivation, and support from their family members. Hence, the study aims at Importance of entrepreneurial development among women and also to analyze the socio-economic framework, problems and prospects of women entrepreneurs in Guntur District, Andhra Pradesh.

Key Words: *Rural women, Self Help Groups, Socio- Economic Status, Women Strategy, Micro Entrepreneurs*

Introduction

The emergence of women entrepreneurs and their contribution to the national economy is quite visible in India. The number of women entrepreneurs has grown over a period of time, especially in the 1990s. Women entrepreneurs need to be lauded for their increased utilization of modern technology, increased investment, finding a niche in the export market, creating a sizable employment for others and setting the trend for their women entrepreneurs in the organized sector. While women entrepreneurs have demonstrated their potential, the fact remains that they are capable of contributing much more than what they already are. Women's entrepreneurship needs to be studied separately for two main reasons. The first reason is that women's entrepreneurship has been recognized during the last decade as an important untapped source of economic growth. Women entrepreneurs create new jobs for themselves and others and also by being different. They also provide the society with the different solution to management, organization and business problems as well as to the exploitation of entrepreneurial opportunities. The micro fiancé is agenda for empowering poor women. The microenterprise is an integral a part of a planned strategy for securing the balanced development of the economy of the poor women. Rural women's participation in agro-based activities in much more than what statistics reveal. This is mainly due to the fact that most of the work done by the women as farm and home is disguised as daily chores. Mechanization and easy availability of labour provide more time to energetic women to engage themselves in self-employment or entrepreneur ventures. Rural women are having human and non-human resources to take up entrepreneurs need one an employment among rural youth. It helps to generate employment for a number of people within their own social system. This is more beneficial for women in rural areas it enables them to add to the family income while taking care of their own home and livestock centred task. Rural women possess abundant resources to take up an enterprise. She has the benefit of easy availability of arm and livestock based raw material and other resources. So it is necessary to empower women socially, economically and technologically to enable them to stand in society on their own with confidence. It includes both contras over resources' and ideology, greater self-confidence and an inner transformation of one's consciousness that enables one to overcome external affairs (Sharma & Varma 2008). In today's competitive world, there are various ways by which women get themselves empowered.

Objectives of the paper

1. To study the Socio-Economic factors of the women entrepreneurship in Guntur District, Andhra Pradesh.
2. To understand the importance of women empowerment.
3. To provide the solution to improve the satisfaction of women entrepreneurship of Guntur district.

Methodology

The study intends to analyze the role played by in women empowerment. In pursuance of the objectives and hypothesis the methodology adopted for conducting the study has been described as follows.

Sources of data

The present study is empirical in nature and is based on the collection of data through survey method. Both primary and secondary data are used to achieve the objective of the study. Researcher intends to collect the primary data needed for the study through the questionnaire and holding the interviews with the respondents and microfinance institutions in Guntur district. Primary data is collected through questionnaires and interviews. Separate and independent questionnaires are prepared to both women beneficiaries and women empowerment institutions. The questionnaires are split into two parts for both types .The first part of questionnaires for women beneficiary consists of the Demographic features, Occupation, Details of association with microfinance like the level of income generation, Source and repayment of loan and other details related to socio-economic development and second part consists of statements of five point scale .As women beneficiaries were less literate.

In this resources paper, the data collection has been mode by primary as well as secondary sours. The primary data was collected through questionnaires, Interview and so, on. The secondary data has been collected through such journals, articles, books and so on.

Sample Size

As our aim is to assess the socio-economic development of women in Guntur district, the researcher approached various SHG's in the district. Stratified random sampling technique is used to draw the sample for present study. Kalaburagi District comprises of six talukas along with Kalaburagi city and Rural. Only those Self help groups have been chosen who had taken loan from banks (As per the data available from guntur district at a Glance-2013-14 &Women & Child dev. Out of the total SHGs in taluk wise who had taken loan, 15% of the sample of SHGs were selected, and Finally out of the selected SHGs 2-3 respondents from each Self help groups were chosen for interview. The total sample size comprised to 600 respondents.

Review of the literature

1. Kumar (1997) made a case study Self-Help Groups in Andhra Pradesh. A total of 21 SHGs were selected for this study after a detailed description of the profile of groups and groups members, the author came to the following conclusions, the groups were mostly homogeneous in terms of their socio-economic background. This homogeneity contributed to the cohesiveness and solidarity of the members. The saving level was reasonably satisfaction because of low-interest rates charged by the banks and the revolving fund.

2. Rama Lakshmi (1998) found that the DWCRA groups take up traditional income-generating activities like dairy, agriculture-related activities like sericulture. Skills worm rearing and silk weaving, grafting of fruit plants, managing orchards, fish rending, prawn processing crop production on leased lands managing tractors, litters and others agricultural equipment, sheep and goat rearing, small business, vending of agricultural production flowers, fruits, artisan activities like pottery, toy making, leather work.

3. Morgan and dharmalingam (2000) opined that empowerment of women through SHGs would to benefits not only to the individual women and women groups but also for the family and community as a whole through collective action for development. Empowering is not just for meeting their economic needs, but also for holistic social development.

4. Gautham and sing (2001) reported the impact of DWCRA in four districts of Himachal Pradesh. A total of 23 types of different economic activities were being pursued under this scheme, with the maximum number of group (126) pursuing milk production activity. In spite of 91 per cent achievement of the target in organizing the unit of groups under DWCRA, the functional units accounted for only 67.17 percent. The reasons for this were improper, the non-availability of raw materials, high cost of raw materials compared to finished product and the lack of local demand and marketing facilities.

5. "Selvaraj" Entrepreneurship the need of the day (1998) emphasized the need for the development of entrepreneurship in rural areas, as it will bridge the required disparities between the rural and fewer development regions. Migration has become a major problem in our country. If the potential migrates are engaged in entrepreneurial activity, this can be minimized and the problem of urbanization can be eliminated.

Table 1: Socio-Economic Factors.

Personal Characteristics	*Category*	*No. of Respondents*	*Percentage*
Age	Bellow 30 Years	17	18.88%
	30-40 Years	35	38.88%
	40-45Years	28	31.11%
	50 Years	10	11.13%
Marital Status	Married	61	67.77
	Single	39	43.33%%
Total		90	100

Sources: Primary and Secondary Data.

6. Data Analysis and Interpretation. This study has aimed the problems and prospects of women entrepreneurs in Guntur districts. For this purpose the study conducted for 90 respondents of the women entrepreneurs. An attempt has been made in this section to analyze the collected data with reference to the activities of the women entrepreneurs a detailed analysis is given below problems faced by women entrepreneurs, by using Rank order
7. Entrepreneurship Development of Rural Women Through Self Help Groups Women comprise half of human resources they have been identifies as key agents' of sustainable development and women's equality is an central to a more holistic approach towards stabilizing new patterns and process of development that are sustainable. The contribution of women and their role in the family as well as in the economic development and social transformation are pivotal. Women constitute 90 per cent of total marginal workers of the country. Rural women who are engaged in agriculture from 78 per cent of all women in regular work. Experience of NIRD action research projects reveal that, the operational aspects, such as the extent enabling that goes into the community self help process and sharpening the mindset of women.

   Men and the project administration are low or critical components that determined their extent to which empowerment may not take place. The role of micro-credit is to, improve the socio and economic development of women and improve the status of women in households and communities. The micro-entrepreneurship are strengthening the women empowerment and remove the gender inequalities. Self-Help Groups micro-credit mechanism makes the members involved in their community development activities. Microcredits are promoting the small-scale business enterprise and its major aim is to alleviate poverty by income generating activities among women and poor.

8. Role of Self Help Groups in empowering Women: Participation in income generating activities helps in the overall empowerment of women. The SHGs had the major impact on the socio-economic life of rural women. It empowers women and trains them to take activities part in the socio-economic progress of the nation and make them sensitized, self-made and self-disciplined. In this regard, Patnaik (2003) has stated that SHGs are continuously striving for a better future of rural women as participants, decision-makers and beneficiaries in the domestic, economic, social and cultural spheres of life. But due to organized properly and effectively. The SHGs have included a great capacity of women in moulding the community in the right perspective and explore the initiative of women in taking the entrepreneurial ventures.

9. Advantages of Entrepreneurship among Rural Women: Empowering women particularly rural women is a challenge. Micro enterprises in the rural area can help to meet these challenges. Micro enterprise not only enhances national productivity, generate employment but also help to develop economic independence, personal and social capabilities among rural women.

   (a) Economic empowerment
   (b) Improved stander of living
   (c) Self-confidence
   (d) Enhance awareness
   (e) Increased political activities
   (f) Engaged in a political and social intersection

10. Improvement in leadership qualities: Economic empowerment of women by micro-entrepreneurship led to the empowerment of women in many things such as socio- economic opportunity, property right, political representation, socio equality, personal right, family development, market development, community development and last the nation development.

Conclusion

The main objective of the scheme is to improve the economic, health, educational and social status of rural women by providing them assistance and creating employment opportunities. The specific objectives of the scheme are: To help and promote self-employment among the rural women, who are below the poverty line, by providing skill training in vocations which are acceptable to the beneficiaries, by encouraging productivity in their existing vocations and by introducing new activities hitherto undertaken; To organize the beneficiaries in groups, activity-wise and promote economic and social self-reliance. To generate income for the rural poor by creating avenues for production of goods and services; To organize production enhancing programmes in rural areas. To provide for care of the children of the workingwomen by providing an improved environment, care and food by establishing crèches / balwadis. The programme called for formation of groups of 10-15 women who could collectively engage in an activity. One woman amongst the members functions as the group organizer who helps in the choice of activity, procurement of raw materials, marketing of products etc.

Women's entrepreneurship is both about women's position in society and about the role of entrepreneurship in the same society. Women entrepreneurs faced many obstacles specifically in the market their product that have to be overcome in order to give them access to the same opportunities as men. In addition, in some countries, women may experience obstacles with respect to holding property and entering the contract. At present women have broken the monopoly of men and proved that they are not inferior men. The SHGs and micro enterprises had the major impact on the social and economic life of rural women. The study concludes that there was an increase in self- confidence, self-reliance and independence of rural women due to the involvement in the entrepreneurial and other activities of SHGs. Now women entrepreneurs are aware of opportunities available to them, but there is scope for improvement and therefore it becomes imperative for the government to frame policies for development of entrepreneur among women.

References

1. Ahmed, A (1999), Women Empowerment, Self Help Groups, Kurukshetra.
2. Bhatia Anju (2000) 'Women Development and NGO" Rawat Publication, New Delhi.
3. Gardon.E. Natarasam (2003), Entrepreneurship Development, Himalaya Publishing House, New Delhi.
4. Ram Naresh Thakur (2009) 'Rural Women Empowerment of Rural Women in India" Kanishka Publishers, New Delhi.
5. Shobana Nelasina & Junofy Antoroza (2009) Rural Women Empowerment through Self Help Groups" in Empowerment of Rural Women in India .New Delhi.
6. Makandar, N.M. & Mulla , I.K.(2003), Self Help Groups: A tool for Inclusive Growth. Excellence International Journal of Education and Research. Vol. 1 (3). pp. 192.204.
7. Pulla Rao. D (2006) "Problems of women Entrepreneurship in India" Paper Presented at the XXIV Annual Conference of Andhra Pradesh Economic Association held during 11-12.

   March 2006 at Department of Economics, Maris Stella College, Vijayawada.

12

Skill Development Programmes to Women SHGs: A Study in Krishna District of Andhra Pradesh

— *Dr M. Sreevidya*

Abstract

Women cooperation and strengthening are major women's rights to empowering women to have control over their lives and set forth impact in society. Women frequently confront separation and sexual orientation imbalances, with a few women encountering numerous segregation and avoidance in view of components, for example, foundation or rank. This paper deals with abilities improvement through professional preparing alongside different measures, for example, Pradhan Mantri Kaushal Vikas Yojna, National Skills Development Corporation, National Skills Development Mission. Service of Labor and Employment has taken various activities in the field of aptitude advancement and business. For example, preparing for mentors, Vocational Training for young ladies is being directed by Advanced Training Institutes and Regional Vocational Training Institutes keep running by the Ministry. Professional Education and preparing are the fundamental component of any procedure to enhance cultivate and nonfarm efficiency that enhances country livelihoods. Expertise is the extension amongst employment and workforce. Women regularly have diverse preparing needs than men, since they will probably function as contributing family specialists, subsistence agriculturists, locally established small scale business people, or low-paid occasional workers, notwithstanding taking care of their household work and care obligations. Skill improvement is a vital component to enhancing family unit profitability, employability and pay winning open doors for women and furthermore to enhance economical rustic advancement and occupations.

Introduction

The women Self Help Groups (SHG) play a vital role in this era. It particularly shows that the other angle of the empowerment and come out of poverty. A programme has been found in the society that makes the changes in the more popular in the southern region and particularly in AP. We can see the change in women from wage and agricultural labourers to entrepreneurs and in other income-generating activities. Women, in particular, rural those belong to the socially and economically weaker sections of society have limited access to resources or employment opportunities that would make them financially independent. They survive in conditions that do not permit them to meet minimum consumption needs. Even the money earned by them from hard physical labour is not controlled by them. Institutional credit is difficult to access as women rarely have any property rights to mortgage or collateral to offer, and they have to depend on rural money-lenders for their production-cum-consumption needs. This entraps them into a vicious cycle of perpetual poverty and indebtedness.

The has qualitative and quantitative data of the positive and negative impacts experienced by SHG members in Krishna district of Andhra Pradesh related to increasing in self-worth, communication skills, and desire to protest social evils, improved response to problem situations and a decrease in family violence. A consistent increased access to various amenities such as water, health and sanitation, schools and markets is also indicated.

Based on the concept of "self-help," small groups of women have formed into groups of ten to fifteen and operate a savings-first business model whereby the member's savings are used to furnish loans. The results from these self-help groups (SHGs) are promising and have become a focus of intense examination as it is proving to be an effective method of poverty reduction and bringing socio-cultural change, particularly among the marginalized communities. Microfinance has evolved over the past quarter century across India into various operating forms and with varying degree of success. One such form of microfinance has been the development of the self-help movement.

Objectives of the study

The main objectives of the study are:

(a) to analyze whether skills development has the impact on the personality of SHG members.

(b) to measure the impact of training and development programmes on the self-help group members in the study area.

(c) to examine the role of SHGs in income generation activities to poverty reduction.

Area and sample

The area of the study consists of two mandals of Krishna district in Andhra Pradesh and the focus is on its Self Help Group members based on the SC population and ST population. The unit of a sample is the member of woman self-help groups and her family. The sample was selected based on multi-stage random method.

Methodology

The data for the study were collected from both primary and secondary sources. The primary data were collected through anthropological field work using interview schedules, observation, formal and informal interviews and case study method. The secondary data collected from APRPRP, DRDA SC Corporation, books, journals, manuals, and articles from websites.

Review of literature

The origin of Self Help Groups (SHGs) is from the Grameen banks of Bangladesh, which was founded by Mohammed Yunus; SHGs were started and formed in 1975. In India, the concept of SHGs was initiated by NABARD during 1986-1987. But the real effort was made after 1991-92 from the linkage of SHGs with the banks. They have been recognized as a useful tool to help the poor and as an alternative mechanism to meet the urgent credit needs of poor through thrift (V.M. Rao, 2002). SHG is a medium for the development of a habit of savings among women (S.Rajamohan, 2003). SHGs ensure the equality of status of women as participants, decision-makers and beneficiaries in the democratic, economic, social and cultural spheres of life, (Rita Jain, 2003). The basic principles of the SHGs are group approach, mutual trust, organization of small and manageable groups, group cohesiveness, spirit of thrift, demand-based lending, collateral free, women-friendly loan, peer group pressure in repayment, skill training , capacity building and empowerment (N. Lalitha, 2000). And many scholars have made their research work on the Self Help Groups.

The activities of DWCRA and Velugu were integrated under a programme called Indira Kranti Patham. The basic objective of this integration is to implement various programmes for a strengthening of self-help Groups with the similar implementation strategy. The new scheme Indira Kranti Patham had been designed by clubbing Women Empowerment with Poverty Alleviation.

It works with 4,76,930 Self Help Groups federated into 28,080 Village Organizations (VO) and 700 Mandal Samakhyas (MS) in Andhra Pradesh. The project mandate is to build strong institutions of the poor and enhance their livelihood opportunities so that the vulnerabilities of the poor are reduced. Community Investment Fund (CIF) is the major component of the project, which is provided to the SHGs/ VOs/ MSs to support the wide range of activities for socioeconomic empowerment of the poor.

The basic function of personnel management is the management of manpower resources by utilizing, directing and developing human energies for attaining individual, group and organizational goals effectively and speedily. Training and development is a vital function in this regard. Development function is concerned with the personnel development of employees by increasing their skill through training so that job performance is properly achieved. It includes preparation and implementation of training and development programmes for employees at all levels of the organization, holding of seminars and discussions, provision of education facilities and vocational counselling, appraisal of employee performance and potentialities (D. Sasi Kumar).

Analysis of Study

The present study was focussed on the impact of human resource development through training on SHG members. Training for the SHG members is organized by the TTDC with the collaboration of the NGOs, Banks, DRDA and other agencies functioning in the district. Training is provided covering various areas like vocational, managerial, financial, marketing skills etc. TTDC also provide training and outreach to members in fields such as health care, awareness about government schemes and occupational skills like tailoring, candle/incense sticks making, perfume making, pickle making etc. The general training given to SHG members includes basic literacy, book-keeping, group formation and group dynamics.

Women self-help groups

A Self-Help Group is defined as a voluntary group valuing personal interaction and mutual aid as means of altering or ameliorating problems perceived as alterable, pressing and personal by most of its participants. Women empowerment is an active, multi-dimensional process, which enables women to realise their full potential and powers in all spheres of life. SHGs are concerned with the development of women in all respects along with a sound knowledge of their rights and duties. Voluntary membership, participatory planning, education and training, resource mobilisation, self-management, anti-bureaucracy, empowerment building, linkage building, process extension and movement building, monitoring and self-evaluation, sustainability are some of the characteristic features of Self-Help Groups.

Personality

The personality of a person is defined as the nature, quality, temperament, spirit and moral attitude of an individual. Certain concepts such as positive approach, level of stage fear, influence on people, sentimental feelings, shyness level, tension, confusion, laziness, frustration, are taken into consideration in this regard.

Self-worth

The self-concept of a women SHG member is defined as the way in which she thinks about the whole environment. Queries were raised with the respondents regarding democracy, equality, dowry, system, child marriage, friendship, optimism, exposure to public etc.

Administration

Administration deals with managing policies, plans, procedures, people, materials, machine, finance and the whole organization. Leadership qualities, resistance power, counselling skills, problem facing capacity etc. are considered here. Knowledge and desire to, improved response to problem situations and a decrease in family violence Knowledge refers to the information, awareness and understanding of the multi-faceted environment. World knowledge, women's rights awareness, study about people are considered here. SHGs are concerned with development of women in all respects along with a sound knowledge about their rights and duties. Communication skills Public relation is the attitude of a person to deal with other people. Communication skills, speaking talent, marketing skill etc. are taken for the study. SHG members have up graded themselves in their public relations scores since they have more exposure to the society.

Protest social evils

Responsibility of a person can be defined as the liability or duty to be performed well in time as per schedule. Job satisfaction, morale, social responsibilities are dealt here. Generally responsibility goes in par with authority.

Attitude

Attitude of a person can be defined as the interpretation about himself. A positive change in the attitude could alter the current submissive image of an Indian woman since she is related as a reproductive tool and a homemaker. Factors like cleanliness, dressing sense, self-motivation etc. are considered in this regard.

Flexibility

Flexibility can be defined as the adaptive nature of a person with changing environment. Generally some sensitive women SHG members are not ready to accept changes. In due course of time, based on their age and experience, they gain this factor. Based on the factor scores before and after joining SHGs (pre and post SHG periods) under four and six point scaling, their empowerment level have been measured.

Women SHGs in Krishna District

The activities of DWCRA and Velugu were integrated under a programme called Indira Kranti Patham. The basic objective of this integration is to implement various programmes for strengthening of self-help Groups with similar implementation strategy. The new scheme Indira Kranti Patham had been designed by clubbing Women Empowerment with Poverty Alleviation.

It works with 4,76,930 Self Help Groups federated into 28,080 Village Organizations (VO) and 700 Mandal Samakhyas (MS). The project mandate is to build strong institutions of the poor and enhance their livelihood opportunities so that the vulnerabilities of the poor are reduced. Community Investment Fund (CIF) is the major component of the project, which is provided to the SHGs/ VOs/ MSs to support the wide range of activities for socioeconomic empowerment of the poor.

Nature of Business

Apart from regular savings, SHGs are engaged in business activities to uplift themselves financially and economically. Women SHG members have taken risky businesses too on par with men. Self-Help Groups in the district are engaged in handloom weaving, palm-products making, livestock rearing, sanitary napkin manufacture, rope manufacture, tailoring and garments, rock collieries, waste management, pickle manufacture, cloth centres, ration shops, grinder stone cutting, sericulture, mushroom cultivation, medicinal plant cultivation, agriculture using natural waste, coconut leaves thatching etc. The DRDA has constructed a marketing complex called 'Poomaalai' at an estimate of Rs.28 lakhs for the purpose of marketing SHGs products.

Entrepreneurship Training

Entrepreneurship training for women is given in order to motivate women to start their own enterprises and proceed successfully. Women had come forward nowadays to start the business of their own for their financial upliftment. The training imparts entrepreneurship qualities like eagerness, utilisation of opportunities, time management, proper planning, quality of work etc.

Membership Training

Membership training teaches SHG women the way of starting and running an SHG, the conduct of meetings, disbursement of loans, accounts books maintenance, social service etc. SHG management, general hygiene, environment consciousness, women and the law etc. are dealt here.

Skill Training

SHG members in Erode district are provided with training programmes to develop their personal / managerial / technical skills. Initially, they are given practice in reading, writing and speaking followed by leadership qualities, computer skills, communication skills, marketing skills, register maintenance skills, collective bargaining skills etc.

Other Training Programmes

Apart from the above training programmes, SHG members are given practical orientation in Desktop Publishing, Photo Shoppe, Embroidery etc. Youth skill training was launched to provide technical skills to rural youth in areas such as typewriting, motor coil rewinding, two-wheeler mechanism, electrical works etc. Stipend and other allowances are also paid in this regard.

Major Findings of the Study

The study is a social cum managerial research and has brought out major outcomes which are depicted in Table-2.

The findings reveal that the mean scores and standard deviation among the sample respondents have shown a positive trend after joining

SHGs. It discloses the role played by SHGs in the district in women empowerment through training and development programmes. Experience and track record in self-employment & poverty alleviation programmes and the Council has been in the field of Urban/Rural Development Programmes, promoting a variety of self-employment schemes and poverty alleviation programmes for nearly four decades. Major features associated with the individual schemes are discussed in the following paras.

Establishment of Rural Marketing Service Center (RMSC)

A government of Andhra Pradesh entrusted the task of establishing Rural Marketing Service Center (RMSC), for specified target groups, to bring them under one roof and to provide skill up gradation as well as to provide backward and forward linkages for production and marketing of their produce. Under this project, 300 BPL (below poverty line) families from the downtrodden community were identified based on their existing artisan skills. The activities involved:

Identification and motivation of rural artisans

Capacity Building

Skills up gradation

Basic Orientation Training Programmes

Preparation of Project Profiles

Liaison and coordination for potential financial assistance

Providing backwards and forward linkages

The successful grounding of units.

The various craftsman covered under the scheme were Basket Weavers, Chappal Making, Carpentry, Silk Weavers, etc.

EDP to Prime Minister's Rozgar Yojana (PMRY) Beneficiaries

The main objective of the scheme is to provide self-employment opportunities to the educated unemployed youth. The Commissionerate of Industries, the implementing agency entrusted the Council, the task of conducting Entrepreneurship Development Programmes for the beneficiaries under this scheme in the State of Andhra Pradesh since 1993. The Council has so far trained about 72,000 number of beneficiaries in Industry, Service and Business sectors.

The candidates are exposed to the concepts of Entrepreneurship skills, motivation, accounting procedures, marketing and managerial aspects of operating their units on the profitable basis. On the basis of the ground level evaluation carried out, the success rate of the above scheme is around 65%. A.P.P.C. was the first organisation to undertake the conduct of EDP's in all the 23 districts during the first year of its inception.

Chief Minister's Empowerment of Youth (CMEY)

The Government of Andhra Pradesh started an innovative scheme to provide self-employment avenues to rural youth. The programme aims at inculcating cooperation and team building among youth, by forming homogenous groups for self-employment. The Council acted as the catalyst in promoting 22000 groups in 8 districts of Andhra Pradesh. Also, the Council organized Entrepreneurship orientation programmes and skill up gradation programmes besides capacity building to the above groups. The programme was launched in the year 1996-97.

During the year 2002-2003, the council was entrusted to organise Entrepreneurship development programme to 2883 CMEY groups. Under this programme, the council besides organising EDP's has provided assistance in identification of Projects, Preparation of Project Reports. Identification of Skills, Establishing backwards and forward linkages.

Facilitating Swarna Jayanthi Gram Swarozgar Yojana (SGSY)

The SGSY is a holistic programme covering all aspects of self-employment such as organisation of the poor into self-help groups, training, credit linkage, skill up gradation. Infrastructure development and forward and backward linkages. Under this scheme APPC has organized various programmes viz., Basic Orientation Programmes to SGSY beneficiaries and SHG's, Skill development programmes to SHG's and Entrepreneurship Orientation Programmes to SHG's in various Districts of A.P.

Basic Orientation Programme to SGSY Beneficiaries

With the Objective the familiarize the Swarozgaris with SGSY objectives, the responsibilities of Swarozgaris as well as the behavioral aspects, the council has organized a number of BOP's to SGSY beneficiaries in Nellore, Nizamabad and Vizianagaram districts successfully during the years 1999 to till date.

Basic Orientation Programme to Women SHG's

The BOP's seeks to introduce the members of SHG's the concept of SHG and its objectives through direct interaction with the members, responsibilities of leaders and members, importance of duties and records maintenance as well as behavioral aspects. The ultimate aim of BOP is to establish linkage with banks for micro credit and micro enterprise promotion.

Skill Development Programmes to Women SHGs

Under the auspices of the Ministry for Rural Development, APPC has established Skill Development centers for multiple trades training like Leather Goods Manufacture, Carpentry, Fashion Designing, Tie & Dye, Ready to Cook foods, Ready to eat foods, Fancy items, etc., in various Districts of Andhra Pradesh. Under this project, women from thrift groups and unemployed youth were selected, trained and provided gainful employment. Some of them have started their own self-employment ventures.

Entrepreneurship Orientation Programmes (EOPS) To SJSRY, TRYSEM & SGSY Beneficiaries

The Council has also organized Entrepreneurship Orientation Programmes followed by skill development programmes to unemployed youth, women thrift groups drawn from urban and semi-urban areas under various schemes such as TRYSEM, SGSY and SJSRY Programmes.

EDP to Rural Employment Generation Programme (REGP) Beneficiaries

The Khadi and Village Industries Commission (KVIC), Government of India has entrusted the council to organise Entrepreneurship Development Programme to margin money beneficiaries under REGP scheme with a view to create awareness about the need and importance of self- employment and entrepreneurial career.

Suggestions

The researcher has given the following concrete suggestions based on the study undertaken in the context of women development through Self-Help Groups in Krishna District of Andhra Pradesh.

- Educational institutions may offer Personality Development Programmes to the SHG members so that they develop a right and positive attitude within themselves and also towards the society.
- Free education could be offered through distance education programmes which will develop the knowledge, attitude and job opportunities of SHG women thereby making them more assertive of their rights and duties.
- It is suggested that the women SHGs of various geographical areas such as rural, semi-urban and urban should have a proper networking system to share their technical knowledge and acquire good public relations scores.
- The NGOs and Government authorities may offer proper HRD programmes to the SHG members to enrich their knowledge and administrative skills and to curtail ego clashes between them.
- It is suggested that adequate technical skills and finance should be provided for the interested women entrepreneurs and the products produced by them should be assisted with proper marketing support through the Government.
- Women should be positioned in large numbers at top levels for significant and effective exercise of power and they need to be equipped with suitable means to shoulder these responsibilities.
- The Government may enact a common legislation for SHGs and women empowerment, which would serve the present scenario needs of women.

Conclusion

SHGs in Krishna district of AP are concerned with development of women in all respects along with a sound knowledge about their rights and duties. Women in the district are to be given more exposure in social, cultural, economic, political, educational and technical aspects. The literacy rates and labour earnings of women are generally lacking behind men. They are in a recessive condition as far as a family is concerned. Training and development programmes offered through SHG operations in Krishna district play a vital role in the economic and personality development leads to income-generating activities of women in the district. The present scenario paves a way for the overall upliftment of women in India.

References

ADB.1997: Micro-enterprise Development: Not by Credit Alone, Asian Development Bank. www.adb.org.

Alexander, 1968: Social Mobility in Kerala, Poona, Deccan College.

Almelu 2008: "Group Formation- Modalities and Objectives" – Encyclopedia of Gender Equality and Development, vol.1 edited by C.P. Yadav, Anmol publications Pvt. Ltd, New Delhi.

Amarthya Sen, 2000: Social Exclusion: Concepts, Applications and Security", Asian Development Bank.

Fisher T and Sriram MS, 2002: Beyond Micro-Credit: Putting Development Bank into Microfinance, Vistar, New Delhi.

Ghurye. G.S 1950: "Caste and Class in India", The Popular Book Depot, Bombay.

J.K Pundir, 1997: Changing Patterns of Scheduled Castes: Rawat Publication, Jaipur.

Lalitha. N., 2004: Rural Development in India, Dominant Publishers and Distributors, New Delhi.

Malik, 1979: The Integration of Scheduled Castes, Abhinav Publication, New Delhi.

Rao V.M, 2003: Women Self Help Groups, Profiles from Andhra Pradesh and Karnataka, Kurukshetra, Vol.50, No, 6.

Sreevidya, M: Thesis submitted entitled "Micro-Finance and Changing Livelihoods among Scheduled Castes in Krishna District of Andhra Pradesh"

Sasi Kumar. D., Krishnamurthy N.A. 2009: Training and development in women self-help groups in erode district of Tamilnadu, Journal of contemporary research in management July - September, 2009.

Thurston, E, 1909: Castes and Tribes of Southern India, Madras Government Press, Cosmo Publication, Delhi.

Websites

1. http://www.erode.tn.nic.in.
2. http://www.tn.gov.in.
3. http:// tncdw.tn.nic.in.

Annexure

Acronyms used in the study:

DRDA - District Rural Development Agency

HRD - Human Resource Development

NGO - Non-Governmental Organization

SHG - Self-Help Group (of Women)

SGSY - Swarna Jayanthi Swarozgar Yojana

13

Inter - Generational Change in Education, Occupation and Income of Puducherry Arundhathiyar

— *V. Pragati*

Abstract

The Scheduled Castes people are lagging behind in the development process for generations due to various historical and social factors. They are backward socially, economically and educationally compared to the other caste groups in India. The poor educational development amongst the Scheduled Castes has been due to the strong caste prejudices of the so-called higher castes against them. The educational backwardness was the main reason for the social and economic backwardness. In the Pre-Independence period, the British rulers recognized the need for special provision to assist the Depressed Castes. In the Post-Independence period, a number of political and social activities were initiated for the benefit of Scheduled Castes to come out of the social, economic and educational backwardness from which they had suffered for generations.

Introduction

After Independence, the makers of the Constitution took special note of the conditions in which these communities lived. Special provisions included to guarantee the promotion of their interests in education, employment and political participation. There are a number of schemes for the development of education amongst the Scheduled Castes people, which include the opening of various types of schools, scholarships, provision of hostel facilities, giving stationary grants, boarding grants, midday meals, free uniform supply etc. The reservation of student places and relaxation criteria for admission is provided for students belonging to the Scheduled Castes in technical and other educational institutions. Education is considered as an instrument of mobility, as a fulcrum to cross over from generation to generation as a key to economic advancement and as a process generating force assuring social equality.

There have been a number of studies on Scheduled Castes in general and a few with particular reference to Madiga or Chakkiliyan, synonyms of Arundhathiyar of South India and Charmers of North India. Reddy (1950), Briggs (1956), Singh (1969), Micheal (1999), Srivasatava (1980), Khare (1984), Saine (1972), Singh (1979).

Objectives

(a) To know the changes in different generation

(b) To understand the reasons for the generation change

Method

Comparative and anyalytical methods are used for the study

Scope

The children are taken into consideration. The generation gap on account of various factors governing the personality of children.

Educational development of the Arundhathiyars has been slow comparatively than the other Scheduled Caste groups. Changes in occupation are also taking place along with educational attainment. Nevertheless, changes in occupation gradual due to the limited educational opportunities available to the Arundhathiyar.

The present study aims to analyze the impact of educational and occupational change among the Arundhathiyar of Pondicherry Union Territory. Three generations i.e., ego's grandfathers, fathers, and sons were taken up for analysis. This study also aims to identify some of the factors, which are constraints for the achievement of education and occupational change by the Arundhathiyar of Puducherry.

The fieldwork for the present study was carried out between 1996 and 2003. For this study, two slum areas were chosen in Puducherry Muncipality (Arundhathipuram and Govindasalai Sakkilipalayam), Periyakalapet in Ozhukarai commune Panchayat and one village namely Karikalampakkam in Nettapakkam commune. In all these areas, the Arundhathiyar distribution is high. Although they are widely distributed in throughout Puducherry, for convenient purpose the above-mentioned four areas are selected. The study households numbering two hundred is drawn from these habitations in Puducherry. It does not mention that Arundhathiyar habitation is not in other villages. They are also in other villages, where there are about ten households in each of the ten villages. The researcher also visited those villages for collecting ethnographic data.

Standard anthropological methods and techniques were used in the field. Keeping in mind, the objectives of the study and the different types of information is collected for different purposes, several methods such as interviewing, observation, case studies and informal discussions were employed for collecting data.

The study concentrates and heavily depends upon inter-generational changes in case studies. Besides the data collected from the 200 households, the researcher had long conversation with a variety of the people in the village. Those conversations proved to be very useful, as they tended to throw valuable light on certain aspects of the problem. The secondary sources such as government records, census reports, data published by the planning and statistically division are supporting data.

The Scheduled Castes population is 16% in the Union Territory of Pondicherry. The Chakkiliyan of this Union Territory prefer their identity to be the Arundhathiyar. The present study hence is done in the name of Arundhathiyar, and the analysis throughout the study uses the term Arundhathiyar. The Arundhathiyar claims that they are spatially the most widespread Scheduled Castes groups in India. According to their understanding, they are distributed all over Andhra Pradesh, Tamil Nadu, Karnataka, Kerala, Maharastra and Orissa. They are called as Maadiga in Andhra Pradesh, Chakkiliyan in Tamil Nadu, Holeya in Karnataka and Pulaya in Kerala.

Migratory History of Arundhathiyar

The mother tongue of Arundhathiyar is Telugu. Even after having been settled in the Tamil country for generations, they still speak their mother tongue at home (South Indian Gazetteer, 1989). Their mother tongue retention shows that the Arundhathiyar would have migrated from Andhra Pradesh. The Chakkiliyans of Tamil Nadu state also could speak Telugu and refer them as Maadiga. Reddy also mentioned that, this fact throws up a compelling suggestion that the Maadiga (Chakkiliyan or Arundhathiyar) migrated in the Southward and Eastward directions from beyond North-western Andhra and found them dispersed in various numerical proportions in different localities (1950).

They are found in all the four districts of Pondicherry Union Territory. Ninety per cent of the Arundhathiyar claims that they are spatially the most widespread Scheduled Caste groups in India. According to their understanding, they are distributed allover Andhra Pradesh, Tamil Nadu, Karnataka, Kerala, Maharashtra and Orissa. They are known as Maadiga in Andhra Pradesh, Chakkiliyan in Tamil Nadu, Holeya in Karnataka and Pulaya in Kerala. At present the Maadiga in Andhra Pradesh, and Chakkiliyan in Tamil Nadu, would prefer to be called as Arundhathiyar.

They are also known by several other names, such as Mathangulu, Kattimadiga, Madiga, Pedda Madiga, Edagaiyavaru, Jambuvalu, Manjigoolu and Chakkiliyan. Nowadays, they prefer to be called as Arundhathiyar. Because they have belief that it gives them relatively better status not only among the other *dalits*, but also among other caste people. The Arundhathiyar traditional occupations is removing the dead animals, tanning, footwear making, drum beating and working as agricultural labourers.

Since, they were settled in Tamil Nadu for long period, so they could also speak Tamil fluently. Even after having settled in the Tamil country for generations together, but still they could speak their mother tongue with the family members and relatives. Majority of Arundhathiyar children has good fluency in Tamil and are giving Tamil medium education to their children. As they are in few in number in totality of Scheduled Castes population, they could not compete with other major Scheduled Castes groups of Pondicherry Union Territory and Tamil Nadu. It clearly mentions that how these groups are excluded from the main stream of reservation. In comparison to other major Scheduled Castes communities, the Arundhathiyar are least developed educationally, economically and socially. The Arundhathiyar of Tamil Nadu jointly fought for increase in reservation quota, as they could not endeavor with other major dominant Scheduled Castes communities in population and strength wise. Recently State Government of Tamil Nadu gave the 3-percentage reservation declaration for the Arundhathiyars in educational institutions and in employments along with inclusive of 18% reservation for all the Scheduled Castes communities. The Arundhathiyar of Puducherry does not have any such reservation to raise their status both educationally and economically. In view of that, they are finding it difficult to develop.

Despite with this struggle, nowadays the Arundhathiyars are striving hard to come up in their lives. The focus of the study is to understand the changing social status of Arundhathiyar of Puducherry. This implicit the inter-generational changes in terms of education, and occupation at the household.

Education

Among the Arundhathiyars in the present study, there is only one boy who is doing engineering degree course. He is the first one to do so. There are 114 students in the age group of 10 to 14 years in the HHs studied and 13, 11.45% of them are receiving Pre-Metric scholarship. Similarly out of the 64 students in the age group of 15 to 25 years, six 9.5% are receiving the Post-Metric scholarship. A special coaching facility is given by appointing a qualified part-time teacher for middle and secondary school students in each settlement of Scheduled Castes. Out of the four settlements covered for the present study, the scheme is popular in only one settlement and well-utilized while in the rest of the three settlements the utilization of this scheme is rather poor. Dr. Ambedkar Memorial Award is granted to the Scheduled Caste boy and one girl student of each district of Pondicherry Union Territory (Pondicherry, Karaikal, Mahe, and Yanam) who scored the top marks in the Higher Secondary Examinations. A lump sum of Rs.1000 is paid to the selected students. None from the Arundhathiyar of the present study has received this award.

In Pondicherry Union Territory, education for Scheduled Castes students up to degree level is free. There are 54, 5.5% people who have done a diploma/degree from among the 976 Arundhathiyar people covered under the present study.

In Pondicherry Union Territory, there is an award of opportunity costs for parents of Scheduled Caste girl students. The value of this is Rs.2, 000/- per academic year, payable to the Scheduled Caste parents for each daughter studying in classes VI to XII standard. Only three of the 200 households covered by the present study are availing this opportunity.

Occupation

The working (earning) population is 431, 44.2% out of the 976. Agriculture is still an occupation for a substantial proportion of the working population 48.7percentage. A small number of people 43(10.0%) are continuing their traditional occupation of leatherwork. It is seen that 79(18.3%) of them are working in private sector, 34(7.9%) in government, 25(5.8%) as daily wage earners and 24(5.6%) are doing petty business .Most of them are in private sector, they are workers in the local textile and leather factories. Majorities of the government employees are working as peons/attendants and only a few are working as teachers and clerks.

Fifty-three children below 19 years are workers. Out of them ten 18.9% are below fifteen years. This is a reflection of the critical nature of the socio-economic conditions obtain in this society.

Income

It is in the past fifty years or so that the positive discrimination opportunities are being used, to a very little extent, one should emphasize, and newer occupations are being adopted. In the latter segment, that one finds that there is a little stable income and livelihood security.

Those who are employed in government and private service essentially salaried class are deriving the advantage of having a regular income, however minimal it is. This factor of stable and certainty of income both in terms of quantity and time certainly has initiated a potential process of educating children, entering newer occupations and having stable incomes. However, it is clearly seen that such a potentiality is not fully utilized by all the households of Arundhathiyar of Puducherry.

There is a clear difference between the male-headed and female-headed households in terms of their monthly income. The average monthly income of a male-headed household is Rs.1621 and that of a female-headed household is Rs.896. The average monthly income of all the households put together is Rs.1519. It is observed here that 81 households fall below this average and the rest of the 119 households above.

Thirty persons have taken up a secondary occupation and have some supplementary income. The secondary occupations include agriculture work, leatherwork and petty business. Essentially the supplementary earnings are not substantial and the average earnings are less than Rs.500 per month.

It is important to note here the average household monthly expenditure, which works out to Rs.1848. It is seen that 85 households fall below this average and the rest of 115 are above. It is a fact that some of the households have expenditure exceeding their income. It is these households, which borrow money to meet their expenditure. Due to low household income, and increasing cost of living some of the respondents are facing acute economic crisis and remain in debt.

It is seen that nearly every month household (24%) is indebted and there is not much difference between the male-headed and female-headed households.

It is seen that most of the respondents i.e., 30 respondents spend their loan amount for productive purpose i.e., to improve their business or to buy agricultural related things. It is also seen that fewer are borrowing for children's education.

Government is the major 31.2% source for borrowing money. Obviously, these loans are given under some specific schemes meant for business and so on. Borrowing for reasons other than this, most of them have turned to their friends and relatives 22.9% or have borrowed from banks 18.7 % or from private money lenders 18.7% or from their employer or landlord 8.3%.

Inter–Generational Change

Using the biological criterion of 25 years as equivalent to one generation, it is seen that the total workers (earners) in the present study of 431 could be classified into the Ego's generation of 212 people (49.2%), parental-generation of 115 (26.7%) and children's-generation of 104 (24.1%). Essentially the present study generated a three–generational data in terms of education and occupation.

The proportion of illiterates has come down from the parental 57.4% to the Ego's (45.3%) and to the children's generation (17.3%). The trend is similar in the sense that there is an increasing proportion of people completing schooling (22.6%, 24.5% and 44.2%) and collegiate education (0.0%,7.5% and10.6%) with each succeeding generation.

There is a definite and almost a direct relationship between the levels of education and levels of income. A majority of the illiterates 75.5% earn Rs.1000 or less, while a majority of the persons completing schooling 66.2% and collegiate education 96.3% earn more than Rs.1000.It is significant to note in this context that 19.4% of the persons completing high/higher secondary education and 37.0% of those completing collegiate education earn more than Rs.2500 a month (TablevI.1).

Out of all the working persons 431,255 (58.8%) are engaged in traditional occupations i.e., agriculture and leatherwork put together. However, a gradual decrease is seen from the parental 65.25% to the Ego's 57.1% and the children's 56.7%. There is a gradual increase in the proportion of parents in private and government employees put together from the parental 15.6% to Ego's 29.7% to the children's 30.8% generation. The income levels indicate that they are higher among the government employees followed by the private employees (Table 1.2).

There is a clear difference in terms of the Ego and children's generation put together on the other in education and occupation. In essence, there is a clear difference between the pre-Independence generation and the post-Independence generations. It is a fact that in the post-Independence period several Constitutional provisions, positive discrimination provisions and their programmatic implementation have initiated, to some extent, perceptible changes. However, again the conditions for utilizing the provisions and program remained uneven. Among the Scheduled Castes, those, which were practicing traditional occupations such as leatherwork and other jobs such as cleaning the night soil, have largely remained untouched by the process of change initiated in the post Independence period. With the result the very inequalities that existed in terms of the so-called higher castes and the untouchable castes, which were supposed to tackle through positive discrimination, have reproduced themselves within the Scheduled Castes. The Constitutional provisions are the spontaneous and are only basic potential conditions for change; a change from the demeaning occupations and a change for better educational attainments. Nevertheless, these potentialities to translate to grass roots level realities, there is need for creating enabling conditions so that these communities could also fully utilize the provisions and programs.

Arundhathiyar of Puducherry is traditionally involved in clearing the animal carcasses, using the animal skins for tanning, stitching, and mending footwear. The practice of this occupation has determined their local social hierarchical position, i.e., at the bottom. In fact the Arundhathiyar of Puducherry were untouchable among the untouchables, i.e., they are humiliated by the Scheduled Castes and the higher castes. This also meant that they required enabling conditions in a double dose fully utilize the opportunities. In spite of the fact the two full generations have come up in the post-Independence period, the changes in terms of their education and occupation are not significant. The Arundhathiyar of Puducherry Districts reflects the hiatus between the potential and the reality.

Table 1: Age, Income and Occupation
(A)

Income (Rs.)	Agricultural workers			Leather workers			Private sector workers			Government servants		
	1	2	3	1	2	3	1	2	3	1	2	3
0-500	4(8.3) (7.5)	12(25.0) (12.2)	14(29.0) 23.0)	-	-	2(4.1) (14.3)	4(8.3) (16.7)	6(12.5) (15.4)	2(4.2) (12.5)	-	-	-
	30(62.5) (14.2)			2(4.2) (4.6)			12(25.0) (15.1)			-		
501-1000	38(19.6) (71.7)	66(34.0) (67.3)	4(2.1) (66.7)	14(7.2) (60.9)	4(2.1) (28.6)	-	7(3.6) (29.1)	4(2.1) (10.3)	2(1.0) (12.5)	-	-	-
	138(71.1) (65.1)			22(11.3) (51.2)			13(6.7) (16.5)			-		
1001-2500	11(75.5) (20.8)	18(12.3) (18.4)	13(8.9) (21.3)	2(1.4) (33.3)	7(4.8) (30.4)	6(4.1) (42.9)	13(8.9) (54.1)	22(15.1) (56.4)	6(4.1) (37.5)	4(2.7) (50.0)	12(8.2) (50.0)	2(1.4) (100.0)
	42(28.8) (19.8)			15(10.3) (34.9)			41(28.0) (51.9)			18(12.3) (52.9)		
2501 and above	-	2(4.7) (2.0)	-	-	2(4.7) (8.7)	2(4.7) (14.2)	-	7(16.3) (17.9)	6(14.0) (37.5)	4(9.3) (50.0)	12(27.9) (50.0)	-
	2(4.7) (0.9)			4(9.3) (9.3)			13(30.1) (16.5)			16(37.2) (47.0)		
	53	98	61	6	23	14	24	39	16	8	24	2
Total	212(49.2) (100.0)			43(10.0) (100.0)			79(18.3) (100.0)			34(7.9) (100.0)		

Table 1: Age, Income and Occupation (B)

<table>
<tr><th colspan="3">Daily wage earners</th><th colspan="3">Petty business</th><th colspan="3">Retired persons</th><th>Total</th></tr>
<tr><th>1</th><th>2</th><th>3</th><th>1</th><th>2</th><th>3</th><th>1</th><th>2</th><th>3</th><th></th></tr>
<tr><td>4(8.3)
(36.4)</td><td>-</td><td>-</td><td>-</td><td>-</td><td>-</td><td>-</td><td>-</td><td>-</td><td>48
(11.1)</td></tr>
<tr><td colspan="3">4(8.3)
(16.0)</td><td colspan="3">-</td><td colspan="3">-</td><td></td></tr>
<tr><td>7(3.6)
(63.6)</td><td>6(3.0)
(60.0)</td><td>2(1.0)
(50.0)</td><td>-</td><td>4(2.1)
(28.6)</td><td>-</td><td>-</td><td>-</td><td>2(1.0)
(16.7)</td><td rowspan="2">194
(45.0)</td></tr>
<tr><td colspan="3">15(7.7)
(60.0)</td><td colspan="3">4(2.0)
(16.7)</td><td colspan="3">2(1.0)
(14.2)</td></tr>
<tr><td>-</td><td>4(2.7)
(40.0)</td><td>2(1.4)
(100.0)</td><td>4(2.7)
(66.7)</td><td>6(4.1)
(42.9)</td><td>4(2.7)
(100.0)</td><td>-</td><td>2(1.4)
(100.0)</td><td>8(5.5)
(66.7)</td><td rowspan="2">146
(33.9)</td></tr>
<tr><td colspan="3">6(4.1)
(24.0)</td><td colspan="3">14(9.6)
(58.3)</td><td colspan="3">10(6.8)
(74.1)</td></tr>
<tr><td>-</td><td>-</td><td>-</td><td>-</td><td>4(4.3)
(28.5)</td><td>2(4.7)
(33.3)</td><td>-</td><td>-</td><td>2(4.7)
(16.6)</td><td rowspan="2">43
(10.0)</td></tr>
<tr><td colspan="3">-</td><td colspan="3">6(14.0)
(25.0)</td><td colspan="3">2(4.7)
(14.2)</td></tr>
<tr><td>11</td><td>10</td><td>4</td><td>4</td><td>14</td><td>6</td><td>-</td><td>2</td><td>12</td><td rowspan="2">431
(100.0</td></tr>
<tr><td colspan="3">25(5.8)
(100.0)</td><td colspan="3">24(5.6)
(100.0)</td><td colspan="3">14(3.2)
(100.0)</td></tr>
</table>

Note: 1. 25 years and below (104 persons), 2. 26-50 years (212 persons), 3. 51 years and above (115 persons)

Table 2: Income, Education and Age

Income (Rs.)	Illiterate			Primary			High School/Higher Secondary School			Diploma & Degree			Total
	1	2	3	1	2	3	1	2	3	1	2	3	
0-500	2(4.1) (11.1)	12(25.0) (12.5)	15(31.2) (20.7)	6(12.5) (20.7)	3(6.3) (6.3)	2(4.1) (8.7)	4(8.3) (8.6)	3(6.3) (5.8)	1(2.0) (3.8)	-	-	-	48(100.0) (11.1)
	29(60.4) (16.1)			11(22.9) (11.0)			8(16.7) (6.4)			-			
501-1000	16(8.2) (88.9)	63(32.4) (65.6)	28(14.4) (42.4)	16(8.2) (55.2)	22(11.3) (45.8)	14(7.2) (60.9)	23(11.3) (50.0)	9(1.03) (17.3)	2(1.03) (7.7)	1(0.5) (3.7)	-	-	194(100.0) (45.0)
	107(55.2) (59.4)			52(26.8) (52.0)			34(17.5) (27.4)			1(0.5) (3.7)			
1001-2500	-	21(14.4) (21.8)	20(13.6) (30.3)	7(4.7) (24.1)	21(14.4) (43.8)	3(2.0) (13.0)	15(103) (32.6)	25(17.1) (48.1)	18(12.3) (69.2)	10(6.8) (90.9)	6(4.1) (37.5)	-	146(99.9) (33.9)
	41(28.0) (22.8)			31(21.2) (31.0)			58(39.7) (46.8)			16(11.0) (59.3)			
2501 and above	-	-	3(7.0) (4.5)	-	2(4.7) (4.2)	4(9.3) (17.4)	4(9.3) (8.6)	15(34.9) (28.8)	5(11.6) (62.5)	-	10(23.3) (62.5)	-	43(100.1) (100.0)
	3(7.0) (1.7)			6(14.0) (6.0)			24(55.8) (19.4)			10(23.3) (37.0)			
	18	96	66	29	48	23	46	52	26	11	16	-	431(100.1) (10.0)
Total	180(41.8) (100.0)			100(23.2) (100.0)			124(28.8) (100.0)			27(6.3) (100.0)			

Note: 1. 25 years and below (104 persons), 2. 26-50 years (212 persons), 3. 51 years and above (115 persons)

Conclusion

It is befittingly concluded thatlegal set up and constitutional safeguards to cheduled caste people are

References

Briggs, George. 1956. *Chamars*. London: Oxford University Press.

Khare, R.S. 1984. *The Untouchable as Himself: Ideology, Identity and Pragmatism among the Lucknow Chamars*. Cambridge: Cambridge University Press.

Micheal, S.M. 1999. Dalit Vision of a Just Society in India. In S.M.Micheal (ed.). *Dalits in Modern Vision and Value*. New Delhi: Vistaar Publications.

Reddy, N.S. 1950. Madiga-Spatial Variance of Customs in Andhra Pradesh. In Bala Ratnam (ed.). *Anthropology on the March*. Madras: Social Sciences Association Publication.

Antony Cyril Francis. 1982. Gazetteers of India. Union Territory of Pondicherry. Vol. II. Pondicherry: The Government of Press.

Singh, N.K. 1979. *Education and Mobility among Harijans*. Allahabad: Vohhra Publishers.

Singh, T.R. 1969. *The Maadiga: A Study on Social Structure and Change*. Lucknow: Ethnographic and Folk Culture.

Srivasatava, S.N. 1980. *Harijans in Indian Society*. New Delhi: S. Chand and Co.

14

Struggle for Social Justice within Scheduled Caste: A Study from the Union Territory of Pondicherry with Special Reference to the Migration Issue

— P. Jayapradaban

Abstract

India, being a republic nation for more than sixty eight years tries its best to ensure that the basic and fundamental rights is not curtailed to any and reaches all the citizens of the nation. Third section of the Indian constitution talks firmly about Fundamental Rights and its security is entrusted in the hands of Judiciary. However, the beneficiaries of Fundamental rights vary from people to people according to their voice and resistance. Fundamental Rights are forcefully denied to the vulnerable groups by those who possess more power in the system. In the caste system followed in ancient India, lower caste was denied its rights by the upper caste people. This power structure existed even within the same caste. India government has implemented reservation system to uplift the lives of such downtrodden people. Today, the question that pertains is whether the reservation system made for the benefit of the Schedule Caste people really serves the purpose.

For more than twenty years the SC Students and Job Applicants, who migrated to Pondicherry from Tamil Nadu, are treated under general

category, denying their rights for reservation. As an educationist and social reformer, I would like to raise a few questions on this issue. a) Can we forcefully change a Schedule Caste candidate to a general category who seeks job or higher education under any circumstance?, b) Is there any law that forbids SC people of Pondicherry seeking matrimonial alliance from neighbouring state of Tamil Nadu with in the SC community?, c) Does the national funds for Schedule Caste Schemes exclude the Migrated SCs?, and d) Finally, could the past twenty years which denied the Fundamental rights of the community, in other words violation of human rights in terms of pursuing education, the basic benefits of government, and Job opportunities of the Migrated Scheduled Caste be recovered at any cost?
Keywords: Fundamental Rights, SC Migration Issue & Certificate, SC origin certificates.

Introduction

The Constitution is the demonstration of the will of the people and also it is the supreme certificate which guides the state and the its subjects to create moral responsibilities and duties by which the state is bound to frames instructions, laws and guidelines for the safety and promotion of the prosperity and equality among the people and the subjects are bound to obey those rules, regulations and laws for harmony to prevail in the country. Our historical experiences inform us that our Hindu society was stratified and non-egalitarian in which the status and identity of an individual or group was determined based on the privileges assigned by one's birth in a particular caste. Aspiring to establish secular, democratic and civil libertarian and egalitarian political and social order, our constitution makers have put up fundamental rights based on natural rights and justice in part three such as right to liberty, equality, right against exploitation, religious-cultural rights and right to constitutional remedies. They all have got judicial enforceability thereby an aggrieved individual or group in case of these rights encroached by state or another individual can approach the court for seeking remedy.[1]

Objectives

(a) To know the extent of social injustice caused among scheduled castes

(b) To understand the reasons for migration

Method

The paper is prepared with use of descriptive and narrative method.

Scope

The paper intends to cover the issue of migration as result of social injustice among scheduled caste people.

With a view to create equality in the society, right to equal opportunity in the matters of education and employment has been given importance under article 16 of Indian constitution.[2] Having realized the fact that the unchanging nature of unequal society was created and sustained by the ideology of caste because of the lack of equal opportunity to access the common resources and public space, the intellectual in an independent India like Dr. B.R. Ambedkar have decided that if equality needs to be achieved in the country, the state must practice positive discrimination towards rich and privileged sections of the society which is very significant for the irradiation of caste-based inequality. Thus, we find article 16(1) of the constitution as fundamental right specifying some relaxation to the scheduled caste and scheduled tribes in the form of special reservations which are further supported by special articles 330[3], 335[4], 338[5] and 338(A)[6] that reserve seats in the Lok Sabha and state legislative assembly, seats in the education and jobs and constituting commission for protection of interests of scheduled castes and tribes. As a result, once those who were considered untouchable are now able to become legislators, good intellectuals and bureaucrats. Moreover, they could raise their voice whenever their rights are violated and atrocities committed on them. The reaction of the upper caste and privileged section of the society against reservation was very enormous, they not only opposed the reservation to the SCs and STs, but also they looked at reservation as stigma of the untouchables.

However, in the present context, particularly, after the Mandal commission report of recommendation for the reservation to the other backward classes (OBC, the reservation itself came to be seen by the upper caste people as a tool to get government jobs. The huge irony is, once those caste and groups, which opposed Mandal Commission's recommendation, they are now on the streets for claiming reservation for their own caste and community. Jhats in Haryana[7], Patels in Gujarat[8] and Marathas in Maharashtra[9] can be sighted as instances in this regard. Reservation, from its focus on means of upliftment of the real disadvantaged section of the society, has been shifted to a violent tool for political mobilization of the socially dominant classes for electoral vote-bank politics. Thus the dilemma prevails over the question of whether social criteria or economic one must be taken to determine who and which community are entitled for the reservation without entering into altruistic analysis of whether those who were entitled for reservation had actually accessed the reservation and promoted their status.

The aforesaid dimension about the reservation is pan-Indian perspective. But, the contrast that prevails in the union territory of Pondicherry is totally different. Here, the fight is not between socially dominant castes and socially under-privileged castes of the society but between the two groups within scheduled caste community. The notion of indigenous and migrant haunt the people and based on this premise, the scheduled caste Pondicherry SC natives claiming to be origins of the land can only enjoy the reservation as the sons of the soil and those who migrated from other parts of the country could not. This kind of narrow interpretation of one's position in the enjoyment of reservation involves in violation of basic entitlements, which the migratory category of scheduled caste are supposed to get as per the constitutional as well as statutory norms.

A short history of Pondicherry

Pondicherry is considered as one of the most important Union Territory of India in terms of history, tourism, water, and coast of living etc. It is comprised of four erstwhile French settlements known as the regions of the Pondicherry, Karaikal, Mahe and Yanam. It is located 169 kilometres away from Chennai (south), and surrounded by the districts of Tamilnadu namely Cuddalore and Villupuram. Similarly, another settlement, Karaikal lies nearly 149 kilometres away from core city of Pondicherry which is located south of Pondicherry. An interesting aspect of which is within Nagapattinam district known as one of the district of the state of Tamilnadu. The region Mahe is situated on the Kerala coast and sharing the borders of Kozhikode and Kannoor districts of Kerala. Finally, the region Yanam is located within the east Godavari district of the state of the Andhra Pradesh. The location of these regions are strategically very important, in terms of educational institutions and employment opportunities in other words, they are very much prosperous regions.

Pondicherry is also admired for two things. For one, Arabindo Ashram is globally renowned institute for spirituality and social service. For the second, it has got Arikkamedu a Roman Settlement which functioned as port-come factory site that revealed several historical truths to the world.

In the 16th and 17th century, Pondicherry had become a place for commercial activities to the European companies namely, the French, the Danish, the Dutch and even the English. When the commercial interests of the east India companies of the English and French grew, subsequently when they started to gain monopoly over trade, the rivalry between them became inevitable phenomenon. Not only this, their unnecessary intervention in the internal politics of the native states particularly Carnatic and Hyderabad states, the rivalry took the colour of gaining significance of who should rule India and finally as result the French were defeated and the English ensured their supremacy as ruler in India. However, as a matter of good-will gesture of the English, the French were given back with five settlements namely Pondicherry, Karaikal, Mahe, Yenam and Chandranagar.

Under the impact of French administrations, a number of developments had taken place in the Pondicherry such as the architectural designs of the town, French Culture, dresses religious practices, food habits, and language etc. unlike other parts of India; Pondicherry got Independence on 1st November, 1954. However, the merger has taken place on 16th August, 1963 with the Treaty of accession signed between India and French. Though, the administrative system and the official duties continue till the date, some policies are modified for the concern of a few groups who dominate the social order in the Pondicherry.

Issue of Human rights Violations in Pondicherry

In Pondicherry, approximately 20 per cent of population belong to scheduled caste community. They belong to different sub-castes such as Paraiyars, Pallars, Vetuvars, Valluvars, etc., and when India got independence; Pondicherry was stilled ruled by the French. Only after 1954, this territory of Pondicherry was acceded to the Indian union as a union territory. As the constitution and its provisions apply bind on the people who live in its territory, the people of Union Territory of Pondicherry also came to be protected by the same constitution. The rights and privileges have also come to be applying on the people in the same manner as applied on the people of entire India. Similarly, the special privileges given and recognized by the constitution to the scheduled caste communities also came to be enjoyed by the scheduled caste communities in Pondicherry.

However, in the recent decade, the people belonging to scheduled caste communities are divided on the imaginary conception of origin and migration. This artificial division in the scheduled caste communities indulge in violation of some fundamental rights accorded by the constitution. The migrant scheduled caste students are unable to get seats in schools and colleges under reserved category. The migrant scheduled caste qualified candidates are not able to get recruited in government services and moreover, all the migrant scheduled caste citizens are denied the basic government services and entitlements. On the contrary, the people claiming to have scheduled caste origins of Pondicherry enjoy all the aforesaid services and entitlements under reserved category.[10]

This kind of artificial watershed divisions kindles our knowledge to raise few theoretical questions and necessarily hypothetical conclusions in the following manner.

Whom does the state belong to? and what is the state meant for? Is the state, as said by Karl Marx that belongs to the dominant class because they often use it to suppress the voice of subordinates? Is the state, as defined by Abraham Lincoln that is of the people, by the people and for the people? the state is the one which is supposed to protect the interests of all the vulnerable sections of the society. It should not be partisan and biased towards somebody and some group has the duty to enforce rule of law whenever somebody or some group with vested interest take law in their hands and demand for unconstitutional agendas.

However In the present case, the so-called migrant scheduled caste people aggrieved and deprived of their basic rights with the denial of education, job and other services by the officials brought their grievances to knowledge of the state, it keeps quiet and does not intend to the interests of aggrieved sections. Moreover, when an individual approached the judiciary for the remedy for the denial of reservation based on the notion of migration, the court guides the government to adhere to provisions of the constitution and provide reservation to all who belong to scheduled caste communities and discord other presumptions such as origin and migrants. Yet, the state has not enacted any law in order to protect the vulnerable sections among the scheduled caste communities particularly the migrant category. It is totally violation of human rights, which are supposed to be enjoyed by the scheduled caste communities.[11] To that extent, the kind of policy and the rules brought by the erstwhile French administrators was so much welfare-oriented.

This situation in Pondicherry make us to presume that the notion of origin and migration are manipulations employed by the political parties to divide the people belonging to scheduled caste communities so that they would never get united. It could be purposefully done by the socially dominant politicians in order to maintain their political as well as social status quo. Thus, it indicates that politicization of scheduled caste communities would be possible when they all are united. The same could have been prevented at the cost of disunity, which I think, has been the legacy of upper caste politicians and parties. It is well borne by the fact that despite being aware of human rights violations resulting from the so-called origin migration dichotomy, no politician and political parties raise their voice there in the legislature both at the state and centre.

It is totally an irony that an oppressed community based on the presumption of origin with selfish economic interest began to suppress another oppressed sections of the society based on migration. If this is the case, none of the scheduled caste communities other than Mahar (the caste to which Ambedkar belong) should enjoy reservation. The father of the constitution fought for reservation of and human rights of all the depressed and not only for the Mahar. Thus, those who are fighting for protecting imaginary and inhuman assumption of origin-based reservation must realize the philosophy of Dr. B. R. Ambedkar of Unity of Dalits as political strength rather than fighting for narrow selfish interests.

Conclusion

State must be present to protect the people and promote equality, liberty and fraternity among them all. The presence of state must be realized by its citizens by obeying to the rules and laws of the land. The laws and regulations must be framed with the consent and participation of the people so that obedience to law could be possible and agreement could prevail. Moreover, laws must be based on the principle of natural rights and justice so that human beings can nurture and promote welfare of entire humanity. On the contrary, states and governments derive and sustain their power by dividing the people based on caste, language and region, humanity would disappear, and human beings will transform themselves into animals. Therefore, reservation given by our forefathers to nurture and promote the equality in the society and that is why it is rewarded to particular sections of the society. If it is furthered and portioned by the depressed communities based on the notion of origin and migration that will lead to creation of unnecessary vacuum for those who oppose reservation.

References

1. Durga Das Basu, *Introduction to the Constitution of India*, 20th edition, New Delhi, 2008.
2. Laxmikanth, *Indian Polity*, McGraw Hill Education, New Delhi, 4th edition, 2013.
3. Madras High Court's judgement, P. Jeya vs Union of India, dated: 16. 08.2004; Supreme Court of India's judgement, civil appeal nos. 10829-10830 of 2010-decided on 7-8-2014 (2014 STPL(WEB) 525 SC)
4. *The Constitution of India, Government of India Ministry of Law and Justice*, modified up to the 1st of December, 2007 (Article 32 in the Supreme Court)
5. The Hindu, Tamilnadu- Chennai, dated: 03.04.2010 (http://www.thehindu.com/2010/04/03/stories/2010040353250400.htm)
6. *The Hindu* (Daily News Paper), other states - Chandigarh, dated: 21.05.2016, 12. 09. 2016, Ahmedabad, dated: 29. 04.2016, 20.09.2016, Mumbai, dated: 28.02.2017.

15

Caste, Ritual and Politics among Yadav Community: An Inquiry

— *Devi Prasad & Savita Yadav*

Abstract

Post-Ambedkarite movements have given a new legacy to Dalit-Bahujan politics, and Uttar Pradesh (UP) had witnessed a political shift emerged during the 1990s. On the one hand, a socialist leader, Mulayam Singh Yadav along with few other leaders formed Samajwadi Party in U.P. with the principle of 'equality' or an ideology of 'socialist society.' The party functions with a 'secular' and a 'democratic outlook.' On the other hand, keeping in mind the ideologies (for uplifting the marginal sections) of great social reformers like B.R. Ambedkar, Jyotiba Phule, Narayana Guru, Periyar E.V. Ramasamy and Chhatrapati Shahuji Maharaj, Bahujan Samaj Party (BSP) was formed by a visionary leader Kanshi Ram in 1984, and later, led by Mayawati Prabhu Das (popularly known as Bahen-ji [sister]).

The crux of this ethnographic investigation is to map out the inter-connected relationship among caste politics, religion, and relevance of the thought of Dr. B.R. Ambedkar. The study is carried out through an analysis of socio-political activism of the last three decades among Yadav community. In addition, the data is collected from primary sources through the interview and the participant observation to understand the grounded reality at village level while secondary sources like local magazines of Yadav community, website (www.yadavhistory.com), blogs,

Facebook, etc. are used for an in-depth understanding of the legacy of iconic figures B.R. Ambedkar, R.M. Lohia and Mulayam Singh Yadav.
Keywords: *Ambedkarism, Biradari Bhoj, Identity Politics, Krishna, Ritual, Yadav Community.*

Introduction

The thoughts of B.R. Ambedkar, R.M. Lohiya, J.P. Narayana (popularly known as 'Loknayak') are also helping millions of 'Backward Classes' including Mulayam Singh Yadav, Kanshiram and Lalu Prasad Yadav who stand up for socio-political rights and become the significant politicians for backward classes in North Indian state. In addition, the vision of Ram Manohar Lohiya, 'Samajwad' (a socialist society) along with the mantra of Baba Sahib Ambedkar, 'educate, agitate and organize' inspired Mulayam Singh Yadav to come forward for the welfare of unprivileged sections like OBCs, SCs, STs, and Minorities after 1990s. Few trajectories such as the 'Emergency', 'Mandal affair', 'Babari demolition', and emergence of Samajwadi Party in UP gave a political shift. These consequences gave a way to middle-lower castes including Yadav community to come forward as a safeguard for the welfare of marginal sections and building a self-respective image for the own community. Especially Yadav community also began claiming as a 'caste of politician' with (self-claimed) a mythological association with a favourite Hindu god 'Krishna' (Michelutti, 2008). Thus, 'identity politics' was a prime concern for Yadav community but if we compare them with Dalit community it can be said that 'dignity politics' and 'symbolic perseverance' were main concerning points for the leaders of this community in late 20th century as well as the early 21st century.

Although for nearly three decades, Uttar Pradesh has had a movement to mobilise the *dalits* and the backward castes of the state. On the one hand, Bahujan Samaj Party (BSP) was primarily supported by scheduled castes as well as most backward classes emotionally keeping in mind the mantra of Ambedkar, be 'organize.' Meanwhile, BSP could not fulfill socio-economic gap, and UP's lower castes had before the mobilization began, and still have, the worst social indicators in the state and country (Mehrotra 2006). The result of which, SP has become an alternative political party for most backward classes. The thoughts of R.M. Lohiya, J.P. Narayana, Janeshwar Mishra and Mulayam Singh Yadav gave a path to backward classes especially Ahir, Kurmi, Koiri, Kuswaha, Kewat, etc. to come under the banner of 'Samajwadi Party' (SP) with the same mantra of B.R. Ambedkar at an abstract level. On the other hand, it appears that after the formation of SP, Yadav community has emerged as an influential caste politically while UP's mobilisers of the dalits have focused exclusively on capturing power, and the gains to the lowest castes have been entire of a symbolic nature (Ibid 2006).

The political consequences and acceptance of suggestion, reservation for backward classes, of Mandal Commission by B.P. Singh government created a nuance in order to attract the OBCs' voters. Moreover, this step helped backward caste to enter in Indian larger bureaucratic system through constitutional means. The result of which, backward classes got a new enthusiasm and support through the constitutional mechanism. Regional parties- SP, BSP, Apana Dal, etc. of marginal sections also timely raised the question for proper implementation of reservation to backward classes. The question of reservation for backward classes became a political tool which also changed the direction of UP's politics during the 1990s. At the same time, Ambedkarite philosophy was also taking shape in new political milieu while 'the rejection of political dominance' by the "manuvadis[1]" became the mantra of new dalit political ideology. Wankhede (2008) points out, "The Ambedkarite Buddhist identity challenges the "immoral," unscientific and regressive mode of the social system and is hopeful of building a modern social order based on human values." The decade was witnessed when Kanshiram was trying to transform the "given identity" into "self-respective" dignified identity with the legacy of Ambedkar, but it was not a very smooth journey for him. It is important to notice here when Kanshi Ram began giving more weight to Mayawati, and projected her as a chief ministerial candidate for Assembly of Uttar Pradesh, his colleague Sone Lal Patel and few other leaders parted BSP because of arrogance nature of Mayawati as well as own outfit in November 1995.

In sum, SP and BSP have been influencing state politics of UP after 1990. Both have become a major political force with certain caste consciousness as hidden truth. The first one, SP, is very popular among

Yadav community who represent about twelve per cent of state population while the second, BSP, is much popular among dalits who represent about twenty per cent of the state population. It appears that for the supporter of SP, caste identity is a major concern while dignity politics and resistance against Brahminical ideology is an important concern for the follower of BSP. Thus, both metrics depends on particular political context.

Objectives

(a) To study the social life of yadav community

(b) To understand the socio economic problems of Yadav community

(c) To suggest measures for their solution

Method

Descriptive and analytical methods are employed for the study. The major idea of this paper is to map out the various strategies which are applied for getting the dominant position by Yadav leaders from local to the provincial level. On the one hand, the paper would examine through certain parameters like active participation, significant behavioural changes, language/slang (used by local people) and the connection of local Yadav leaders with state/central level leadership at the grassroots level. The primary data have been collected from Rajanpur and Tandawa village in Sultanpur district of UP during November 2016 to January 2017. The respondents are leaders, *Chaudharis* (heads of a caste), *Mukhiya* (head of the family), *Gram Pradhan* (elected leader in village Panchayat), organizers and participants of *biradari bhoj*. The multi-sited ethnography, oral history, interview schedule and interactive discussion with research participants have been used to enrich the in-depth understanding. On the other hand, the debates discussed in this paper are based on the basic consequence of UP politics. A comparative approach has been used for data analysis.

Scope

The paper makes an attempt to deals with only socio-economic life of yadav community.

Politics and Caste Identity

Both term are closely associated with each other and very relevant to the present context because identity of members of a caste is formed when the caste has certain features, for instance, a common name which symbolizes the uniqueness of the community and distinguish to one from others. To some extant, a caste also shares a common political ethos because few myths on common origin relates them with the common ancestors, birthplaces, foundation, and a shared history (i.e. the shared memories of successive generation of the collective community) etc. Some cultural characteristics such as institution, customs, or language build a sense of solidarity (Green, 2010; Smith, 1993). The sense of capturing political power along with socio-cultural practices are interlinked with an identity, which is also reconstructed, reproduced or reshaped as well as reconfigured as a new avatar over a period continuously.

For getting in-depth understanding, let me exemplified Yadav community. The umbrella term 'Yadav' is a political category which represents several allied castes/sub-castes. In this case, the idea of 'identity' denotes the 'fusion' of different 'cognate castes'[2] (Ahir, Goal, Gop, Dhandor, etc.) who claim a broader caste identity through reformulating some new myths from religious texts of 'Mahabharta'. It is referred that Yadavs were traditional, a low-to-middle-ranking cluster of pastoral-peasant castes that have become a significant political force in Uttar Pradesh. Rao (1978) writes that 'the umbrella term 'Yadav' denotes few 'cognate castes' and these castes associate themselves with a traditional occupation of cattle-herding. Their speculation of 'Yadav' identity is based on historical facts and cultural similarities.' Apart from a common mythical and cultural understanding, a specific folk theory emphasizes that all pastoral castes of India as descendants of king Yadu (a mythic figure) to which a popular god Krishna[3] belonged' (Michelutti 2008). The association with Krishna of Yadav community provides a cultural understanding of the nexus between politics and historical past because Krishna played an important role in whole political episode of Mahabharata. In Weberian sense it can be called as 'calling' because Yadavs feel that they are sons of 'Krishna,' and they must come forward for politics (Michelutti 2002). The idea of single larger group hints at several pre-existing endogamous groups, whose distinction seems to be erased in the process of coming together as a larger community of Yadav because numbers run democracy. Therefore, several allied cognate castes of Yadav community decided to form a larger organization, All India Yadav Mahasabha, in early twentieth century.

Although ideologically the principle of caste and the politics quit dissimilar each other: first one stands for 'fragmentation' while the second one is for 'unification of society' theoretically. Meanwhile, the nexus between caste and politics has a long history as a distinct reality of Indian social system. The nexus is also continued in rural India which is witnessed for rigours caste practices from a span of time. While talking to villagers in Tandwa village of UP, it appears that there are three types of connotation exist between caste and politics. At village level politics especially in 'village panchayat', personal relation with voters plays important role rather than caste factors. Meanwhile, at the level of District Panchayat, socio-economic as well as political background plays very important role in mobilizing the voters. Although for state assembly, caste of a candidate for MLA seat becomes a significant factor because the candidate becomes 'reference man' (man of respect) for the whole community. It also provides a prideful identity for a group of people from which the candidate belongs.

Caste and Dignity Politics

Formulating a dignified social and political identity for marginal sections is perceived as one of the essential tasks, and progressive thinkers have been putting their heart through various social movements as well as through constitutional provision. Keeping in view of various socio-cultural and religious disabilities, the chairman of the drafting committee, Ambedkar, of Indian constitution has provided liberty, equality, justice, and human dignity to Indian citizens through various articles of Indian constitution. The result of which, the phenomena of second decade of Indian independence indicates towards imitation process of ritual activities: ritually higher strata's castes used to perform some religious offering and ritual sacrifices like wearing the *janeo* (sacred thread), *pind-dan* (ancestral worship), *brahm-bhoj* (feasting to Brahmin) etc., and ritually lower strata castes began following the religious symbols and cultural practices of higher castes. This emulating process shows a kind of inter-connectedness and also a gap (in reciprocity) between two (strata's) castes. In this regard, prominent social thinker Srinivas (1952) coined a term "*Sanskritisation*" to map out for this socio-cultural process. The concept "*Sanskritisation*" indicates such social change that was happened during the first decade of India independence in caste and religious route.

However, relative deprivation was the reason behind the imitating for social mobility because from a long time especially during colonial period such citizens who belong to ritually lower strata's castes including Yadav community could not get legal rights to perform such ritual activities (Prasad 2015). If we examine to such effort, our attention also goes to the politics of '*janeu movement*' which was inspired by the thought of Dayanand Saraswati. The wearing of Janeu was a radical effort of Arya Samajis[4], and it also became popular among Kurmi, Ahir and Goala castes in U.P. and Bihar in the beginning of the twentieth century. This cause is also responsible for the conflict with upper castes like Brahmin, Bhumihar, and Baniya because these castes wanted to maintain ritual hegemony over Hindu ritual as a part of their tradition (Rao 1979: 134). The idea of wearing *janeu* was a symbolic protests among allied castes of Yadav community same as "Mahad Satyagraha" and "Kalaram Temple Satyagraha" of Dalits for getting a self-respective identity. Now people have fundamental rights to perform ritual sacrifice, religious offering, etc.[5] by which one can worship, follow and demonstrate any religion accordingly his/her choice.

Heredity and Political Consensus

Sociologically, first, it is paramount to interrogate about the process of building self-respective identity because it appears, certain socio-political ethos is get created through ritual sacrifices and religious offerings. Therefore, we must know how these practices help for building a larger caste network. Both questions are crucial to elaborate here because a consolidated caste network provides backup for political parties, for instance, traditional supporters of SP is backed by Yadavs while Apana Dal and BSP by Kurmis and Dalits. These caste based backups gave a way (after Mondal commission) to emerge an alternative regional politics in Uttar Pradesh. However, politics and ethnic identity are mutually supplementary in India because *dharma* (set of beliefs) gives a moral authority to both by which Indian democracy is idealized in certain circumstances for the reason that gods (in present context, Krishna) is perceived as ancestors, and by the same token ancestors can become gods (Srivastava 1997: 53). Each caste defines them according to convenient. There are also some popular beliefs in the rural society which blur the relation between human beings and gods, for instance, Yadavs trace a direct line of descent from the god Krishna, and there is no conceptual problem in defining him as 'an ancestor' (Mechelutti 2002). Yadav community, for instance, used to go to Gaya (a district of Bihar) for performing '*pind-dan*' (ritual sacrifice) with certain beliefs. They believe that their ancestors (forefather including Krishna) and '*kuldevta*' (demi-gods) are waiting for '*pind-dan*'.

Moreover, few Yadav families still worship Raja Bali (a powerful/ protector demi-god) but their social status is considered lower than such families who worship god Krishna. Often, the higher gods are also linked to the lower god in relations of control, by what Wadley call 'genealogical gap,' which are detailed in the myths of origin and songs of praise to the deities and ancestors (Moffatt 1979). On the one hand, Raja Bali is considered regional and lower than Krishna in ritual hierarchy among North Indian Yadav community. On the other hand, Krishna is seen as universal, 'democratic' and ritually higher than Raja Bali. Therefore, at the core of the formation of the Yadav community lays a tendency to 'emulate' and 'duplicate' the Krishna, at the regional and national levels, the ideology of descent this legitimises local lineages (Fox 1971: 23). Over a period of time, such castes who seek social mobility create some mythologies as well as show their genealogy with well-known king or deities. The creation and changes in beliefs help them for continuous existence in the socio-political world with a dominant position.

In sum, after independence, India chose the path of democracy which runs by numbers. Therefore a caste/community seeking political power tends to enhance its numerical strength. Upbringing cognate castes might fulfil the idea of enhancing the numerical strength within an umbrella term 'Yadav.' This polarization could be possible when a caste reshapes itself with a certain new socio-cultural atmosphere for its continuous survival as a dominant caste/community.

Reshaping Caste with Ritual

Few scholars also notice it that religious beliefs and ritual practices are prominent among rural families. A well-known scholar M.N. Srinivas (1952) points out to this process as "Sanskritization." It denotes the process by which castes placed lower in the ritual hierarchy seek social mobility by emulating the rituals and practices of the upper or 'dominant castes'. Historically, the ethnography of caste in the pre-Independence period was also replete with discussion of the rules of purity and pollution and their use in maintaining social distance between castes/sub-castes. Most notable among these rules were the rules of commensality and endogamy (Dumont 1970; Beteille: 1996), and both factors have been playing very efficient role to consolidate caste network form span of time. However, there are certain irregularities in both practices, which have occurred after independence, and it can be seen in various writings of social scientists, for instance, Khare (1970) points out that land position, education and governmental job help to enhance the ritual status of Kanyakubj Brahmins in order to make 'Hypergamous' relations with higher ritual status Brahmins in Lucknow (Uttar Pradesh) areas.

In terms of the nexus between caste and ritual, there is a rite in Hinduism called '*pitryajna*'/ *pind-dan* or *sharaddh* (ancestor worship), which gives legitimacy to community feast. It shares kind of similar beliefs, culture, and procedure. It is said that there are three main goals of this rite: *Santi* (destruction of evil influences), *pusti* (a well-nourished condition) and *moksha* (salvation) (Sayers 2013). It is performed in some standard formats, for instance, these performances can be seen in fallowing orders likewise prayer, water for washing the feet, water for hand-washing, water for sipping, bathing of the ideal, dressing, offering of the flower, offering incense, offering food, sacrifice, light, oblation through fire, daily festival, music, listening to religious tales, dancing, throwing *akshat* (coloured rice), etc. (Appadurai 1981; Hanchett 1888). These ritual performances have been an inevitable part of rural life from over a period among the believers of Hinduism. Although in particular, it is also associated closely with Yadav community.

It appears that this rite is helping them to consolidate a larger caste network by which leaders of Yadav community seek to achieve their political ambition from local to the provincial level. In other words, *sraddha/pind-dan* is gratitude for ancestors or *gotra* (lineage or ancestry)[6], which can be thought of as a 'day of remembrance.' It is performed collectively during the *pitru-paksha* (literally, the fortnight of the ancestors)[7]. Accordingly Hindu mythology, people perform various rites from *purnima* to *amavasya* (during fourteen days, mostly in the month of September) and collectively these performances are known as *sraddha* (Sayers 2013). The core beliefs behind these performances can be understood by the following statement: first, 'the cycle of rebirth[8] can be ceased (and soul receives salvation) if these sacred rituals would be performed'. Second belief is that 'performers will be relieved from *'pitru-dosha'* (from a curse of forefathers) after performing *sraddha* rite' (Moghe 1994). Chedilal Yadav[9] , a respondent, believes that 'the *pitru-dosha* may be resulted in the form of 'chronic illness,' 'failures in life,' 'debt,' 'repeated miscarriage,' 'consistent death of children,' as well as some problem may be occurred related to 'conceiving pregnant''. However, to fulfill the aim of *sraddha,* at last, people perform a ritual called '*bhoj'*. It is an inevitable part of '*sraddha*'. People believe that after celebrating this last rite the basic aims of the whole ritual process can be fulfilled.

In Durkheimian sense, these ritual processes act as a source of solidarity and identification for the individual within a society, especially as a part of 'mechanical solidarity' systems, and to a lesser, but still substantial extent in the context of 'organic solidarity' (Durkheim, 1915). Also, Durkheimien's idea of 'social solidarity' can be implied to understand the association of ritual practices with caste solidarity. As it is pointed out above, democracy is run by numbers and the idea of *biradari bhoj* is closely linked with rituals, gives space to get together where an aspirant may get some links to flourish his/her political ambition. Although whole debate of community consensus can be based on multi-dimensional including regional, economic, psychological, etc. but in the present research, only a triangle shape (caste, politics, and ritual) would be examined.

For getting adequate the answers, let me explain (a familiar ritual based) a commensal practices, *bhoj* or *biradari bhoj* (community feast), of eastern UP. *Biradari bhoj* (community feast) of which *shradh/pind-dan* (ritual performance), *birha* (a traditional folklore), *chitta* (a special congregation of the head of caste), etc. are essential constituents show a well-organized social system by which the process of articulating a pan Yadav identity becomes possible.

Biradari Bhoj and the Ambedkar's idea of 'Organize'

B.R. Ambedkar has given powerful mantra, 'educate,' 'agitate,' and 'organize,' to the backward sections in the mode of development (Ambedkar, 2005). Meanwhile, the idea of 'organize' is very significant in a popular democracy especially when caste based forces becomes as a part of larger democracy. It is claimed around UP political elections that 'you, not only cast your vote but also vote your caste.' Therefore, this paper discovers and discusses a significant issue *'biradari bhoj'* for examining how Ambedkarite's idea (organize) functions in rural society. *Biradari bhoj* is a commensal practice which is validated through ritual performances and myths. *Biradari* is a Hindi word which is used openly for showing particular caste identity. It also denotes a group of people who demonstrate a collected identity and shared commensal relation while '*bhoj'* means 'feast' or commensality. In combined, the idea of *biradari bhoj* can be referred to such larger commensal practices which are celebrated in the name of the own community. It is a ritual based commensal practice and celebrated in Eastern Uttar Pradesh. It has become a medium of a social congregation and social expression in rural society. It is also known with few other names like '*Gaya-Jagannath ji ka bhoj,' 'biradari bhoj*,' '*Gaya-ji ka bhoj,'* and '*brahm bhoj*,' etc. This grand feast[10] is held for two days in Yadav community. The first day of celebration is called '*kachchi'* while the second day of the celebration is known as '*pakki*.' On the one hand, local villagers from deferent castes are invited in *kachchi* ceremony. On the other hand, people from the same caste are main participants for *pakki* ceremony in which five to ten thousand people get together and discuss on various issues (Prasad, 2016: 186-87).

The primary purpose of explaining here about *biradari bhoj* is to indicate how Yadav community in the rural area is trying to find out a political space where they renew their relation for socio-political ambition because this larger congregation gives sustainability for caste network. It is important to notice here a consolidated caste network is built by strong leadership then question arise here who are leaders behind the grand celebration of *biradari bhoj* because leadership is a necessary function of management which helps to maximize efficiency and to achieve organizational goals at large. Although during the conversation with the research participants, it was countered, '*Chaudharis* are considered as community leaders among Yadavs.' Thus, each caste has its own (male) *chaudhari* which is assigned in each village. The work of a *chaudhari* is to take care of community relation and harmony. *Chaudhari* as a leader takes the initiative and motivates his community fellow in order to unite, and come forward for the welfare of *biradari* (cognate castes of Yadav). These *chaudharis* play very important role in moral building, co-ordination and caste network. Occasionally, they get together for discussing various issues related to Yadav community. This congregation is popularly known as '*chittha*.'

Chittha is a special occasion for *chaudhari* (caste head; a male member) where they get-together and discuss some issues, for instance, inter and intra-caste conflicts, misunderstanding among *biradaris* etc. Throughout those meetings[11], it appears that *chittha* system also creates a 'collective consciousness' in the long term. In the Durkheimian sense, 'collective consciousness is the set of shared beliefs, ideas, feeling, conception, and moral attitudes which represent entire group of people with common acceptance. It is constituted through individual consciousness, interaction as well mutual perceptivity' (Fish, 2005). It appears that the idea of get-together in predetermined place gives scope for collective consciousness. It is found that 'Yadav community holds this function before one week of the *biradari bhoj*. The primary aim of this function is to manage the *biradari bhoj* in systematic way in which *chaudhari* takes responsibility to distribute '*chitt*' (invitation) among his *biradari* (community members) while the second aim[12] of this function is to maintain caste network and community relation smoothly.

However, if we see the nature of *chitt*, it is a hand-made card, but the idea of *chitt* plays very vital role in upbringing Yadav community together. The structure of *chitt* system can be understood with its functional aspect. The main purpose of this scheme is to invite collectively for *biradari bhoj* because each *chitt* may be equal to hundred invitations or more than that but it depends on the proportion of the families in a village. Each card, for instance, may represent to such heads of the family (within caste fabric) who reside in a village. In other words, a *chitt* may represent to the entire village, if the village is occupied with the same caste. Mostly, the *chitt* is given in the name of a *chaudhari* who informs each head of the family who belong to his (Organizer) caste (Prasad, 2016: 542). Suppose that in Tandwa village in which nine families has been living; a *chitt* represents each family, and Durga Prasad Yadav (a *chaudhari* of Yadav community in Tandawa village) represents to whole caste-fellows, therefore, the *chitt* is sent by the name of Durga Prasad Yadav. Moreover, it is functioned with the idea of collective participation. In other words, the same caste of families who live in Tandawa village; after receiving the *chitt* for the *bhoj*, they collectively participate. It means that *chitt* gives space to show community concern because the idea of inviting gives a platform to discuss such problems that are related with their community. It seems that *chitt* is used as a tool to mechanize caste network.

In sum, the socio-ritual practice has also gone into undermining the divisions among different sub-caste units of Yadav community. They have started practicing inter-marriages. In other words, several endogamous groups within Yadav community who never to have marital exchanges to maintain their own boundaries which orchestrated through certain hierarchal arrangements of rural superiority and inferiority has now given up this practice of difference in northern India to some extent because of this community feast. The result of which, these cognate castes has become a 'numerous community' and a stronger political force in UP.

Samajwadi Party and Caste Formulas

Yadav community is considered as 'vote bank' of Samajwadi Party at present but there are few consequences such as 'emergency' (from 25 June 1975 to 21 March 1977), 'Mandal Commission' (1979), 'Babari demolition,'[13] (On December 6, 1992), etc. which are also responsible for it. Meanwhile, the legacy of socialist leaders, Karpuri Thakur, Ram Manohar Lohiya and Raj Narayain also gave way to detached from Congress (a dominated political party after independence). The detachment also led to Mulayam Sigh Yadav, Lalu Prasad Yadav, Kanshi Ram to initiate dalit-bahujan (SCs, OBCs and Minority based majoritarian principle) politics especially in the state like Uttar Pradesh and Bihar. The decade of 1989-90 was very important for dalit-bahujan politics because many events took place during that time, for instance, in 1989, Mulayam Singh Yadav became Chief Minister of Uttar Pradesh but two years later his government was felled down when the Congress withdrew support to his government but the year 1992 became turning point for Mulayam Singh Yadav and backward castes when Samajwadi Party came into being (see. samajwadiparty.in). Moreover, the unrest among backward castes could be one of the major reasons for initiating a new political party because there was no proper representation of OBCs in both parties: Congress and BJP. In 1993, SP and BSP allied for the elections to UP assembly which was scheduled in November 1993. The primary motives behind this alliance were to give voice to dalit-bahujan (marginal sections) as well as to prevent the return of BJP to the power in the state.

In addition, if we go little back during 1970 in order to see the caste orientation in UP politics, AJGAR (Ahir, Jat, Gujar and Rajpur) formula was used by Charan Singh (former prime minister of India). The idea of caste politics took place when he tried to break the monopoly of Indian National Congress. However, Samajwadi Party has been attracting Yadav community as well as other backward castes with iconic figures Ram Manohar Lohiya since its foundation while BSP has been attracting dalit votes with the legacy of Ambedkar. The first was initiated by Mulayam and Janeswar Mishra with socialist ideology while second was led by Kasi Ram and Mayawati Prabhu Das. Meanwhile, 21st century is witnessed when most of political parties have adapted Ambedkarism as an ideology to attract dalits' votes. Although the idea of 'vote-bank' also became prominent among political parties and the result of which many castes based socio-political activities took place including *bidari bhoj*.

Apart from the above discourse, Post Mondal era (after 1990s) is being witnessed when major political parties are assuming their future on dalit-bahujan's votes. Therefore, politicians have kept remembering the great legends like B.R. Ambedkar, Mahatma Jyotiba Phule, Narayana Guru, Periyar E.V. Ramasamy, Chhatrapati Shahuji Maharaj, Karpuri Thakur, Dashrath Manjhi, etc. in order to convert the legacy of these leaders into votes. Although the most popular leaders from backward classes are also vary in their ambitions; as Shaibal Gupta put it, "Leaders like Karpuri Thakur represented a more Sanskritized section of the backward those with a certain level of education and economic power. It was a section that had achieved a certain economic empowerment and wanted to convert it into political empowerment through the socialist movement of the 1960s and 1970s. But with Lalu [Prasad] Yadav, we saw the emergence of the cockney backwards[14] to the forefront, a non-Sanskritized, earthy, rustic section that spoke the local dialect and existed on the fringe of the market…He, in a sense, reversed the process that leaders like Karpoori Thakur had begun. Under Lal[u]oo Yadav, electoral and political empowerment happened first, economic empowerment later (Witsoe, Jeffrey 2013)." Thus, leaders like Lalu Prasad Yadav in Bihar and Mulayam Singh Yadav in Uttar Pradesh have cleverly converted the legacy of above leaders by putting timely required agendas of 'social-justice' and later 'socio-economic development.'

The Idea of 'Educate' and Respondents

Education is an important variable that plays very important role to build a good image in society. From the field, it has been encountered that the consciousness for education is being developed. It is found that half of the inhabitants are below the 5th standard (education), but often they justified that '*hum padh-likh nahi payein lekin hamare bhachche kafi jagrook hain*' (we could not attain education, but our children are very aware of education). It can be predicted that illiteracy is one of the leading cause for aspiring towards celebrating the *biradari bhoj* because an Organizer of *biradari bhoj* spends around one or two lakh rupees for this feast but he/she is not able to provide quality education for infants.

The idea of organizing a *biradari bhoj* is also associated with 'occupations' closely because it can be seen that rural area is dominated by agriculture as well as few other related occupations like fishery, milk-productions, etc. It appears that people could not get time to come out from their daily routine. It means that commensal practices give space for social interaction. It is noticed that more than fifty per cent of the organizers is engaged in agricultural activities. Due to engaging in agricultural works, they are not able to maintain frequent relation with such inhabitants who mostly live in urban areas. It also appears that these organizers are still carrying their traditional thought which is ascribed from the old generation.

Educational Profile of the Respondents

Education of the Respondent	*Village of the Respondent*		*Total*
	Tandawa	*Rajanpur*	
Illiterate	10 (12.5%)	22 (27.50%)	32 (40.00%)
Up to Primary	14 (17.50%)	15 (18.75%)	29 (36.25%)
Up to Secondary	4 (5%)	2 (2.50%)	6 (7.50%)
Up to Sr. Secondary	5 (6.25%)	3 (3.75%)	8 (10.0%)
Up to Graduation	2 (2.50%)	3 (3.75%)	5 (6.25%)
Total	35 (43.75%)	45 (56.25%)	80 (100.0%)

The above table shows educational attainment of the respondents. The respondents are active participants of *biradari bhoj* and other socio-political activities. In Rajanpur, 27.50 per cent of the total respondents are illiterate whereas in Tarawa village 12.50 per cent respondents are below the literacy criteria. The total respondents up to primary standard are 36.25 per cent. The percentage of the respondents in secondary level remark 7.5 per cent meanwhile 10 per cent of the respondents have attained about Sr. Secondary level. Only minimal percentages of the respondents i.e. 6.25 per cent of the total respondents have attained higher education. Moreover, above given table clearly shows that majority of the respondents have attained school level education while very minimal respondents have achieved higher education.

Visibility in Public Places and Yadav Community from Both Villages

For appropriate understanding of politics and its affiliation with inter/intra-caste relation in local settings, both villages are very remarkable because of its social nature, understanding of politics and existence of several castes together. Geographically, both villages are located in northern parts of Sultanpur district in Eastern Uttar Pradesh.

As for concern of Sultanpur, it is situated at south corner of Faizabad in which a popular place Ayodhya is well-known for the birth place of lord Ram [a Hindu deity]) and controversial figure for 'Babri-demolition'[15]. Sultanpur is dominated socially by Thakur, Brahamin and Muslim community but its neighbouring districts like Jaunpur and Ajamgargh are equipped with Yadav Community as a 'dominant caste'. Thus, another neighbouring district at the south corner of Sultanpur, Pratapgarh is dominated by Thakur caste and Raghuraj Pratap Sigh (from Thakur caste) an MLA of Samajwadi Party has become an iconic but controversial figure. Sultanpur district has consisted with four tehsils and fourteen blocks including Kurebhar block from where Rajanpur and Tandawa villages have been identified for the purpose data collection of the current study. The distance between both villages is about 2km, but junction point for people of both villages is Sudnapur-market. Sudnapur market has become a political space for backward classes because the majority of the shopkeepers are from the same section.

Two Significant Remarks[16]

There are fifty-five families in Tandwa village. The total population of this village can be divided into three factions. Duraga Yadav has been leading one progressive largest faction for twenty-years. The term 'progressive' means here the way of working for the welfare of entire village for the sake of satisfaction of 'worthy-life.' Popularly he is called 'Yadav-ji', but new generations call him '*bhaiya*' or '*chacha'* (by adding '*ji'* [a respectable word]). At the age of thirty, he joined 'Communist Party of India (CPI) in headquarters of Sultanpur district, but after working several years, he felt that the primary objective (development of Tandwa village) of his political career cannot be fulfilled. Therefore, he worked independently with '*gram-pradhan*' (elected representatives of village *panchayat*) namely, Ram Surat Vishkarma and Ram Kirat Vishkarma. In addition, it is very important to point out here that Tandawa village was a very remote village where, just three decades back, lacks of proper road, electricity, school, proper drinking water, etc., people had been living in pathetic situation because in rainy season inhabitants had to pass through shallow lake, if they wanted to go for livelihood or attending the classes.

However, with the support of Ram Surat Vishkarma and few volunteers, under the leadership of Durga Prasad Yadav, first a bridge and link-roads (*kachcha*: made by soil) were built. Later on, he got some fund from local M.L.A. namely Ram Ratan Yadav for building semi-*pacca* road. However, at present, there are availabilities of school (till the eighth standard), well-connected *pacca*-road, electricity, water facility, etc. Durga Yadav made a great attempt for fulfilling the standard of 'Nirmal Gram Puruskar' (NGP) in Tandawa village, and finally Tandawa village got selected for NGP in 2010, and the result of which each household of this village awarded a separate latrine-room.

In term of community concern, he also keeps little interest for the welfare of Yadav community. Therefore, he often expresses his experiences about '*bhoj*'. According to Durga Prasad Yadav, "It (*bhoj*) is a very expensive feast which leads the people of Yadav community into poor and backwardness." He also keeps sharp view about the local (ritual based hierarchal) situation, and pointed out that 'due to the concept of impurity, Ahir, Kurmi, Gaderiya, etc. castes were not participating in the commensal practices of Thakur caste because they were non-vegetarian'. Moreover, he is a very respectable member of Yadav community. Most of the Yadav *chaudharis* keep close social relation with him because of his polite nature. Therefore, if someone from Yadav community needs to find a suitable bride/groom for his daughter/son, Durga Yadav is always ready to help the needy people. In the case of 'Amedkarism', he says, "Amedkarism can be a key for resolving caste related issues which often encounter in day-to-day life."

Another essay is from Rajanpur village: Jagdambika Prasad is 60 years of age and is illiterate. His wife is also illiterate, but his children have attained education till higher secondary level. He works as a peasant and living with his wife and children. He also has four buffalos, a tracker, one two-wheeler/motor bike and good irrigation facility. As a peasant, whole days he works in the field, but every evening he often goes to Sudnapur market where he usually meets with his '*biradari bandhu*' (caste fellows) and few *Chaudharis*. He uses to wear *kurta* and *dhoti* (Indian ethnic clothes), and always keeps '*gamchha*' (traditional towel) on his shoulder in public place to show 'politically aspirant.' If we see his educational background as he is illiterate, it means there is very limited space for social mobility, but *bhoj* provides a 'space' where he can extend his social network. However, his son works with him in the field for fulfilling economic needs, but due to financial crisis, new generation is unable to get the quality education. As I have mentioned above, his father organized a *bhoj* in which he spent around two lacks of rupees in the whole process of this commensality. Fallowing the footsteps of his father he has also become an active participant of *bhoj*, and has been receiving respective 'community honour' from his *biradari*.

In sum, the logic behind to point out these two instances is to justified how the idea of 'politics' is understood among Yadav community in the local context as well as how their active engagement in socio-political activities help them to connect with state leadership. As I have pointed above a remote village (Tandawa), which is attaining a new height of development. It was possible because of active participation in politics of Durga Prasad Yadav and his great effort and close connection with MLAs.

Concluding Remarks

Let me summarise with frequently quoted words of Dr. B. R. Ambedker (1891-1956) which have become a source of inspiration for millions of marginal sections:

> *"Educate, agitate and organize; have faith in yourself. With justice on our side, I do not see how we can lose our battle. For ours is a battle not for wealth or for power. It is a battle for freedom. It is a battle for the reclamation of human personality."*

From the perspective of a local unit of Yadav community, Ambedkar's idea of 'educate,' 'agitate,' and 'organize' seems to be very significant. Yadav's leaders often advocate for 'education' because as a tool of empowerment it has become a way for the marginalized section to move forward. Just a few decades back, the idea of empowerment through 'education' was adapted by extending reservations for backward classes in educational institution and administrative services of Uttar Pradesh by the Janata Dal state government (1989-91), led by Mulayam Singh Yadav (Hasan 2000: 150-151; Michelutti 2002 35). The provision of reservation in education has given a chance to enter into the governmental institution for the backward section. Meanwhile, Yadav community is still carrying their 'past' (political rhetoric), which have found their best display and use in modern politics. They have made their identity project through kinship and corporate local and national power because they believe in caste substance and descent (Ciotti 2006: 908-9).

Moreover, the thought of Ambedkar has become an 'ideology', and major political parties have adapted it. In the same page, Samajwadi Party is also trying to justify the legacy of Ambedkar by concentrating on the main issue of social justice for Muslim, dalits (to some level) and OBCs in the politics of Uttar Pradesh. On the birth anniversary of Baba Saheb Ambedkar, Shivpal Yadav (SP's [UP] ex-in-charge) alleged, "Mayawati has nothing to do with B.R. Ambedkar. She has ruined his mission and is only concerned about Dalit votes."[17] On one hand, Yadav community also adapted Ambedakar's first mantra 'educate' for social mobility after independence. Although at the same time and even before, Yadavs were also trying to fallow the second idea, 'agitate', of B.R. Ambedkar, and they began 'janeo movement' with influence of Arya Samaj but failed badly because it led towards a 'caste conflict' (Rao, 1979: 134; Jassal, 2001: 53). On the other hand, the third message of Dr. Ambedkar, 'organize', is also captured by Yadav community. In this regard, Jaffrelot (2003) noticed, "Yadav leader succeeded in their social fusion project science they persuaded their fellow caste member to downplay the endogamous units into which they were divided: there were even some inter-regional marriages… (pp. 189)." The whole consequences from Mondal commission to Babari demolition as well as active participation of Yadav community led them to wielded political power especially in the north Indian states like U.P. and Bihar. At the grassroots level, the idea of *biradari bhoj* among Yadav community of which 'birha-folklore' (traditional song of Ahir/Yadaav) provides valuable information related to policy and political activity of Samajwadi Party. It can be predicted that the traditional folklore of Yadavs is bridging the gap between rural and rulers.

References

1. The followers of 'Manuavada' are called 'Manuvadis.' In other words, Manuvada denotes the ethos of a society governed by Manusmriti (a religious text, written by Manu), with the term Manuvadi denoting a proponent of such an ethos.

2. The umbrella term 'Yadav' covers many localize castes such as Ahir, Goala, Ghosi, Ghurpita, etc. in UP and Bihar; Panwar, Dabre, Jangade, etc. in Maharashtra; Golla, Kurwa, Peragolla, etc. castes in Andhra Pradesh and Telangana (see. www.yadavhistory.com).
3. According to Hindu philosophy, god Krishna spent his childhood in Mathura as a cow herder, and supposedly he was a Kshatriya because he ruled Dwarika.
4. Dayanand Saraswati was a founder member of Arya Samaj. He was inspired by Indian religious text, 'Vedas.'
5. The right to freedom of religion has been covered in articles 25, 26, 27 and 28 of the Indian Constitution which provides religious freedom to all citizens of India.
6. It is important to notice here that each caste has their special 'gotra' and ancestor. For instance, Yadav community follows 'atriy gotra' and 'Yadu' (a famous king) and Krishna legendary give them a way to move into popular democracy.
7. It is fifteenth lunar day's period of Hindu calendar when Hindus pay homage to their ancestor, in particular through food offering.
8. Hindu philosophy assumes that the soul exists and is eternal, passing through cycles of transmigration and rebirth. After death, reincarnation into a new body is asserted to be instantaneous.
9. He is a fifty-five years old farmer and considered as a Chaudhari in his village. He takes an active part in community feast.
10. It is a family based celebration in which head of the household takes the initiative with particular beliefs. Although relatives also contribute in order to receive bless of Lord Krishna/Vishnu.
11. The initiative for meeting (*Chittha)* is taken by aspirant of *biradari bhoj* because he/she bears the aggregate expenditures.
12. After talking to few participants and Organizers of *Bhoj*, it can say that community feast cannot be bound within certain aims. Thus, the primary objective of this research is to find out the relation between community feast and caste network. Therefore, I am pointing above about 'second aim' of the feast.
13. A large crowd of Hindu *kar sevek* (volunteers) demolished the 16th-century Babri Masque in the city of Faizabad, U.P.
14. The term 'cockney backwards' is used by the author in order to relate the backward sections of Bihar with white poor of Europe.
15. The demolition of Babri Masque has become central figure of UP politics, and sometimes it also changes the direction of national politics (see. the Liberhan Commission report).

16. The two observations have been pointed here is part of another paper (written by the first author). It seems meaningful to say here about two local leaders Durga Prasad Yadav and Jagdambika Prasad Yadav.
17. Retrieved from NDTV on 03/02/2017: http://www.ndtv.com/india-news/mayawati-has-ruined-ambedkars-mission-alleges-samajwadi-party-1395572.

Notes

1. Ambedkar, B.R. (2015). *Annihilation of caste: The annotated critical edition*. New Delhi: Navayana Publication.
2. Appadurai, A. (1981). *Worship and conflict under colonial rule: A South India caste.* New York: Cambridge University Press.
3. Beteille, A. (1996). Caste in Contemporary India'. In C.J. Fuller (Ed.), *Caste today.* Delhi: Oxford University Press.
4. Ciotti, Manuela (2006) 'In the Past, We Were a Bit "Chamar"': Education as a Self- and Community Engineering Process in Northern India, The Journal of the Royal Anthropological Institute, Vol. 12, No. 4, pp. 899-916.
5. Dumont, Louis (1970). *Homo hierarchicus: The caste system and its implication*. New Delhi: Oxford University Press.
6. Durkheim, Emile (1915). *The elementary forms of the religious life* (translated by Joseph Ward Swain). London: George Allen & Unwin LTD.
7. Fish, Jonathan, S. (2005). *Defending the Durkheimian tradition: Religion, emotion, and morality (rethinking classical sociology)*. New Delhi: Routledge.
8. Fox, R.G. (1969). *Kin, clan, raja and rule: State-hinterland relations in pre-industrial India.* Berkeley: University of California Press.
9. Green, Elliott D. (2010) Ethnicity and Nationhood in Pre-Colonial Africa: The Case of Buganda, retrieve from online http://personal.lse.ac.uk/greened/NEP.pdf.
10. Hanchett, Suzanne and Regelson, S. (1988). *Cloured rice: Symbolic structure in Hindu festivals.* Delhi: Hindustan Publishing Corporation.
11. Hasan, Z. (2000). Representation and redistribution: The new lower caste politics of north India. In F.R. Franket, Z. Hasan, R. Bhargava and B. Arora (eds), *Transforming India, social and political dynamics of democracy*. New Delhi: Oxford University Press.
12. Jaffrelot, Christophe (2003). *India's silent revolution: The rise of the lower castes in North India*. London: C. Huest & Co, pp.187-189.
13. Jassal, Smita Tewari (2001). *Daughters of the earth: Women and land in Uttar Pradesh.* New Delhi: Manohar Publication.

14. Khare, R.S. (1970). *The changing Brahmans associations and elites among the Kanya-Kubjas of North India.* Chicago: University of Chicago Press.
15. Michelutti, Lucia (2002). *Sons of Krishna: The politics of Yadav community formation in a North Indian town* (doctoral thesis). Retrieved from website of 'London School of Economics and Political Science', University of London on 12 January, 2017.
16. ________(2008) *The vernacularisation of democracy: politics, caste and religion in contemporary India. New Delhi: Routledge.*
17. Mehrotra, Santosh (2006) Well-being and caste in Uttar Pradesh: Why UP is not like Tamil Nadu, *Economic and Political Weekly*, Vol. 41, No. 40, pp. 4261-4271, October, 2006.
18. Moghe, S.G. (1994). Sraddha-Sagara of Kullukabhatta with a critical exposition and introduction. New Delhi: DK Prindworld (P) Ltd.
19. Moffatt, Michel (1979). Harijan religion: Consensus at the bottom of the caste. *American Ethnologist*: Vol. 6, No. 2, May, 1979, pp. 244-260.
20. Prasad, Devi (2015). Thinking against caste hierarchies: An analysis through Yadav community. *Man in India,* Vol. 95, No. 3, October, pp. 527-539.
21. _____(2016). Symbiosis, reciprocity and village exogamy in two villages of Uttar Pradesh. *South Asian Anthropologist,* Vol. 16, No. 2, September, pp. 185-194.
22. Rao, M.S.A. (1978). *Social movement in India*. New Delhi: Manohar Publication.
23. ______(1979) *Social movement and social transformation: A study of two backward classes*, New Delhi: Macmillan.
24. Sayers, Mathews R. (2013). Feeding the dead ancestors worship in ancient India, New Delhi: Oxford University Press.
25. Smith, Anthony D. (1991) National Identity, United State: University of Nevada Press, pp. 21.
26. Srinivas, M.N. (1952). *Religion and society among the Coorgs of South India.* New Delhi: India.
27. Srivastava, V.K. (1997). *Religious renunciation of a pastoral caste*. New Delhi: Oxford University Press.
28. Wankhede, Harish (2008). The political and the social in the dalit movement today, *Economic and Political Weekly,* vol. 43, No. 6, pp. 50-57.
29. Witsoe, Jeffrey (2013). *Democracy against development: Lower-caste politics and political modernity in post colonial India.* Chicago: The University of Chicago Press, pp.54.

16

Social Roots of Honour Based Violence (Honour Killings) Against Women:

With Special References From Tamil Nadu

— *S. Genani*

Abstract

Violence against women manifests itself in different forms such as domestic violence, marital rape, honour killings, sexual assault, dowry violence and denial of opportunities for girls and women Recently, many deaths are witnessed as killing human beings in the name of so-called 'honour' is to protect caste pride. Especially women in our society are killed in the name of family and caste honour. Now India has registered a nearly 251 cases of honour killings in 2015. Now Tamil Nadu witnessed 81 incidents of honour killings and notorious for many deaths of honour killings go unreported as passed off as suicides. Honour killings are an extreme of violation of the human rights of main women who are perceived to have brought shame or dishonour. This paper tries to analyses certain major honour killings occurred between caste groups in Tamil Nadu and discuss some ameliorative solutions and strategies in policy level.

Keywords: *Honour killing, Violence against women and Honour-based violence.*

Introduction

Honour based violence is a team frequently used to differentiate a particular form of violence against women on the basis of honour, it transpires within the framework of the family and community sphere. It is an act deliberately intended to restore 'honour' to the family and is rooted in men's efforts to control women's sexual and social lives.

Objectives

1. To assess the status of women in india
2. To evaluate the concept of Honour killing and its effects on society

Scope

The paper deals with social norms and system that create an awareness among women.

Method

Descriptive method has been adopted to present the idea.

Violence Against Women

Violence against women is not a new phenomenon. It has plagued communities around the world and continues to subject innocent women and girls to physical, mental and emotional harms. Violence against women manifests itself in different forms such as domestic violence, marital rape, honour killings, sexual assault, dowry violence and denial of opportunities for girls and women. But in this context, the new way of violence imposed on women is a violence-based honour.

Honour based violence (Honour killings) against women

Honour-based Violence (HBV) is a form of initiate, intrafamilial (agnatic, spousal, occasionally community based) behaviour that infringes upon personal liberties through a collection of practices that encompass a broad range of social, financial, emotional and physically abusive and coercive acts in order to protect and uphold a value system predicated on norms and traditions concerned with honour.

The concept of 'Honour' is vital for comprehensive why men in certain societies backlash any real or perceived breach in their honour in such extreme fashion.

Honour killings refer to a family member, close relative or a self–appointed community leader killing another person when they perceive that the person in question has brought dishonour to the family or community by breaking from traditional social conduct. Most often than not, the person in question is female because girls and women are seen to uphold or embody the family or communities honour.

Honour based violence is understood to derive from a desire to control the behaviour of women and girls within a community. Most often with an emphasis on her sexuality, there are many forms of behaviour under scrutiny including dress, communication with men and sexual relationships. Victims of honour violence are targeted because their behaviour is seen to violate cultural or religious norms, where their assailant feels the only way to prevent such behaviour or restore family honour is to harm or kill the victim so-called honour killings are part of a community mentality. Large sections of society share traditional conceptions of family honour and approve of 'honour' killings to preserve that honour. Even mother's whose daughters have been killed in the name of honour often condone such violent acts. Such complicity by other women in the family and the community strengthens the concept of women as property without personal worth. In additions, communal acceptance of 'honour' killings furthers the claim that violence in the name of 'honour' is a private issue and one to be avoided by law enforcement. Community acceptance of these killings stifles accurate reporting of the number of violent crimes against women in the name of 'honour'. As a result, the true extent of the prevalence of 'honour' killings is still not fully known. The tradition and customs of South Asia are so rigid that it comes in way of women to exercise their rights and fundamental freedom. In some cultures, honour killings are considered less serious than other murders because they arise from long-standing cultural traditions and are thus deemed appropriate or justifiable. Reports on honour killing show that each year hundreds of girls and women were killed by their own family members to protect the 'honour' considering that many such cases go unreported and several cases do not end in the killing but brutal assault and restrictions are put on the women, the problem assumes much significance and concern. According to the Evidence, an NGO involved in the protection of Dalit and Tribal rights based out of Madurai had come across 81 honour-based violence are unreported and prevalence for long, the culture of mob violence against women.

These deaths show that racism still prevails in our society despite all the rationalist preachings of our Dravidian leaders. It is very unfortunate that the caste and patriarchal system in India have turned into a social evil for many. It is horrible that many young people have lost their lives in the name of protecting family and caste honour, and there are much more who are at the gunpoint of the rigid system. Especially women in our society are killed in the name of family and caste honour. In order to protected men's shame and honour, women are expected to behave to behave modestly.

Social Roots of Honour-based Violence (Honour killings)

After 80 years of Independence, India has still not been able to get rid of regressive social practices like honour killings and caste-related violence. The nation so helpless in fighting this problem that shows no signs of abating and the youth continues to be both aggressor and victim of this vicious circle of violence even to the day itself. Caste pride and treating women as men's possession are the prime factors behind honour killings, say some activities often, thus killings are committed because women are considered as a preserver of the purity of progeny, a feudal concept. A 'polluted' progeny is unthinkable. Particular issues in Hindu communities are caste and gotra (patriline). Marriage opportunities are very restricted and there may be particularly fierce opposition to any contact between a women and a male of lower caste; it is often the case that it is the man who is the primary victim of violence by the family of the women has approached while it may be required that any partnerships do not lose caste, marriages within a gotra are condemned as incestuous, despite their rarely being any close consanguinity between any members of the same Gotra. Panchayats have actively policed gotra restrictions and called for the deaths of couples who have contravened such norms when a female member is seen to violate an honour norm, the whole family experiences shame killing a wayward women is seen as an act of purification for the family and sometimes, even not doing it quickly enough is perceived to be damaging to the family honour. Women are constantly under threat because any action on their part can bring shame and dishonour to the male members of a family.

"Intermediate communities cannot stomach the idea of transferring their genes to other communities through their women. That is why they resort to violence when their women fall in love with Dalit men but would not mind their men marrying a Dalit Women", says Tamil writer Imayam. In the last three years, the state had witnessed so many honour killings, but most of these cases were "covered up" as suicides. Even if inter-caste marriages had the blessings of parents of the bride and groom, humiliations, social boycott and ostracisation force them either to break the marriage or encourage them to eliminate the newly married in the name of honour killings.

Conclusion

Honour violence is committed across the world, often with impunity; and despite the widespread and severe nature of the violence, cases remain underreported. There is no specific law in India which deals with this gruesome act of honour killings and any punishments regarding the same. Honour killings derive strong sanctions from the society. Though every religion condemns honour killings yet the cultural set up portray such practices as an integral part of religion. Thus, honour killings have one of the strongest supports of masses i.e. through religion. Honour killings are homicide and murder which are serious crimes. More attention needs to be paid to the concept of "honour", how it is perceived and the issues need to be investigated and confronted. The change of human mind will be the better solution to stop this kind of crimes in future.

References

1. DECCAN CHRONICLE, Nov 28, 2016.
2. The Times of India, March 16, 2016: Padmini Sivaraman.
3. Tehelka Magazine, Vol 7, Issue 42, Dated October 23, 2010.
4. S. Murugananthan, " 'Honour Killing' the Menace - A case study in Tamil Nadu", International Journal of Management Research and Social Science

(IJMRSS) ISSN 2394-6407(Print) Volume 1, Issue 1, October - December 2014 ISSN 2394-6415(Online)

5. http://www.youthkiawaaz.com/2010/07/honour-killing-in-india-an-in-depth-study
6. http://yapi.org/wp-content/uploads/2014/01/cmgirlchild.pdf
7. Soli J Sorabjee, Customs never over Constitution, The New Indian Express, 12 the September 2010.
8. http://www.justice.gc.ca/eng/rp-pr/cj-jp/fv-vf/hk-ch/p3.html
9. http://www.theglobaljournals.com/ijar/file.php?val=January_2014_1388584173_ee 78c_75.pdf
10. Gokul Vannan, The story of Madurai Veeran, The New Indian Express, dated 18th July 2010 S. Genani, Assistant Professor, Centre for Women's Studies, Gandhigram Rural Institute – Deemed University, Gandhigram – 624 302. Dindigul District, Tamil Nadu.

17

Plagued with Prejudice: Subjugation of Dalit Women in Rajasthan

— *Sunita Meena*

It is the education which is the right weapon to cut the social slavery and it is the education which will enlighten the downtrodden masses to come up and gain social status, economic **betterment and political freedom."**

— Bharat Ratna Dr. B.R. Ambedkar

Abstract

Caste based discrimination remains a cliché in India even at the dawn of 21st century. Women in India, particularly in a state like Rajasthan, which has a long feudal history, are not only plagued with the prejudiced mindset on the basis of Gender but also by other factors like community and religion. State of Rajasthan has emerged with the highest incidents of registered atrocities against Dalit women in the whole country. In 2010, the state recorded 51.4 cases of atrocities against Dalits per Lakh population under the Scheduled Castes and Scheduled Tribes Prevention of Atrocities Act. The status of Dalit women in Rajasthan is one of the worst in the country. The majority of Dalits in Rajasthan are concentrated in following districts: Sriganganagar, Bhatatpur, Jodhpur, Pali, Tonk and Kota. Dalit women in those districts face violence and humility not only from Non-Dalits but also from her own community. The Dalits are also not socially united. For example Raigar community is still into the profession of shoe making. In Dausa district, economic status, resources and other things are still controlled by the Upper Caste. Dalit women are not allowed to take water and face a lot of health problems.

*The strong impact of caste even on the judicial system has been witnessed in the case of **Bhanwari Devi**. It is a typical case of rape of a lower caste woman as a weapon of retaliation used to punish and silence women's rights activists. This paper will explore the dynamics of discrimination which has subjugated the Dalit Women of Rajasthan. On the other hand it would also examine the issues like the level of education among Dalit women and Political Participation in the state politics in comparison to the upper caste women in Rajasthan. Humiliation and Isolation of Dalit Women in Rajasthan from every aspects of life, forces them to remain in the medieval dark ages when upper caste woman went on to achieve highest political status of the state.*

Keywords: Dalit Women, Caste, Isolation, Gender, State of Rajasthan.

Introduction

Caste based discrimination remains a challenge in India even at the dawn of 21st century. Neither our society nor the states in India are able to resolve this problem. The Indian society is still based on caste system and divided along the lines of class such as Brahmins, Kshatriyas, Vaishyas and Shudras (Untouchables) and Dalits constitute more than 67% of the Indian population. The social status of Dalits is as lower as the Varna System is; no solid changes have a taken place even after the 68 years of India's independence. The Dalits are still marginalised in the society and the caste system is embedded only in Hindu religion. The upper caste is politically, economically, and socially well-off and dominating right from the independence of India. In India, the status of every human being is more or less decided to a great extent fined by their birth, not by their work or talents, whether they belong to upper caste or lower caste. Caste is a concept which was made by the Caste Hindu Brahmins to use it as a weapon against lower caste. As scholars like P.V. Kane argue that 'There were no people who called Dalits or untouchables during the Vedic period"[1]. There are different concepts about the origin of the caste system. Some argued that it originated from Aryans when majority of scholars considers that the origin of caste system is from Manusmriti. But according to Ambedkar, "caste system was there even before the age of Manu, who only articulated the institution of the caste system"[2].

Dalits are the mixed population consisting of a number of social groups from over all India. The word "Dalit" originated from Sanskrit root dal which means broken, ground-down, downtrodden, or oppressed[3]. They are also known as Untouchables, Depressed Classes, and Harijans and they know themselves as Dalit. Dalits are 'outcaste' outside traditional fourfold caste system hereditary within the Brahmin, Kshatriyas, Vaishyas, and Shudra classes. According to Manusmriti, Dalits are untouchable due to the extreme impurity and pollution concept with their traditional occupations, that's why they are socially and physically excluded and isolated from the rest of society[4].

Objectives

Method

Scope

Dalit Women and Hindu Texts

The condition of Dalit women in India is worsening. According to Manu, women should be treated unequally as a woman should be kept under the control of her family, never should be allowed any sort of freedom. Before marriage, she should be kept under her father's control, after marriage under her husband and during old age, she should live under her son's mercy. In other words, women should live under restrictions or boundaries which were drawn to regulate their whole life, from birth to death (*Manusmitri* IX.25). On the other hand, Dr. B.R Ambedkar, Chief architect of Indian Constitution clearly told in his article 'The rise and fall of Hindu woman' that the 'Hindu religious books are responsible for the sufferings of the women [5]. As Manusmriti divided society along stratas of upper caste and lower caste and encouraged the gap of inequality between men and women and women child marriage, for instance women do not have the right to education, independence or wealth. A Brahman, Kshatriya, or Vaishya Man can sexually exploit any Shudra woman (*Manusmitri* IX.25). It is a minor offence for a Brahmin if he kills Dalit women as considered equal to the killing of an animal. Thus, we can imagine the situation of Dalit women, how they faced violence and got discriminated. The Hindu scripture only favoured upper caste and considered them as superior in society in comparison to lower caste who were termed as Rakshahs and Asuras. The word Dalit was first used by Mahatma Jyotirao Phule, a Marathi social reformer. In short, Dalits are oppressed in all spheres.

There used to be a time where if a Hindu touches a Dalit even by mistake, then he would be punished. Dalit Women were no exception in getting treated by the notion of Caste System. Manu's views about women are totally rejected by Ambedkar who was struggling against the marginalization of Dalit Women and emphasised on the concept of gender equality.

Status of Women within Dalit Communities of Rajasthan

The Dalit women in Rajasthan are not simply suppressed due to lack of poverty, education but they are tortured and exploited by the upper caste in every aspects of life as it is legitimized by Hindu religion[6]. The society considered women as an object of sex and sex exploitation. In Rajasthan, there are a large number of Dalit communities which contributed one fifth of the total population of Rajasthan. The major Dalit communities in Rajasthan are Meghwals, Jatavs, Bariwas, Khatik, Chamar, Bunkar, Raigars, Balai's, Jatias, and Gingar, a brief discussion about these communities are following[7]:

Jatav community is mainly residing in the eastern Rajasthan particularly in the districts Alwar, Dholpur, Bharatpur, Sawai Madhopur and Karauli[8].

Raigars (Jatia): This community mostly residing in Alwar, Jaipur, Ajmer, Jodhpur, Barmer Dausa, Sawai Madhopur, Karauli, Tonk, and Pali districts. They are still engaged in their traditional occupation of shoe-making, agricultural labour or own small farms[9].

Bairwas: Bairwas are mostly living in Alwar, Jaipur, Dausa, Sawai Madhopur, Karauli, Ajmer, Kota, Bhilwara and Tonk districts. Their economic condition is better off than other Dalits in Rajasthan.

Khatik: This is the richest community among the *Dalits*. They residing mainly in Jaipur, Bhilwara, Bharatpur, Tonk, Alwar, Ajmer, and Kota and are engaged in cattle business[10].

Chamar, Balali, and Bunkar: These communities have started to call themselves as Meghwals. They mostly live in the Central and Northeastern parts of the Rajasthan. They are still work leather related work, small farmers and labourers[11].

The status of Dalit women is worse than Dalit men in Rajasthan and they are not only facing violence by the upper caste but also state sponsored violence, at home and outside. All over India, including Rajasthan, landless Dalits are helpless to work at landlord's farm where they are forced to do hard work with minimum salary. In Rajasthan Dalit women mostly work as leather workers, street sweepers, cobblers, agricultural workers, and manual scavengers[12]. The process of Globalization of modern time also reduced the means of occupations, particularly the Dalit community has been affected by this process very much. As a result, Dalit men are migrating into urban areas, while Dalit women are left at home to take care of domestic works as well as family, which is why Dalit women easily become the target of rape, murder, and sexual harassment, in the absence of a male in the family, by higher caste in Rajasthan[13]. Lack of any safety nets or works, Dalit women are forced to take loans in emergency such as illness, marriages, death etc, at a high rate of interests by the upper caste and after that this indebtedness becomes as an excuse to exploit them[14].

Dalit women are playing an important role in the contribution of Indian economy as well as in society. They often work as agricultural labourers, Safai Karmchari, sweepers and disposers of human waste (Source: Ministry of Labour). Approximately 80% Dalit women in Rajasthan are engaged in industrial work, road construction with minimum salary. They do hard work under the burning sun with no protection or benefits. Thus, 85% of the Dalit women in Rajasthan have the most formidable occupations, while working in traditional sectors of economy, for example, Dalit women are working as manual scavengers' everyday even today particularly in Rajasthan mainly in the districts of Sawai Madhopur, Tonk, Karauli, and Dholpur, etc[15]. In a family also, Dalit women play a significant role such as getting up early and engaging in domestic works like cleaning home, cooking, and getting ready for her children etc which is strictly followed in Rajasthan or rather imposed on the Dalit women by the male members of the family. On top of this, at night, Dalit Women are tortured and beaten up by their husband as it is seen everywhere, particularly in rural areas of Rajasthan. During the day, they are exploited by higher caste, and rest of time by their own community and husband. Thus we find that Dalit women are facing a large number of discriminations as well as challenges in society such as:-Gender discrimination – patriarchy Social /caste discrimination - untouchability Violence - domestic, at work place and in society, economic deprivation – poverty, unemployment, landlessness, Political powerlessness – non acceptance and participation in decision making[16]

Marginalization of Women: Cases from Rajasthan

Rajasthan has emerged as the state with highest number of atrocities against Dalits and occupied the second position in the top 10 atrocities committed states in the country with has the increasing rate of 7.4%. Madhya Pradesh, Rajasthan and Andhra Pradesh are at the top in the cases of atrocities against Dalits. Approximately 60% cases of the whole India are registered from these states[17]. In 2010, the state of Rajasthan recorded 51.4 cases of atrocities against Dalits per Lakh population under the Scheduled Castes and Scheduled Tribes Prevention of Atrocities Act[18]. According to the National Commission for Scheduled Castes and Scheduled Tribes 2000 Report, around 75% Dalit girls leave primary school at an early age[19]. Besides this, 85% Dalits are landless so Dalit women are helpless and end up in occupations such as agricultural labourers, scavengers, sweepers, and disposers of human waste[20]. Brahminical society interprets Hindu scriptures against Dalit to maintain their superior status in the society and also to fulfil their interests by exploiting Dalits rights. For instance, the *Devdasi system* (also known as temple prostitution) was introduced by the upper caste and it still be found in some parts of India. In this system Dalit girls are considered as "female servants of god", they married to god and left in the temple where they are sexually exploited by upper caste, after a certain date the girl becomes unable to marry. After a living at the temple for lifetime as a prostitute, they are sold to brothels. So it is quite clear even after the sixty seven years of independence the Dalit women are still badly suffering from atrocities from the higher caste Hindu groups.

Rajasthan is the largest state of India in terms of Geographical area. As a largest state, it has its own unique geographical, historical and cultural features that affected the activities of Dalits. Even, the culture restricts women's space and they are not allowed to go in public place. The Situation of Dalit women in Rajasthan is characterised by multiple marginality. Prejudiced mindset among male members of the family against the women members is still prevalent in the rural areas[21]. Rajasthan was a focal point of the feudalistic society by various caste and communities were in hierarchical order with class domination. The state was divided into princely areas ruled by the royal clans such as Rathore of Marwar, Kachhawaha of Jaipur, Chauhan of Sirohi, Bhatti of Jaisalmer, Sisodia of Mewar, Hada of Kota etc; these feudal states had their own administration[22]. They were predominantly powerful and exploited all economic resources, social and political activities. The lower caste depended on the mercy of these feudal class and they were called as "Ochhi Jat" (lower caste).

According to Census 2001, Rajasthan has 17.2% of SC and 12.6% of ST population. Ganganagar district has highest SC population (33.72 percent) and Dungarpur district has the lowest (4.15 percent). Banswara has the highest percentage of ST population (72.3 percent) followed by Dungarpur (65.1 percent) and Udaipur (47.9 percent)[23]. The above three districts have the highest ST population. The district with the least percentage of ST is Nagaur (0.2 percent). Rajasthan is at the bottom in terms of female literacy. The literacy rate of women is 52.1% in Rajasthan. Rajasthan which is home to over 6.1% of the total SC population of the country, literacy rate of SCs is 59.7%, in which male literacy is 68.99%, while female literacy is 33.87%. According Census report, 2001, ST male literacy in Rajasthan is 62.10% while female literacy is 26.16%. This exposes the huge gap between male and female literacy. The education level of Dalit women is much lower than Upper caste women. Dalit women are vulnerable for rape, murder, kidnapping, and sexual harassment. The reasons behind the illiteracy of Dalit women in Rajasthan are following; restriction from her family to send her to school, distance of school from her home, fear of insecurities in village, due to poverty, humiliation, bullying and isolation by classmates, society and even the teachers, they are not allowed to drink water from common water pots, discouraged from studying ,the girls are forced to take care of their siblings when their parents go to work to earn for family, marriage in the early age also prevents them from access to education etc, factors are responsible for this[24]. Due to lack of education, Dalit girls are married in early ages which badly affect their health. Due to the process of Sanskritisation by Hindu, Dalit have started to adopt Hindu's rituals and customs. Dowry is one such custom.

Interpreting the Case of Dalits from the Constitution

The right of equality is fundamental to everyone. Article 14 of the constitution guaranteed "equality before law". State should assure equality before the law or the equal protection of laws to every its citizens. Article 15 of the constitution provides states that "State shall not discriminate against any citizen on grounds only of religion, race, caste, sex, place of birth or any of them". The Scheduled Castes and the Scheduled Tribes (Prevention of Atrocities) Act also made to prevent violence against Dalits. There are two legal laws that have been made at national level to protect SC/ST.

1. Protection of Civil Rights Act 1955
2. SC/ST (Prevention of Atrocities) Act 1989

The main objective of PCR Act was to encourage of Art 17 of the constitution to abolish untouchability and its practice in any form and also brought social equality in the society[25]. After the reservation and quotas, the situations of Dalits women are improving in terms of education, employment and in politics also. But caste problem is still in the state and these reservation policies are still not implemented in a proper way. Due to this, again Dalits are becoming soft targets of exploitation by upper caste. If Dalits got high level job then they are tortured and considered as second citizens of India by upper caste as it is seen in the whole country including Rajasthan.

Struggle of Dalit Women: Instances from Rajasthan

Though the government has introduced a large number of constitutional reforms and government development policies but caste system is still having a great impact in all spheres even in the judicial system of Rajasthan as in the case Bhanwari Devi. It is typical case of rape of lower caste women which was using *as* a weapon to suppress the women's right activities. Bhanwari Devi, a lower caste woman belongs to a low caste *Kumhar* (potter) family live in Bhateri, a small village located 55 km from the state capital, Jaipur. She worked as a Saathin (Friend) which was a part of the Women's Development Project

(WDP) complaining against child marriage. As a result, she was gang rapped by five upper caste persons who belong to Gujjar community and Sharma. After rape, when she went police station for FIR, then she was told that she was too old and was not attractive, so no one would like to rape her. Secondly, a Dalit girl was raped by upper caste in the national capital in Delhi in 2012. She is from Alwar and sexually assaulted by upper caste men for trying to attend college. Another violence event regarding to Dalit women took place in the same year in Dangariya village, Karauli district in Rajasthan where Dalit women are forced to remove footwear while passing through upper caste neighbourhoods[26]. Recently on March, 2014, Fatehpur town in Sikar district a 14 year Dalit girl was raped by an upper caste boy.

Besides this, Dalit are forced to spend their life in dirty places, for example Jhalana Doongri and Kacchi Basti are a settlement colonies located in the outskirts of Jaipur where majority of population are Dalits as 300 out of 500 families. They are living in small plots allotted by the government. The slums are illegal and don not have any legal (Patta) title. So these Dalits are living there only on the mercy of government which can vacate or demolish the Basti as depending on the government's wish[27]. The Jaipur Development Authority has thrice demolished the part of *Kacchi Basti,* over the last decade[28]. Beside this, Dalits are living in bad condition with complete lack of basic amenities. There is no drainage system, foul smelling water flows in the streets in which children play. Because of this, numerous of diseases are spreading including Malaria, Dengue[29]. In the absence of toilet facility, Dalit people are forced to use the road as toilet and Dalit women use when it is dark which contributes to the health hazards and sexual harassment events and thus, Dalit women are raped everyday by upper caste. Thus, there is no proper law and order in Basti.

The Western Rajasthan is otherwise known as Marwar including districts as Bikaner, Jodhpur, Pali, Barmer, Jalore, and Nagaur which is dominated by historical feudalistic upper caste. It is a home of a large population of Dalits and Adivasis who continue suffering from the dominant class. The basic resources are controlled by the upper caste as there is separate matka for drinking, separate line for stand and separate space for sitting all indicates the status of Dalits in the society. Thus, violence against Dalit community is very common in the feudalistic society. When Dalit women go police station for lodge a FIR, they are humiliated, sexually abused, refused to file FIR, misguided, threatened and sometimes they are sexually and mentality harassed by police. Police officers mostly belong to upper caste, and sometimes they ask for bribe from the lower caste, so in this situation Dalit women regret being themselves thrice due to gender, caste and class. She fights alone; with no one help her, and sometimes even her family and her own community blame her. Study of 500 Dalit women's cases of violence conducted by Centre for Dalit Rights stated that majority of the cases are not spoken out in the public by women themselves, or not registered by the police or not reported by media, or most of the times hidden by women's family or suppressed by the society or upper caste[30]. Even to this date, there are a lot of similar cases from all over India. Thus, there is a strong social prejudice against Dalit women who face all the way to the top of the judicial system. Apart from this, the Dalits are also not socially united. As Meena, a dominant tribal community in Rajasthan which is also divided into two categories as Zamidar Meena (upper class) and other Chokidar Meena (lower class). Zamidar Meena is like landlords because they have much of the land, so they are well educated and have more representation in politics, government job as well as in other fields as compared to Chokidar Meena. Also, they are influenced by and have adopted all brahminical rituals while Chokidar Meena are deprived and still living in natural form and believing in folk deities such as Bhairu Baba, Jeen Mata etc. Thus we find the huge gap in customs and rituals within the same community in spite of the same title.

Political Participation of Dalit Women

Age, education, caste, economic status, social status of family, political background of family is the basic determinant of political participation.[31] But 77% Dalit women are illiterate that prevents them from access to political participation. Dalit women are generally excluded from political power and decision making process. The upper caste women dominate a large number of seats in the local, state as well as central level politics. Rights assert by Dalit women as elected representatives of the Panchayat and local governing bodies seen as insult of the dominant class, caste and honour. Dalit women in Rajasthan are mostly affected by various factors such as caste, class, gender, family, political parties, and access to learning and also of regional variation. Besides this, Brahmincal ideology based political parties do not want to see Dalit women as vote bank or as political leader and she should be kept out of these opportunities.

The 73rd and 74th amendment provides opportunity of reservation for Dalit women and other women to be elected in rural and urban governing bodies. The entry of Dalit women in politics has brought some changes in Rajasthan, but still these links come through male family members, and not directly to women. The Dalit woman Sarpanch (head of the village) especially in Rajasthan are mostly wife or daughter in law of the old Sarpanch who was made to sign, while the power is used by her husband or father in law. The Dalit women cannot take their own decisions freely; they have to take their husband's permission before taking any decision. In Rajasthan, Dalit women Sarpanch cannot sit on the chair in front of the upper caste and she have to respect all upper caste people. For instance, a Dalit woman elected representative in Jaipur is being harassed and even subjected to violence and not allowed to perform their duties by upper class in village. Thus, we find that the education level as well as political participation of Dalit women is much lower than the women of upper caste women.

Conclusion

Though Indian constitution guarantees equality, liberty and justice to everyone, but not only Rajasthan but also the whole country is still suffering from traditional caste system and patriarchal system. Besides this, Social and economic inequalities are still dominant almost all over India, including Rajasthan. The Dalits women are still politically, economically, socially and educationally deprived. The state made many provisions for upliftment, particularly for deprived people, but this class is unable to enjoy such privileges due to the lack of education and also they are unable to understand policies of the brahminical modern government. Thus, education is the main key to escape all these violence and discriminations as Dr. Ambedkar also said before. To reduce drop out of girls from school, the government should introduce some scholarships and also introduce strict laws to prevent all type of discriminations. The government should also make new provisions for the protection of Dalit women rights as well as of gender equality. There is also a need to change the mindset of upper caste and they should treat equal to Dalits as they are also Indian citizens and human being.

Notes

All India Dalit Mahila Adhikar Manch :AIDMAM", [Online Web] Accessed on 18th March 2014 URL: http://allindiadalitmahilaadhikarmanch.blogspot.in/p/dalit-women-status-in-india.html

Daily Bhaskar.com (2012):" Rajasthan leads country in atrocities against

Dalits",[Online Web] Accessed on 15th March 2014 URL: http://daily.bhaskar.com/article/RAJ-JPR-rajasthan-leads-country-in-atrocities-against-dalits-3216409.html

"Dalit women sarpanches a harassed lot", *The Hindu*, Jaipur, 1 April 2011

Debnath, Debashis (1995), "Hierarchies within Hierarchy : Some Observations on Caste System in Rajasthan", *Indian Anthropologist, Vol. 25, No. 1 (June 1995),* page no 23-30

Fact Finding Mission Report 1: "Dalit women in Rajasthan: Status of Economic,

Social and Cultural rights", [Online Web] Accessed on 17th March 2014 URL: http://www.pwescr.org/Dalit_Report.pdf

Mahey, Sonia (2011), "The Status of Dalit Women in India's Caste Based System",

[Online Web] Accessed on 15 March 2014 URL:http://roundtableindia.co.in/index.php?option=com_content&view=article&id=3 201:the-status-of-dalit-women-in-indias-caste-based system&catid=120:gender&Itemid=133

Michal, S.M (2007), "*Dalits in Modern India: Vision and Values* ", Los Angeles

[Calif.]: SAGE Publications.

Mimroth, P.L(2011), "Discrimination against Dalit women in India :With special

context of Rajasthan State", [Online Web] Accessed on 18th March URL:http://idsn.org/fileadmin/user_folder/pdf/New_files/IDSN/Consultations/Cases/Dalit_women_in_Rajasthan.pdf

Morris, Alice et al. (2009), *"Making Space: Women's Participation in Local Politics in Rajasthan"*, Ahmadabad; UNNAATI.

Narayan, Badri (2006),"*Women Heroes and Dalit Assertion in North India : Culture, Identity, and Politics*", New Delhi :In Cultural Subordination and the Dalit Challenge ;SAGE Publications.

National Campaign on Dalit Human Rights; who are Dalit? What is untouchbility? [Online Web] Accessed on 16 March 2014 URL: http://www.ncdhr.org.in/ncdhr/general-info-misc-pages/wadwiu

NAVSARJAN; who are Dalit? http://navsarjan.org/navsarjan/dalits/whoaredalits [Online Web] Accessed on 18 March 2014.

Online Campaign against 'Untouchability' in Rajasthan", *News India Times,* 12 July 2012

Rakesh, Renu (2012)," Justice still evades Dalits finds public hearing in Rajasthan", [Online Web] 18th March 2014 URL:http://southasia.oneworld.net/news/dalits-narrate-tales-of-atrocities-police-inaction-at-public hearing#.UyjuHvmSyls

Shukla, Diwakar (2011), " Dr B. R. Ambedkar Vision Towards Gender Equality",[Online Web] Accessed on 17th March URL:http://www.lawyersclubindia.com/articles/Dr-B-R-Ambedkar-Vision-towards-Gender Equality 4144.asp#.UykxsvmSyls

Status of Dalit Women : A Review [Online Web] Accessed on 16th March http://shodhganga.inflibnet.ac.in/bitstream/10603/8562/8/08_chapter%203.pdf

Varma, Sudhir, "Violence against Dalit women in Rajasthan: national Commission for Women", [Online Web] Accessed on 16th March 2014 URL:http://ncw.nic.in/pdfReports/Violence_against_Dalit_Women_in_Rajasthan.pdf

References

1. "Status of Dalit women: a review", [Online: Web] Accessed on 16th March 2014 URL: http://shodhganga.inflibnet.ac.in/bitstream/10603/8562/8/08_chapter%203.pdf, p.2
2. *Ibid.*
3. "National Campaign on Dalit Human Rights: who are Dalit? What is untouchbility?", [Online: Web] Accessed on 16 March 2014 URL: http://www.ncdhr.org.in/ncdhr/general-info-misc-pages/wadwiu
4. *Ibid.*
5. Mahey, Sonia, "The Status of Dalit Women in India's Caste Based System", [Online Web] Accessed on 15th March 2014 URL: http://roundtable-india.co.in index.php?option=com_content&view=article&id=3201:the-status-of-dalit-women-in-indias-caste-based-system&catid=120:gender&Itemid=133, p.150
6. *Ibid.* p. 149
7. Fact Finding Mission Report 1: "Dalit women in Rajasthan: Status of Economic, Social and Cultural rights", [Online Web] Accessed on 17th March 2014 URL: http://www.pwescr.org/Dalit_Report.pdf
8. *Ibid.*
9. *Ibid.*
10. *Ibid.*
11. *Ibid.*

12. "NAVSARJAN; who are Dalit?", [Online Web] Accessed on 18th March 2014 URL:http://navsarjan.org/navsarjan/dalits/whoaredalits.
13. *Ibid.*
14. *Ibid.*
15 *Ibid.* p. 4.
16 *Ibid.*
17 Daily Bhaskar.com (2012):" Rajasthan leads country in atrocities against Dalits", [Online Web] Accessed on 15th March 2014 http://daily.bhaskar.com/article/RAJ-JPR-rajasthan-leads-country-in-atrocities-against-dalits-3216409.html
18. Nichenametla, Prasad (2012), "Rajasthan tops list of atrocities against Dalits", *Hindustan Times,* New Delhi, 03, May 2012.
19. 'Mahey, Sonia' Op. Cit 151.
20. *Ibid.*
21. Mimroth, P.L(2011), "Discrimination against Dalit women in India :With special context of Rajasthan State", [Online Web] Accessed on 18th March 2014 URL: http://idsn.org/fileadmin/user_folder/pdf/New_files/IDSN/Consultations/Cases/Dalit_women_in_Rajasthan.pdf
22. Debnath, Debashis (1995), "Hierarchies within Hierarchy: Some Observations on Caste System in Rajasthan", *Indian Anthropologist,* Vol. 25, No. 1, p. 23
23. Government of Rajasthan (2011): DISE, *Directorate of Economics and Statistics* 2010-11, Yojna Bhawan, Jaipur.
24. "All India Dalit Mahila Adhikar Manch: AIDMAM", [Online Web] Accessed on 18th March 2014 URL: http://allindiadalitmahilaadhikarmanch.blogspot.in/p/dalit-women-status-in-india.html
25. Varma, Sudhir, "Violence against Dalit women in Rajasthan", [Online Web] Accessed on 16th March 2014 URL: http://ncw.nic.in/pdfReports/Violence_against_Dalit_Women_in_Rajasthan.pdf, p. 13.
26. DECCAN HERALD, "Online Campaign against 'Untouchability' in Rajasthan: 2012, (Online web) Accessed on 14 March 2014 URL: http://www.deccanherald.com/content/263762/online-campaign-against-untouchability-rajasthan.html
27. *Ibid.*
28 *Ibid.*
29. *Ibid.*
30. Mimroth, P.L (2011), Op. Cit. p. 4.
31. "Morris, Alice et al. (2009), *"Making Space: Women's Participation in Local Politics in Rajasthan"*, Ahmadabad; UNNAATI. p. 7.

18

A Study of Education Among Lambada Tribes in Krishna District, Andhra Pradesh

— *Mr. Balraju Rajaram*

Abstract

India is a huge diversified cultural heritage country, which is widely spread with various cultures, traditions, castes based on their profession. Banjara or Lambada, a best known tribe in India migrants from one place to another for merchandise, with their Pack-Bullocks. They made the path to several kingdoms from North to South and they are meant to be the outstanding service providers to the Kings. The Global Education for All Meeting (2014) is revealed that above 57 million children and 69 million adolescents does not access to effective basic education in 2011. GEA meeting made sufficient targets to reach the education for by the year 2030. According to the Census 2011, the overall literacy rate of the Schedule Tribes is recorded as 58.96.

There are a number of problems like lack of traveling facilities, school accessibility, sometimes girls have to take care of her siblings and boys has to work in the agricultural field instead of parents. The Infrastructure of the school is very poor, with no basic facilities. The assumption of the researcher is to study about the Lambada Tribe culture and the economic circumstances. And most crucially to understand the available facilities for Education, close availability of schools to their places for attaining the regular education.. The "National Policy on Education" is also given special priority to tribal education and provides the facilities needed.

Key words: Lambada Tribe, Facilities for Education, Availability of schools.

Introduction

The Indian schedule Tribe having large number of population, which is recognized by the constitution of India order 1950. The order mentioned there are 744 tribes across 22 states in its first schedule, in earlier Andhra Pradesh has 33 types of Schedule Tribes living across 8 districts. These Tribes having their own cultural heritage and innocent lifestyle, they are living in hilly or forest areas for fulfill their needs of the forest. In Telangana most of the Lambada communities are engaged collection of dry sticks, seasonal fruits they'll sell it in town, to buy there necessary things for the home. Now days also they following this method that's why in Telangana people used to call them as "Adavi Thalli Biddalu". So there is another part of about Lambada Tribes people in earlier days, they were used to engage in agriculture activities and other activities. There is restricted to school going children in earlier days, but now Lambada Tribes are empowered. Although immobile is taking place in their Education like lack of traveling facilities from home to school, sometimes girls have to take care of their siblings, boys used to go for agriculture and allied works.

Objectives

- *To find out the Literacy status of respondents in the study area.*
- *To understand available facilities for regular Education in Lambada Thandas*
- *To recommend the effective solution to obtain regular education*

Methods for Data collection

The present study was collected through primary and secondary data sources based on the needs. The data collected through primary sources consist of the respondents mainly parents who are sending their children to school. Participatory scientific observation and Interview schedule are the tools for collecting the primary data. Secondary sources include census reports, articles, newspaper reports, journals and books.

Sample size

The respondents have been selected by random sampling method; total sample size is 60 respondents for this study. Three Mandals namely Gampalagudem, Vissannapeta and Mylavaram each Mandal covers two Thandas and every Thanda covers 10 samples will be collected for this study. The study is only based on the parents' perspective; the ultimate respondents are parents who are living in Thandas and sending their child's school.

Design of the study

At this juncture, for this study descriptive design was undertaken to describe the data. Descriptive design is a scientific method which involves observing and describing the behavior of a team without influencing it anyway.

Collection of Data

The collection of present data was analyzed and discussed with the help of descriptive and simple percentage method.

Analysis and Interpretation

Table 1: Literacy Status of Respondents

S.No	*Particulars*	*No of Respondents*	*Percentage*
1.	Illiterate	08	13
2.	Primary	13	21.6
3.	Secondary	27	45
4.	Intermediate and above	12	20
	Total	**60**	**100**

Source: Primary Data from Field.

The above table shows that Illiterate respondents in the study area is 13 percent, primary education is 21 percent, secondary education respondents are high that is 45 per cent and Intermediate and above respondents 12 per cent in the study area.

So, here Illiteracy is low level in the study area that is only 13 per cent and a majority of the respondents, 45 per cent of them were studied secondary education in the study area.

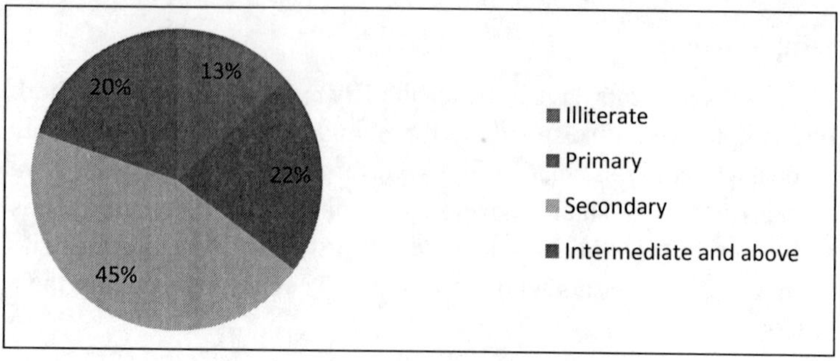

Fig. 1: Literacy Status of Respondents

Table 2: Status of Primary school availability

S.No	Particulars	No of Respondents	Percentage
1.	Yes	54	90
2.	No	06	10
	Total	60	100

Source: Primary Data from Field.

The table 2 shows that the majority of the 54 per cent of the respondents expressed that their Thandas having the facility of Primary school and merely 06 per cent of them are told that not having the primary school facility.

Table 3: Teacher of Primary school presence

S.No	Particulars	No of Respondents	Percentage
1.	Timely presence	33	55
2.	Late presence	27	45
	Total	60	100

Source: Primary Data from Field.

The above table reveals that majority of the 55 per cent respondents expresses that the Teachers of the primary school not coming on time and 45 per cent of the remaining respondents said that teacher are coming late to the schools.

So, here most of the school teachers not coming to the school on time.

Table 4: Facilities available at primary school

S.No	*Particulars*		*No of Respondents*	*Percentage*
1.	**Play Ground**	**Yes**	38	**64**
		No	22	**37**
		Total	60	100
2	**Toilet**	**Yes**	34	**57**
		No	26	**43**
		Total	**60**	**100**

Source: Primary Data from Field.

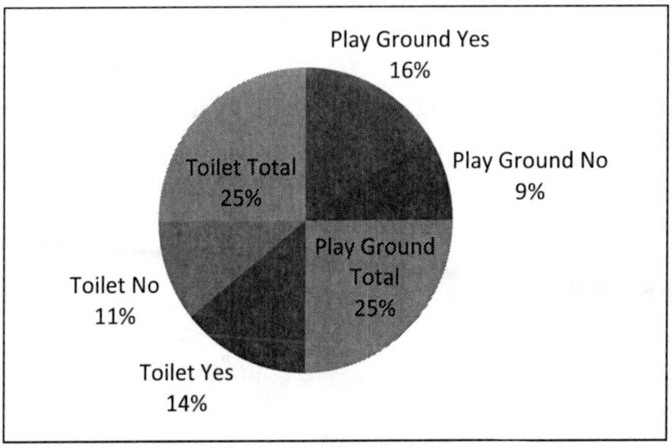

Fig. 2: Status of available facilities at Primary School.

Here, in the above table 63 per cent of the respondents reveal that there is no playground for primary school children and 56.6 per cent of the children are not having the facility of the toilet.

Table 5: Attention of the students at primary school by Teacher

S.No	*Particulars*	*No of Respondents*	*Percentage*
1.	Good attention	20	**33**
2.	Average attention	13	**21.6**
3.	Partial attention	27	**45**
	Total	**60**	**100**

Source: Primary Data from Field.

Table 5 explains that teacher attention towards the students' active participation in the class is 45 per cent of respondents accept that partial attention of the teacher, 33 per cent said good attention and 21 per cent revealed average attention.

Therefore, here the majority of the 45 per cent of the respondents getting partial attention in primary school and 33 per cent of them are getting good attention.

Table 6: Availability of High school facility within five km from Thanda

S.No	*Particulars*	*No of Respondents*	*Percentage*
1	**Yes**	24	**40**
2	**No**	36	**60**
	Total	**60**	**100**

Source: Primary Data from Field.

The above table reveals that high proportionate of 60 per cent of the respondents accepted, they don't have the High school facility within 5 km and 40 per cent of them accepted having High school within 40 percent.

Table 7: Traveling facilities available from Thanda to School

S.No	*Particulars*	*No of Respondents*	*Percentage*
1.	Regular Bus Facilities	05	08
2.	No proper bus facilities	31	51.6
3.	Depends on Private vehicle	24	40
	Total	**60**	**100**

Source: Primary Data from Field.

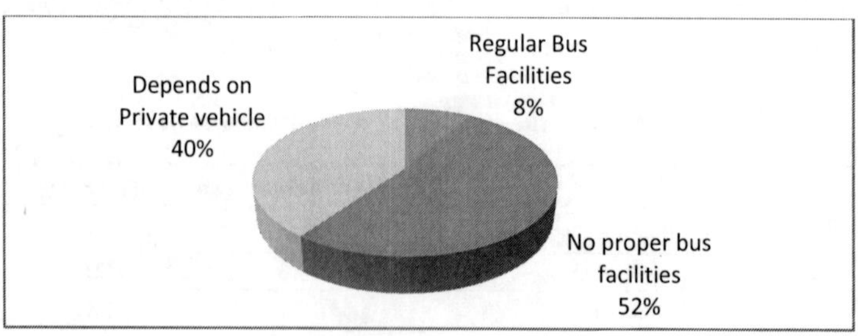

Fig. 3: Traveling facilities from Thanda to school.

The above table shown that the greater part of the respondents, 51.6 per cent of them accept they do not have proper bus facilities, 40 per cent of them said that they are depending on private vehicles to send their children to school and only 8 per cent of them said there is no regular bus services.

Table 8: Remedies to Increase the Facilities for Education at Thandas

S.No.	*Particulars*	*No of Respondents*	*Percentage*
1.	Recover travel facility	12	20
2.	Provide good Infrastructure facility in schools	22	36.6
3.	Form monitoring committee for Lambada Education	04	6.6
4.	Improve the quality of Teachers	16	26.6
5.	Establish High School within 5 km from Thanda	06	10
	Total	**60**	**100**

Source: Primary Data from Field.

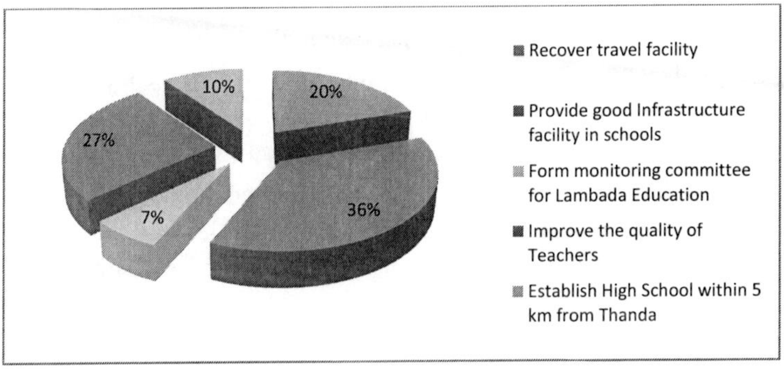

Fig. 4: Ideas to improve the facilities for Lambada Tribe Education.

In the above table 36.6 per cent of the highest respondents suggesting that to provide the proper infrastructure facilities for the schools, 26.6 per cent of the respondents suggested to improve the quality of the teachers and 20 per cent of them like to recover the travel facilities properly.

Findings

- The majority of the 45 per cent of the respondents was studied secondary level in the study area and there is low per cent that is 13 are the Illiterate in the study area.
- Ninety per cent of the respondents accepted the status of the availability of primary school at their Thandas.
- Fifty five per cent of the respondents accepted primary school teacher coming in right time and 45 per cent of them not accepted.
- The greater part of the 45 per cent of the respondents getting partial attention in primary school and 33 per cent of them are getting good attention.
- Sixty three per cent of the respondents reveal that there is no playground for primary school children and 56.6 per cent of the children are not having the facility of the toilet.
- Forty five per cent of the respondents getting partial attention in primary school and 33 per cent of them are getting good attention.
- High proportionate of 60 per cent of the respondents accepted, they don't have the High school facility within 5 km.
- The greater part of the respondents, 51.6 per cent of them accept they do not have proper bus facilities.
- Thirty six per cent of the highest respondents suggesting that to provide the proper infrastructure facilities for the schools, 26.6 per cent of the respondents suggested to improve the quality of the teachers.

Recommendations

- Increase the traveling facilities to through Lambada Thandas
- Install proper infrastructure availabilities at every primary school of Lambada Thandas.
- Enhance regular monitoring committee to execute primary schools.
- Establish High school within 5 km distance from every Thanda.

- Build playground and toilet facilities for every primary school.
- Arrange the moral sessions like personality development and yoga for primary school teachers to give good education to children.
- Thanda head should be the chairman of the primary school to scrutinize the welfare of the school.
- Tracking progress in access to primary and upper primary schools in Lambada affected areas.
- Identify and promote best practices in the area of Tribal education.

Discussions

India is the largest country in population and also in problems there many social problems which make us underdevelopment, India has large Tribal communities and many of the communities still in this 21 century, they don't know what is education and how the education will be, but in this context Lambada Tribe is in developing stage in terms of education. Although, still this Tribe facing lot of exploitation from the society and they could not able to get the proper infrastructure facility to earn a proper education in Thandas. Almost all Thandas having Primary school facility, but the huge per cent of them not have the facility of the toilets and playground, primary school children must have the entertainment with playground and needed infrastructure for playing activities. Every school is getting sufficient funds for school development, but we don't know where this fund is going and what is going on. Telangana Government appointed Cluster Resource Person (CRP), Mondal Resource Person (MRP) for every Mandal, but what is the implementation progress and their working status towards school development.

Conclusion

Education is the greater part of the every development in the rural grassroots level. The indigenous population is very essential to take attention and improve their educational facilities and availability of education, proper infrastructure facilities must be provided by the government. Please join the hands to improve their educational, institutional facilities and proper traveling facilities. Tribal people are Naturally, having the knowledge of intelligence for that if the education is added to them it will be more fruitful.

References

1. Kabita Kumari Sahu (2014) *" Challenging Issues of Tribal Education in India"* OSR Journal of Economics and Finance (IOSR-JEF) e-ISSN: 2321-5933, p-ISSN: 2321-5925.Volume 3, Issue 2. Ver. II (Mar-Apr. 2014), pp. 48-52.
2. P. Subramanya chary (2013) *"Status of Schedule Tribes in Andhra Pradesh"* The Down Journal, Vol. 2, No. 1, January-June 2013.
3. Motkuri Venkatanarayana (2013) *"Scheduled Castes (SCs) and Tribes (STs) in Andhra Pradesh: A Situation Assessment Analysis.*
4. Banoth Lal (2013) *"Community organizations of Telangana Lambadas: Transition from Gwar Panchayat to Modern Political Institutions"* International Journal of Political Science, Law and International Relations, ISSN 2278–8832, Vol. 3, Issue 4, Oct 2013, 23-28.
5. *Statistical Profile of Schedule Tribes in India 2013.*
6. *Statistical Profile Of Scheduled Tribes In India* (2010) by Ministry of Tribal Affairs, India.
7. M. Gopinath Reddy & K. Anil Kumar (2010) *"Political Economy of Tribal Development: A Case Study of Andhra Pradesh"* pp. 1-5.
8. Planning Commission (2007) *"Research study on livelihood options, assets creation out of Special Component Plan (scp) &Ttribal Sub Plan (TSP) schemes and its impact among SCs and STs in India* pp1-10.
9. A.V. Yadappanavar, (2003) *Tribal Education in India*, ISBN 81-7141-672-1.
10. Sujatha, K. (2002) "*Education among Scheduled Tribes. In Govinda, R. (ed.), India Education Report: A Profile of Basic Education"*. New Delhi: Oxford University Press.
11. Jha, J., Jhingran, D. (2002), *Elementary Education for the Poorest and Other Deprived Groups, Centre for Policy Research*. New Delhi.
12. Sujatha, K. (1999) *Education of Indian Scheduled: A study of community schools in the district of Vishakapatnam, Andhra Pradesh*, UNESCO: International Institute for Educational Planning in 1999.
13. *Education of India schedule Tribes: A study of community schools in the district of Visakhapatnam, Andhra Pradesh*, Unsco Report, 1999.

19

Socio-economic Conditions of Women Tea Plantation Workers in the Nilgiris District in Tamil Nadu - A Sociological Study

— *Dr. S. Vedapurieswaran*

Abstract

Women today are being gradually recognized as important powerful and meaningful contributors to the life of men, but till a few decades back, their condition was pitiable. Women are active partners in the development of the country and work for it. In fact, women constitute the vital part of the workforce in any business establishment and even in industries. Now, they are joining those professions as well, which were earlier considered to be the domain of males only. The ideologies and institutional practices and norms existing in society contributed much to their humiliation harassment and exploitation. These behaviour patterns thrive even today.

This Attempt is being made to probe into the problem of women workers, the extent to which their dual roles act and react on each other, the difficulties faced by women workers with family responsibility, the steps that could be taken to ensure to women their due share in the gains of industry with determinant to their safety, health, welfare and similar issues consequently. This has led to a continual transformation in sympathy with the changes in the social and economic sphere of the nature and type of employment they would like to undertake.

The present study deals with the socio-economic conditions of the Tea plantation workers household, the migration factors and living condition of the women workers. The major focus of the present study is employment pattern of women tea plantation workers in the village of Kakchi comes under Huilcal town panchayat at Coonoor block of the Nilgiris district in Tamil Nadu.

Introduction

> *"You can tell the condition of a nation by looking at the status of its women".*
> — Jawaharlal Nehru.

Every known economic system, from time immemorial has heeded and utilized the work of women. From the primitive times, when men hunted animals, down to the present day, when thousands are employed in factories, women are found to stand shoulder to shoulder in all the occupations.

Women today are being gradually recognized as important powerful and meaningful contributors to the life of men, but till a few decades back, their condition was pitiable. Women are active partners in the development of the country and work for it. In fact, women constitute the vital part of the workforce in any business establishment and even in industries. Now, they are joining those professions as well, which were earlier considered to be the domain of males only. The ideologies and institutional practices and norms existing in society contributed much to their humiliation harassment and exploitation. These behaviour patterns thrive even today.

In the early days of the present century, only women folk belonging to the lower sections of the community, sought employment in the plantations, factories and mines. In a sense, they were pushed into the factory, through sheer economic necessity and not pulled by any lure of factory / employment.

More and more women began to enter the field of gainful employment. In the initial stages, the factory owners, taking advantage of the poorer classes, recruited women and children on a large scale at low wages and made them to work under inhuman conditions Gradually, however the pressure of public opinion impelled the state to enact legislation to safeguard women workers against some of the major ills such as night work, excessive hours of work, employment during maternity and immediately after confinement and termination of employment on the first signs of pregnancy.

This Attempt is being made to probe into the problem of women workers, the extent to which their dual roles act and react on each other, the difficulties faced by women workers with family responsibility, the steps that could be taken to ensure to women their due share in the gains of industry with determinant to their safety, health, welfare and similar issues consequently. This has led to a continual transformation in sympathy with the changes in the social and economic sphere of the nature and type of employment they would like to undertake.

The Problem

The present study deals with the socio-economic conditions of the Tea plantation workers household, the migration factors and living condition of the women workers. The major focus of the present study is employment pattern of women tea plantation workers in the village of Kakchi comes under Huilcal town panchayat at Coonoor block of the Nilgiris district in Tamil Nadu.

Women Workers in Plantation

Women have worked in the tea industry from its very inception. Tea garden labour is recruited from the tribal population of Bihar, Madhya Pradesh, Orissa and West Bengal. There was heavy emigration of labour to the tea gardens in the middle of the 19th century. In the tea gardens "the workers hoped to build a new life for themselves and the fact that they did so is borne out by the comparison which can be found today between the comparatively well off plantation workers. In duecourse women found a niche in the tea estates on account of her more skillful fingers in relation to plucking and the attractive garden pluckers' became famous throughout the tea drinking countries of the world. It is in fact difficult to think of an industry in which woman has played so important a part. The plucking of tea is not, however, a female prerogative, and men have always undertaken this work as well as women, particularly in the busy season. There has never been any differentiation between the plucking rates of males and females and thus we see an early implementation of the principle of "equal pay for equal work". The presence of women on the plantation and the co-ordinated family life, there has been little labour trouble" (L.S.Yadav, 1998) Prior to her emigration she had been used to taking important responsibilities in her village. She transplanted the grain, she harvested the grain, she pounded the grain into rice and lastly she cooked the rice for her man and her family.

The data compiled by labour Bureau, Government of India from annual returns under the Plantation Labour Act, 1951 show that nearly 10.9 lakh persons were employed in the plantation sector, comprising 10.2 lakhs in Tea, 30680 in coffee, 27032 in rubber, 3463 in cardamom, 2696 in cinchona and the remaining in other plantations. At all India level, 50 per cent workers in tea and coffee plantations, 34 per cent workers in rubber,62 per cent workers in caradamom,38% workers in palm oil and 45 per cent in cinchona were women. (Indian Labour year Book, 2002). In the plantation sector, nearly 80 per cent are small holders, having less than 20 acers each. Workers in smaller estates are by and large unorganized and their levels of employment are relatively lower than their counterparts in large plantation estates. It has been known through personal interviews of coffee and rubber planters in kerala and Karnataka that workers in small plantation estates receive Rs.10 to Rs.20 less per day (1987) as compared to those working in large estates. Also they do not adequately get the benefit of minimum wages, bonus and other facilities such as housing medical care, maternity benefit etc.

The tea plantation sector is the largest provider of industrial employment in the Niligiris district. More than 25 per cent of the working population is engaged in the plantation sector. The fall in coffee and tea prices is stated to be the basic cause of the plantation workers crisis, which has ostensibly forced plantation owners to increase the workload, reduce wages, mechanize plucking or even abandon plantation operations.

In the early phase of liberalization there is decline in the growth rate both type of workers i.e. contracts and casual labour. In the later phase, though there is some growth it is more towards the casualisation of work force.

Contracts and casual labour recruiting mechanisms in the tea plantation sector was quite different during the early period of the industry. The casual workers get job for 5-6 months in a year whenever there is need of extra manpower in the plantations message is sent to them. This is the most common route to the entry to the job market by the casual workers.

As compared to the estate workers many basic amenities are not available to the casual workers who work under the small growers. Most of them are not getting accommodation. They are not provided with sanitary and health facilities by the garden owners. The concern for health is reflected among the workers as about two third of the workers have vaccinated their children against diseases.

The monsoon failure had affected the living condition of both small growers and their workers forced them to switch over to some other cropping pattern, Incase of their workers who are unable to find any other avenue for their livelihoods, since they are trained (or) specialized other than plantation. In such conditions or situations their future is questioned.

Based on the above study focuses attention on the socio economic conditions of women plantation workers in the Nilgiris District of Tamil Nadu. (This study was carried on March to June-2004)

Objectives of the Study

- To study the socio-economic background of women workers in the study area.
- To assess the employment and income generation through tea plantation works in the study area.
- To highlight the problem faced by the women workers in tea plantation in the study area.
- To study welfare amenities for workers in plantation.

Area of the Study

The study village of kakchi is located in Hulical town panchayat at Coonoor taluk in The Nilgiris district of Tamil Nadu.

Udagamandalam, is the district headquarter, and Coonoor is the nearest town (15 KM) of the study village in the South East. For higher studies and medical treatment, the Kakchi village people depend upon Udagamandalam and Coimbatore.

The study village is connected with coonoor and woodland road in the South by motorable road. Kakchi the study village has 868 households with population of 5193, Hulical town panchyath has total population of 17048.

The study village is inhabited by the caste groups such as Gounder and Adi-Dravida. The major occupation in the study area is plucking tea leaves. The facilities such as education (primary school), panchayat building, balwadi, health sub center, water taps, transport and communication etc, are available in the study village.

Sample Size of the Respondents

The Kakchi village comes under the Hulical town panchayat was selected as the study area in view of availability of more number of tea plantation women workers.

Many of the villagers are employed in nearby tea plantations, which include 500 casual women workers, by using simple random sampling method one fifth of the casual women workers one hundred in number were selected for the purpose of this study.

Accordingly 100 casual women workers were selected from the Kakchi village the study area.

Analysis and Interpretation of Data

Table 1: Educational Status of the Respondents' family members

S. No	*Category*	*No of Respondents*		*Percentage*
1.	Illiterate	29(16.86)	27(32.54)	56(21.96)
2.	Primary	35 (20.35)	16(19.27)	51(20.00)
3.	Middle	43 (25.00)	19(22.89)	62 (24.32)
4.	High School and above	65(37.79)	21(25.30)	86(33.72)
	Total	**172 (100)**	**83(100)**	**255 (100)**

Source: field data.

Table 1. reveals that educational status of respondents family. Out of total respondents (multiple) 86 (33.72 %) of them had High school and above level education 62 (24.32 %) belonging to the category of middle school level, 51 (20.00%) belonged to the category of primary level of education and remaining 56 (21.96 %) belonged to illiterate people

It was understood from the table that majority of the respondents family (33.72%) belonged to High school and above level of study.

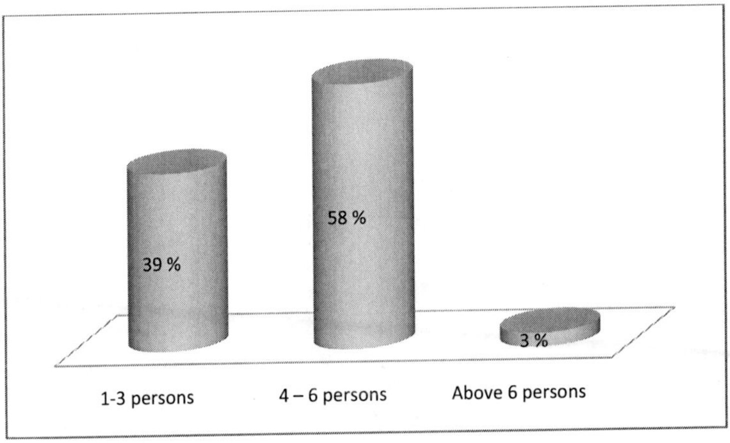

Source: field data.

Figure 1. Distribution of the Respondents According to their Family Size.

The figure 1. percents distribution of the respondents according to their family size. More number of persons in a family leads to more family size. The present study reveals that majority (58 percent) of the respondents had 3-6 members in the family, and 39 per cent of the respondents had 1-3 members. Whereas remaining 3 per cent of the respondents had above 6 members in the family. Thus, a majority of female respondents families are medium size (4-6 persons).

Table 2. Distribution of Respondents According to their no. of Family Members Working in Plantation.

S.no	*Category (Persons)*	*No.of respondents*	*Percentage*
1.	1	15	15
2.	2	85	85
	Total	**100**	**100**

Source: field data.

From table 2. Shows that number of family members working in plantation. 85 per cent of the respondent families two members each were working in plantation. Remaining 15 per cent of the respondent families have one member working in plantation.

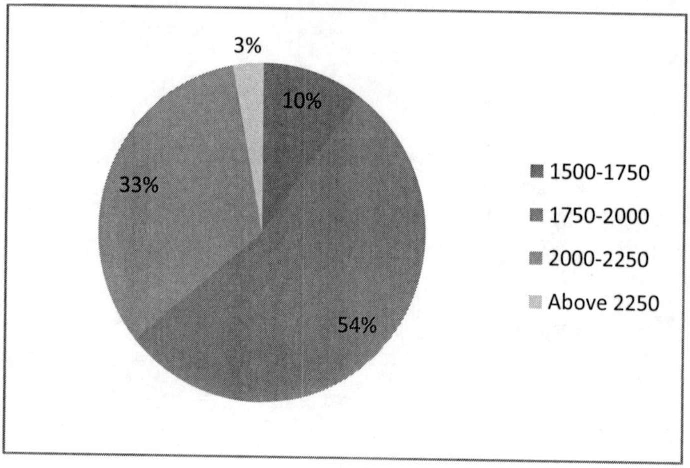

Source: field data.

Figure 2. Monthly income of the Respondents.

The above figure presents the monthly income of the respondents. From this table it is clear that 10 per cent respondents were getting monthly income of Rs. 1500-1750 followed by Rs. 1750-2000 per month, 54 per cent remaining 36 per cent earning Rs. 2000-2250 and above 2250.

Majority of the plantation women workers were earning income of Rs. 1750-2000 in a month.

Employment and Income

Most of the women worked on temporary basis (more than five years) in the tea garden and from the age of 14 or 15 years and learned the art of tea plucking. These labourers are divided into two, as daily wagers in estate and who work under small grower. Here there is no overtime work. Besides, these work, they don't know any other work. They should pluck about nearly 25 Kg of tea leaves per day. The wage is fixed on the basis of the number of kg tea leaves plucked by the workers. They are given Rs.4 per Kg as wage. As per the estate rules they should work 8 hours duty apart from one hour lunch interval. The trained workers alone selected for the work by the estate and they were provided tea at least two times a day. The casual workers got the same wage, wherever they were i.e., with estate or with small growers. The Estate labourers avail the transport arranged by employer. The average distance of working places was 15 Km for estate labourers, but small growers labourers go to the work place by walk. Small growers labourers suffered by unemployment, minimum 15 day, during off seasons. The estate workers were given compulsory leave by the estate management. Though the estate workers are named as daily wage earner, the distribution of wage took place once in a week through supervisor. The plantation women workers report their work spot by 8 am after completing household activities. In the evening, the workers watch T.V., hearing the radio as their rest time activity. There was no exploitation in economic front.

Problem faced by women workers

The plantation workers play a dual role. Early morning as a household role and breadwinning supporting role. They could not pay much attention on their children and aged at home on account of reporting to the work spot at 8.00 a.m. During evening, they fetched water from far away places and stored it for next day household purposes. The study area, There was not sufficient transport and cabs facilities for the plantation workers during emergency. At the time of illness they have to walk down around 3 Km for consulting the doctor. On the part of education, only minimum numbers of students were enrolled in the nearest primary school and the parents were hesitating to send their children to school. The ration shop under public distribution system is 2 Km away from the workers residential area. The working time of ration shop and the plantation workers was same. So that they did not get their ration materials on time from ration shop. There is an allotment of working segment to each worker. There was a verbal attack from supervisors when the workers skip certain segments. If they skip, then there is a loss to the estate.

Occupational demerits

A common form of injury caused to workers is during weeding of the plants. The reason for skin diseases to be common among the estate workers is attributed to lack of awareness in the use of pesticide and medicines. Lack of proper sanitation facilities and the ignorance of the need to maintain high standards of personal hygiene are contributing factors for the health of the women workers. They are often done in the same clothes during their working hours and thereafter at home until the end of the day and this causes serious skin exposure many of these workers do not obtain medical treatment of these skin irritations, which may spread rapidly among other members of the community there by causing epidemic situations. Unless proper care and prevention is taken, this may result in a serious occupational problem among the plantation workers in the future.

Welfare measure of the women workers

Majority of the people living in Kakchi village are employed as casual labourers in tea plantation. Some of them are employed as temporary daily wage labourers in tea estates and few works as casual labourers with plantations of small tea growers. Estate labourers get welfare measures as per Plantation Labour Act like, crèche, Balwadi, Toilet, Canteen, Rest Room and Bonus. Those who work at small growers avail bonus alone not other benefits. But both workers get their wages promptly. The workers are neither organized as trade union members to fight for their rights nor does the government take up their concerns seriously. Amidst their vexed struggle with their employers to become permanent employees of the plantations, the labourers seldom find time/energy to think of an association to fight for their cause. Moreover this employment being the only source of survival the labourers are least interested to sacrifice their jobs for the sake of association.

Based upon the study the findings are as follows:

1. Majority (62 %) of the respondents belong to the productive age group of 21 – 40 years.
2. More than half of the respondents (52 %) are illiterate.
3. 75 % of the respondents are married.
4. Majority (62 %) of the respondents belong to nuclear family.
5. More than half of the respondents (54 %) monthly income is in between Rs.1750-2000.
6. Majority (58 %) of the respondents families are medium size (4- 6 persons).
7. 85 % of the respondents' families have two to three earning members in the family.
8. (33.72%) of the respondents family members had their education up to High school and above.
9. Most members of the workers family (52 .94%) were adults.
10. 67 % of the respondents have own house.
11. 68 % of the respondents were living in the tiled house.
12. Total asset value of respondents (47 %) is in between Rs.40,001- 60,000.
13. Majority of the respondents (67 %) don't have saving habits.
14. 37 % of respondents have debts.
15. 31 % of respondents replied that money lenders are the main source of their credit.
16. 43 % of respondents spent most of their income on the medical treatment
17. More than half of the respondents (52%) reached their work spot by walk.
18. It is found that, illiteracy (24 %), poverty (12 %) and family need (28%) were the main causes to prefer this occupation.
19. Majority (62 %) of the responders said that 6 – 10 days are non working, unemployment days in a month.

20. It is stated that, seasonal work (27 %), failure of monsoon (51%) and Compulsory leave (22 %) were main reasons for unemployment.

Suggestions

Development is a group effort. To improve the condition of women Tea plantation workers Government, NGOs, Panchayat and the plantation owners should join together the ameliorate the socio-economic condition of women Tea plantation workers.

This is not an overnight work. The following steps may be taken on a peace meal manner.

Government

- To enhance the condition of women workers in Tea plantation the awareness should be created through education. The non formal education may be offered effectively.
- The Government and the private companies should come forward to promote their projects in this area. It will provide employment during off-seasons.
    - The Plantation labour Act Should be enforced by Government departments to provide labour welfare facilities to all.
    - The Government should direct the institutionalized credit agencies to provide special attention and distribute loans to them for milk animals and sheep, etc.,
    - The Government comes forward to open for employment in this area.
- The general awareness about opportunity to improve their economy and health conditions with the help of Radio, TV, Newspapers, Mass media and local school teachers.

Non-Government organisation

- Training programme should be organized for small scale and cottage industries.
- To enhance economic position of the plantation women workers through the concept of self help group should be introduced and strengthened.

- The non-Governmental organizations may adopt this village for their various projects. It may ventilate their handicaps.
- National and International philanthropist organizations like Lions club, Rotary club etc., should come forward to take these areas as command area for their projects.

Panchayat Boards

- Panchayati Raj Institutions ensure the minimum basic needs like Sanitation and Drainage facilities
- Foot path
- Street light
- Library
- Canal

Tea plantation owners

- Should provide of ambulance and other medical facility for workers emergency needs.
- They can offer permanent employment to any one member of every family.
- Provide loan for their emergency need.

Conclusion

'A cup of tea' has its own style of refreshment. It is a sign of respect and hospitality shown to guests, a relaxation to a tired mind. But the people behind this refreshing tea are ailing, their life is not as refreshing as the tea, the flavour is bitter for them and the future is darker than the essence of tea leaves. The women tea plantation workers are still under privileged, alienated and isolated. Inspite of working hard and sincere their voice for a permanent employment remains unheard. Their dreams for facilities like education, housing, transport, and medical care are yet to see the dawn of the day. These unorganized classes of tea plantation women workers are in dire need of a helping hand from the Government to save them from their sorry state of affairs. A paradigm shift in the policy of government towards these unorganized women workers of tea plantation is essential. Not only in framing policies the government must also ensure proper implementation of the same in letter and spirit to help the women tea plantation workers see the light of the day. The government should necessarily intervene and provide the necessary 'healing touch' to the hundreds of ailing hearts of women tea plantation workers.

References

Afanu Thakur, "A Post Modernist enquiry into women's work force participation", The Indian Journal of labour Economics, Vol. 42(4) July-Sep. 1999, p. 56-60.

Agarwal, C.M, "*Indian women*", Vol. III, New Delhi, India publication, 2001, p. 12-13.

Anita Arya, *"India Women Work and Development*", Vol. III, New Delhi, Gyan publishing house, 2000, p. 58-59.

Asha Adhikaram and Vasantha, "Women labourers in selected plantation", Social welfare, Vol.50 (12), March 2004, p. 24.

Banerjee, N. *"Women Workers in the unorganized sector: The Calcutta Experience",* Sanjam Books, Hyderabad, 1985, p. 55.

Banerjee. N. "Women Workers in the unorganized sector: The Calcutta Experience", Sanjam Books. Hyderabad, 1985, p. 55.

Barooah. N.C. "Hands Behind Tea: Plantation Labour in North East Tea News", July – Sep. 1999, p. 34.

Bedi M.J. "*Protection of women in moral Dangers*", New Delhi, Himanshu Publisher, 1992, p. 272.

Chaudhari, C.D. and Ganorkar, P.L, "Involving fram women in agricultural activities", Kurushetra, Vol. 11(4), Jan.1992, p. 25.

Gulat, "Women's development in India with special reference to rural women", 1995, p. 17-19.

Kalyan Das, *"Labour Contracts and work agreements in Tea plantations of Assam"*, V.V. Giri National Labour Institute, Noida 2002, p. 1-2.

Manimekalai. N. "A comparative study on working women & House wives", Social Welfare, Vol. 49, August, 2002, p. 24-25.

Mita Bhadra "Plantation women workers and their commitment to industrial workman in India", Vol. 66 (3), Sep. 1986, page. 233-234.

Padmini Sengupta, *"Women workers of India,"* Bombay, Asia publishing House, 1960, p. 34-35.

Prafulla Kumar Das and Niranjanes Pardhan, "Fisher women of Chandrabhaga", Social welfare, Vol. 50 (12), March 2004, p. 26-29.

Rachel Kurian, *"Women workers in the Sri Lanka plantation sector"* Geneva, International Labour Office, 1982, p. 34.

Rajeswari, "Socio-economic conditions of workers in Ambanadu Tea Estate at Kerala", Southern Economist, Feb. 2002, p. 19-21.

Ram Ahuja, "*Crime Against Women*", Jaipur, Rewart publications, 1987, p. 1.

Ram Nath Sharama, "*Labour Problems Social Security and Welfare*", Meerut (u.p), Rejhans publication, 1987, p. 58.

Remachandran,V.K. "Wage labour and un freedom in Agriculture: The Indian Case study", Clare don press, Oxford, 1990.

Renuka, C. "Plight of women workers: A Case study" Southern Economist, Dec.2002, p. 6-8.

Saraswati Mishra, "*Status of Indian Women*", New Delhi, Gyan publishing house, 2000, p. 39-40.

Satya Sundaram. I, "Violence Against women", Social Welfare, Vol.49 (4) July, 2002, p. 13-14.

Sharda Rath, Navaneeta Rath, "*Women in India A search for Identity.*" New Delhi, Anmol Publisher P.Vt, 1999, p. 133.

Shobhan, V. Vimala Devi and Jothi, "Socio-economic status of women in sericulture", Kurushetra, Vol. 46 (9) June 1998, p. 46-48.

Sudharani, K Uma Devi, D and Srilath Kishori, "Awarness of women about their Rights", Social Welfare, May 2003, p. 20-23.

Talwar Sabanna, Doddanogouda Patil, Bhagwantappa Bulla, "Women workers and globalization", social welfare, Vol. 49 (3) June 2002, p. 30-34.

Tripathy. S.V, and C.R. Dasy, "*Migrant labour in India*", New Delhi, Discovery publication, 1997, p. 19-20.

Udayan Misra, "Assam Tea: The Bitter Brew", Economic and political weekly. July 2003, p. 3029-3031.

Ursula Sharma, "Women Work and Property North-West India", Tavistock publications, New York, 1983.

Vats. S, Shakunthala Mudgal, "*Development of women in modern India*", Vol III, Faridabad, Om publication, 1998, p. 16.

Yadav, L.S. "*Mechanisation of tea plantation practices of women worker,*" Social Welfare, Vol 44(11), Feb-1998, p. 39-40.

Reports:

District Census Hand Book, Census of India, 2001.

Provisional Population Totals, Census of India, 2001.

Tamil Nadu and Economic Appraisal, The Government of Tamil Nadu, 2002.

Tamil Nadu Human Development Report, The Government of Tamil Nadu, 2003.

UAPSI, KVK Annual Report, Coonoor, 2002.

Women And Men in India, The Government of India, 2001.

20

Contribution of Tea Gardens in Uplifting Socio-Economic Status of Women Workers in Tea Industry of Dibrugarh District, Assam

— *Himadri Dutta, B.S. Mipun*

Abstract

Tea plantation plays important in the socio-economic development of Assam by creating a huge labour market and work participation for women. Women are working as wage labour from early 19th century till date. The present research has analysed the contribution of tea gardens in uplifting the socio-economic status of women workers in tea industry of Dibrugarh district which has the highest number of tea garden in Assam.Five tea estates were selected for the survey to show the spatial variation of socio-economic status of the women. A sample size of 30 per cent households from each of five tea estate is taken by using simple random sampling. The Study decomposed the socio-economic status of women into three dimension viz.,demography, socio-culture and economy, each of which comprises few parameters.It is found from the study that median age of the women workers is 35 years and socio-economic status of those women workers is varying significantly over places depending on the infrastructure, health and leisure services given by the tea industry. Comparatively, women in Basmatia tea estate are way better than the rest of the surveyed tea estate.

Keywords: *Tea garden, Women work participation,Socio-economic status.*

Introduction

The concept of status is one of the key factors in any reading of social behaviour and in the workings of a society. It is regarded as a multidimensional concept consisting of societal, legal and attitudinal attributes. Research indicates that Socio- economic status (hereafter SES) is a key factor in determining the quality of life, with resulting effects on the lives of children and families. Inequities in wealth and quality of life for women are long standing and exist both locally and globally.

Growth of tea industry mainly concentrated in both the Brahmaputra and Barak Valley in Assam. Tinsukia, Dibrugarh, Sivasagar, Jorhat, Golaghat, Nagaon, Sonitpur are the districts where tea gardens are mostly found. Dibrugarh has the world's largest area covered by tea gardens. The entire district is surrounded by tea plantation area and factories. Dibrugarh district has the highest numbers of tea gardens- 144 in all and some of them are more than 100 years old. It also has the largest production and average yield rate of tea in Assam (Majumder, 2012).Women workers are the most potential labour force in the Tea industry of Assam. They are the victim of circumstances and they are struggling for their existences.Women workers have all along been an integral part of the labour force engaged in the Plantation Industry in India. A majority of the plantations labourers are women workers. Owing to the very fact that soft hands and nimble fingers are suited especially for tea leave plucking and picking of coffee seeds, women workers dominate the employment scene in these Plantations.

Objective

(i) To evaluate the contribution of tea gardens in uplifting socio-economic status of women workers in the district.

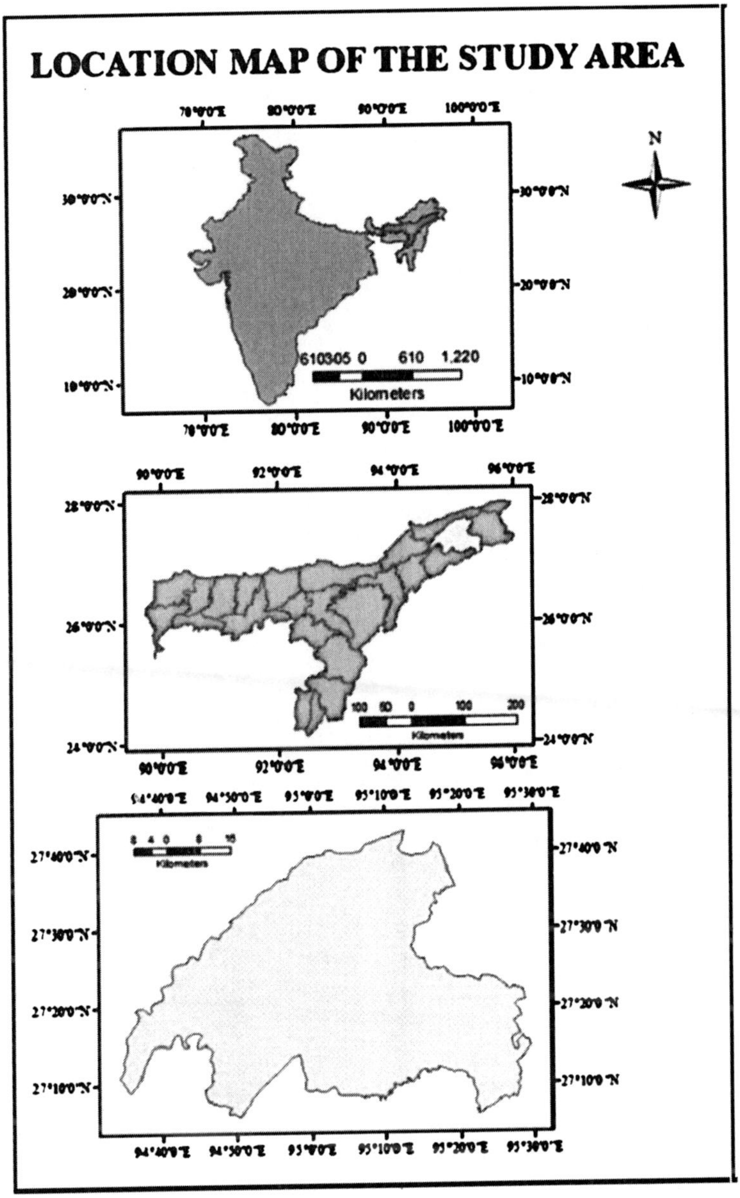
LOCATION MAP OF THE STUDY AREA
N
610305 0 610 1,220
Kilometers
27°40'0"N
27°30'0"N
27°20'0"N
27°10'0"N

(A)

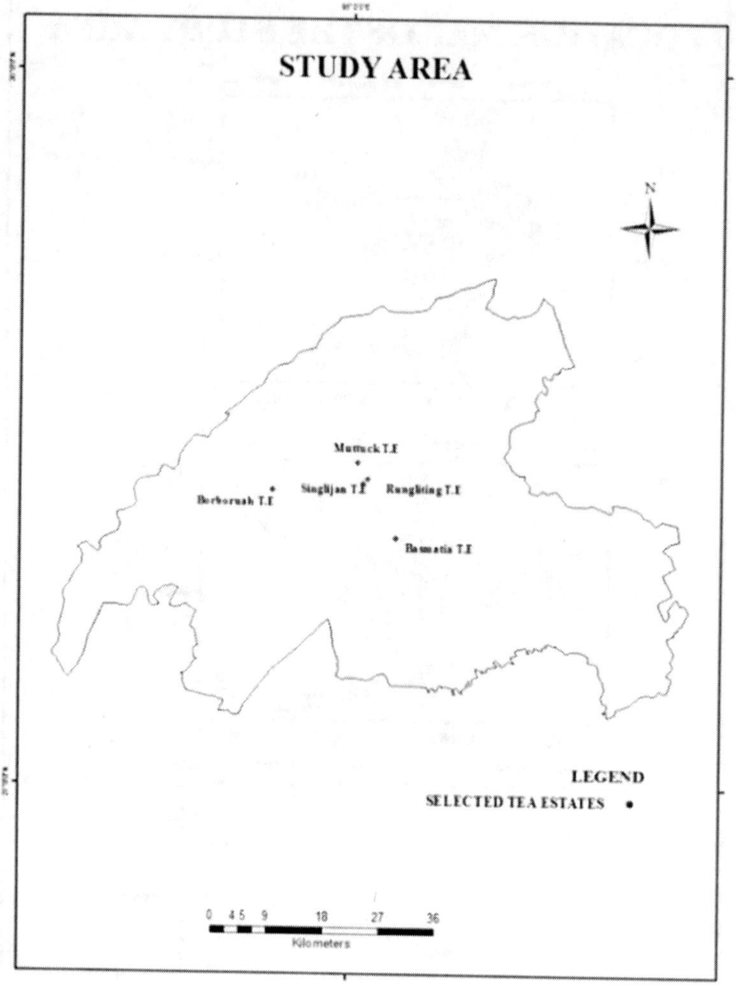

(A)

Fig.1: Location map of the study area (A) and (B).

Database and Methodology

The study is basically a comparative research to examine spatial variation in socio-economic status of women and to analyse the potential contribution of tea estates to sustainable livelihood of women workers.

The work is based in data collected through primary survey regarding socio-economic status. The Universe of the study is five Tea estates viz. Barbaruah Tea Estate, Muttuck Tea Estate, Singlijan Tea Estate, Rungliting Tea Estate and Basmatia Tea Estate of Dibrugarh district of Assam.The socio-economic status of women categorised into three dimension viz.,Demography: age, type of family, size of family, caste, marital status; socio-culture: religion, participation in festivals and rituals, literacy rate and level of education, access to safe drinking water, access to sanitation, access to safe fuel for cooking, percentage of household having good quality house, number of services provided by tea estates; and economy: number and type of secondary occupation (other than wage labour in tea estate), monthly income, savings,value of household assets. Each of the variables under these three dimensions contributed equally to build aggregate socio-economic status of women. Variables chosen for this study has different measurement unit. Therefore, these indicators has been transformed and standardised by assigning weightage through Eq.1. This is done by subtracting the minimum value from each indicator and then dividing it by the indicator-range i.e. maximum value subtracted by minimum value for each indicator.

$$index_{s_w i} = \frac{S_a - S_{min}}{S_{max} - S_{min}} \quad \text{.......................... (Eq. 1)}$$

Where S_a is the actual value of the variable of the area *a*, S_{min} and S_{max} are the minimum and maximum values, respectively, for each variable determined using dataset.

After each was standardized, dimensions were averaged using Equation (2) to calculate the value of each major component.

$$M_{w_a} = \frac{\sum_{i=1}^{n} index_{s_w i}}{n} \quad \text{................. Eq. (2)}$$

Where, M_{wa} is the average weighted of one of the three dimension for area ‘a’[demographic status, Socio- cultural status, Economic status] and ‘n’ is the number of indicators in each component.

Sampling Design

Stratified sampling was applied to create a stratum and was classified depending on the number and area of tea garden spread all over Assam. Then, purposive sampling technique has been used to select the district. The Dibrugarh district was chosen because it has the highest number of tea garden and coverage area. Barbaruah, Muttuck, Singlijan. Rungliting and Basmatia tea estate was chosen using simple random technique.A sample size of 30 per cent households from each selected garden was taken for the survey by using simple random sampling.

Data Collection and Analysis

Household information regarding socio-demography and livelihood was collected with the help of structured schedules through personal interview. Simple frequency, percentage, average were calculated to quantify the variables relevant to objectives of the study and qualitative description has been given to answer direction of relationship of the variables with socio-economic status of the women working in tea estate.

Results and Discussions

It is seen that the demographic aspects of Barbaruah Tea Estate shows the lowest value with 0.43, Muttuck Tea Estate has a higher value of 0.65 ,whereas in Singlijan, Rungliting and Basmatia Tea Estate the value is found to be low with 0.42, 0.47 and 0.44 respectively

Table 1: Socio-economic status of the five tea estates

Dimensions of Socio-economic status	*Barbaruah tea estate*	*Muttucktea estate*	*Singlijantea estate*	*Runglitingtea estate*	*Basmatiatea estate*
Demographic status	*0.43	0.65	0.42	0.47	0.44
Socio- cultural status	0.59	0.36	0.4	0.4	0.66
Economic status	0.68	0.61	0.67	0.65	0.63
Composite index	0.56	0.54	0.49	0.50	0.57

Source: Field survey 2015.

* All the variable is converted into a single composite value which ranges from 0-1. Value 0 is pooreststatus and 1 is better off status.

(table. (1) Muttuck Tea Estate has the highest number of women workers working under the age group between 30 to 40 years of age, 88.63 per cent of the women workers are married, it has the highest number of nuclear and small familes.76.51 per cent of the women workers are literate in this Tea Estate.

Infrastructural aspects show huge differences in score values. Basmatia Tea Estate has the highest value of 0.66 in infrastructural aspects because infrastructural facilities are more accessible to this Tea Estate. Next is Barbaruah Tea Estate with 0.59, Muttuck Tea estate has the least value of 0.36 which is a very low percentage. Singlijan and Rungliting Tea Estate have a score value of 0.4 of infrastructural facility provided by the Tea estates. For Infrastructural aspects, sanitation(Paccka), tube well (supplied), quarter, firewood, medical facility and electricity are taken.

In economic aspects,occupation (permanent), savings, income(Medium income) and work participation rate of women are taken into consideration. The value of Barbaruah Tea Estate is found to be of more value in economic aspects with 0.68. This Tea Estate has the highest percentage of women work participation among the five Tea Estate surveyed with 75.24 percent, 74.86 per cent of them are

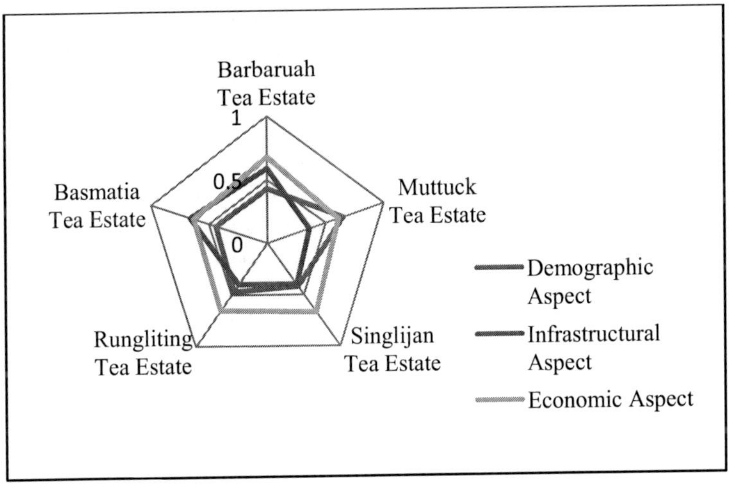

Fig. 2: Socio-economic status pentagon of five tea estates.

permanent workers and 86.63 per cent have a bank account. Next is Singlijan Tea Estate with 0.67, here the work participation rate of women is 61.48 percent. The economic aspect of Rungliting is found to be 0.65, Basmatia Tea Estate is found to be 0.63 and in Muttuck Tea Estate its 0.61. To understand the socio-economic status, the score values of five Tea Estates are diagrammatically representedby socio-economic status pentagon (Fig.2).

It is found that the value of composite index for Barbaruah Tea Estate is 0.56, for Muttuck Tea Estate the value is 0.54, Singlijan Tea Estate has the lowest value of 0.49, Rungliting Tea Estate has a value of 0.50 and for Basmatia Tea Estate the value is 0.57, which means the socio-economic status of the Tea Estate surveyed have moderate socio-economic status. Although the differences in value is very low but as the score value of Basmatia Tea Estate is found to be the highest it can be concluded that the socio-economic status of the women workers of Basmatia Tea Estate is better than the rest of the Tea Estate surveyed. Because among the five Tea Estates surveyed Basmatia Tea Estate has the highest number of permanent workers. Almost 81 per cent of the women workers stay in tea garden quarters with electricity facility which is also highest in percentage among the other Tea Estates surveyed. A large number of women workers are engaged in good posts in Basmatia Tea Estate. The literacy rate of the women workers in Basmatia Tea Estate is also high i.e. 42.5 percent. Basmatia Tea Estate also has the highest number of women workers having a bank account.

Conclusion

The tea plantation workers are found to be paid wages much below the minimum wages for agricultural workers so they cannot afford the minimum need of livelihood. They get an amount of Rs. 100 irrespective of permanent or casual and male or female labours. The average monthly salary of worker is Rs.2400 which is very nominal. So their standard of living is extremely low. In present day of high prices, they are not able to meet the demands of the family due to their low wage rate.The festival bonus they get is also very nominal based on the amount of salary they get. It can be seen that most of them have a bank account and a few are also engaged in self-help groups. Early marriage is still widely prevalent in tea estates. In the five tea estates taken for survey about 87.28 per cent of the women are married which live mostly in small families (1 to 5 members). Most of the tea garden labourers now live in nuclear families in the surveyed tea estates. Literacy can be considered as acid test of socio-economic and cultural improvement of a society. The literacy rate of the women workers are seen to be very low in the surveyed Tea Estates. Out of the five tea estates surveyed, 73.24 per cent of the total women workers are illiterate, 24.41 per cent are under metric, 1.62 per cent is under graduate and rest 0.71 per cent are graduates. So, it can be seen the illiteracy rate is more than the number of literates.

As far as infrastructural facilities are concerned, the present study reveals that 72.22 per cent of the workers of the five tea estates reside in rent free labour quarters in the residential colonies called as *cooli line* made of semi-brick materials without good sanitation facilities. Other basic facilities such as electricity most of them don't have the electricity connection facility and some have not taken the electricity connection because of high bills which is deducted from their salary. For medical facility there is a hospital provided by the tea estate authority to each of the tea estates. These hospitals are small and not well equipped or modernized to cater to all medical needs of the workers. In case of emergency they have to go to Assam Medical College. There are also no maternity benefit schemes for the tea garden women workers. It was observed that even during pregnancy and post-natal period they continue to engage in hard work. For source of water a tube well is provided by the Tea Garden Authority to 4 to 5 families at an average. Tube wells are the most common source of water supply in the Tea Garden. Almost all of the women workers use fire wood as their source of energy for cooking which is supplied from the Tea Estates.

Despite of the poor living condition, these people preserve their socio-cultural status. The labourers enjoy most of the puja festivals like durga puja, manasha puja, kali puja etc. in all the five tea estate. Each festival is celebrated in the garden with dance and music. Jhumur is the most outstanding tune of tea garden culture. Recreational facilities are also provided by the tea garden authority. The nature of work is hard they are engaged in eight hours of work a day. The present salary is not adequate to run their family. They are not able to provide proper education to their children. The only thing they appreciate is that they have free rented houses and tax free water facility.

Reference

Bhattacharjee A & Nirmolia L. (2015).*Role of Tea Industry in Rural Development of Assam:Issues and Challenges in respect of Human Resources*. Paper presented at the *XVI Annual conference Proceedings on Jan. 2015,* Delhi, India.

Borah, K. (2013). Tea cultivation on small holding: A new business opportunity for the indigenous people of Assam. *EXCEL International Journal of Multidisciplinary Management Studies*, *3*(1), 123-131.

Borah, N. (2013). The rights of women workers in the tea gardens of Assam. *The Clarion*, *2*(2), 128-131.

Borah.A C. (2012). *Small tea cultivation and land use change, Sivasagar district, Assam,(1st ed).*Guwahat: Geophil Publishing House

Borah, A. (2014). Women empowerment through self-help groups – A case study of Brahmaputra Development Block in Nagaon district of Assam. *Journal of Economic and Finance,* 4(3), 56-62.

Borah, K. (2013). Entrepreneurship in small tea plantation: A case of Assam. *International Research Journal of Interdisciplinary & Multidisciplinary Studies 1(1), 9-18).*

Chakraborty, B. G. (2005).Small tea growers of North Bengal.*The Assam Review and Tea News.*

Das, S. (2012). Women at the 21st Century: A reflection on the status and security of women in Assam. *Journal of Alternative Perspectives in the Social Sciences,* 3(4), 111-138.

Deka .A. (2001).*Agriculture of Assam.* Jorhat, Assam: Directorate of Extension Education, Assam Agricultural University.

Devi, P. (2014). Socio-economic status of the tea garden women workers in Assam: A case study with special reference to Sonitpur district. *Reviews of Literature*, *2*(2), 1-7.

Ganguli, P.(2014). Small tea growers of Assam: Theories, practises and challenges of an indigenous entrepreneurship. *International journal of Informative and Futuristic Research,* 2(1), 21-27.

Ghosh, J. K., Godbole, P. N., & Ghosh, S. K. (2000).Mapping of tea gardens from satellite images: A fuzzy knowledge-based image interpretation system. *International Archives of Photogrammetry and Remote Sensing*, *33*(B7/1; PART 7), 460-468.

GoA. (2015-16). Economic Survey of Assam, 2015-16. Assam: Directorate of Economic and Statistics.

GoA.(2011). *District census handbook,* 2011, Assam: Directorate of Census Operation.

Hazarika, K & Borah, K.(2013). Small tea cultivation in the process of self-employment: A study of the indigenous people. *International Journal of Latest Trends in Finance and Economic Sciences, 3(2), 502-507.*

Hazarika, M., &Muraleedharan, N. (2011). Tea in India: An overview. *Two and a Bud, 58*, 3-9.

Hossain, M. (2012).Smallholder tea Cultivation for poverty alleviation in Banglades. *Two and a Bud, 59(2), 14-18.*

Iyengar, N. S., &Sudarshan, P. (1982).A method of classifying regions from multivariate data. *Economic and Political Weekly*, 2047-2052.

Kurmi, P.(2014). Problems of educational attainment of children: A case study of the tea garden labourer's households in Derby tea estates. *Research Journal of Language, Literature and Humanities,* 1(4), 1-7.

Majumder, Basu, A., Bera, B. &Rajan, A.(2012). *Tea statistics: Global scenario.* India, Kolkata: Directorate of Research, Dept. of Statistics, Tea Board of India.

Nath, D. (2000). *Importance of small tea gardening and utilization of human resources in Assam.*Minor research project sponsored by UGC (NER).

Nath, S., & Sen, D. (2012).Role of small tea growers in the socio-economic development of Udalguri district of Assam.*International Indexed and Referred Research Journal, 4(44).*

Pal, B., &Goswami, A. (2014). A study on the socio-economic conditions of tea garden labours in Jalpaiguri district of West Bengal, India. *International Journal of Advanced Research in Management and Social Sciences*, *3*(8), 84-90.

Palihakkara, I. R., Mohammed, A. J., & Inoue, M. (2014). Current livelihood condition of and futurity of tea farming for marginal small tea farm holders (MSTH) of Sri Lanka: Case study from Badulla and Matara District. *Environment and Natural Resources Research*, *5*(1), 11.

Prodip, B. D. (2008).*The tea industry of Assam: Origin and development.* Guwahati: EBH Publisher.

Roy.S. (2011).Historical review of growth of tea industries in India: A study of Assam Tea, *International Conference on Social Science and Humanity,* 5, 166-170.

Saikia.B. (2008).Development of tea garden community and adivasi identity politics in Assam.*The Indian Journal of Labour Economics,* 51(2).

Sarkar, S. (2013). Closure of tea gardens and displaced livelihoods: A study of women plantation labourers. *Journal of Exclusion Studies,*3(1), 57-61.

Sharma, P., Borua, S &Talukdar, R. K. (2013).Agriculture based livelihood options of inhabitants of tea gardens in Jorhat District of Assam. *Journal of Academic and Industrial Research,* 1(8), 497-500.

Singh, S. N. &Narain, Amarendra. &Purnendu Kumar. (2006). *Socio-economic and political problems of tea garden workers : A study of Assam*. New Delhi, India: Mittal Publications.

Index

R

S

T

U